W9-DDL-040

Working in Social Work

SAGE SOURCEBOOKS FOR THE HUMAN SERVICES SERIES

Series Editors: ARMAND LAUFFER and CHARLES GARVIN

A source is a starting point, a place of origin, information, or payoff. The volumes in this series reflect these themes. For readers they will serve as starting points for new programs, as the place of origin of advanced skills, or as a source for information that can be used in the pursuit of professional and organizational goals.

Sage Sourcebooks are written to provide multiple benefits for both professionals and advanced students. Authors and contributors are recognized authorities in their fields or at the cutting edge of new knowledge and technique. Sourcebooks deal with new and emerging practice tools and current and anticipated policy issues, transforming knowledge from allied professions and the social sciences into information applicable to the human services.

1. **MANAGING THE HUMAN SERVICE ORGANIZATION**
   by RICHARD STEINER (out of print)
2. **MASS MEDIA AND HUMAN SERVICES**
   by EDWARD A. BRAWLEY
3. **DESIGNING INTERVENTIONS FOR THE HELPING PROFESSIONS**
   by EDWIN J. THOMAS
4. **THE TRAPPED WOMAN: Catch-22 in Deviance and Control**
   edited by JOSEFINA FIGUEIRA-McDONOUGH & ROSEMARY SARRI
5. **FAMILY THERAPY WITH ETHNIC MINORITIES**
   by MAN KEUNG HO
6. **WORKING IN SOCIAL WORK: Growing and Thriving in Human Services Practice**
   by ARMAND LAUFFER

Armand Lauffer

Working in Social Work

Growing and Thriving in Human Services Practice

SAGE SOURCEBOOKS FOR THE HUMAN SERVICES SERIES
VOLUME 6

SAGE PUBLICATIONS
The Publishers of Professional Social Science
Newbury Park Beverly Hills London New Delhi

For information address:

SAGE Publications, Inc.
2111 West Hillcrest Drive
Newbury Park, California 91320

SAGE Publications Inc.
275 South Beverly Drive
Beverly Hills
California 90212

SAGE Publications Ltd.
28 Banner Street
London EC1Y 8QE
England

SAGE PUBLICATIONS India Pvt. Ltd.
M-32 Market
Greater Kailash I
New Delhi 110 048 India

Printed in the United States of America

Library of Congress Cataloging-in-Publication Data

Lauffer, Armand.
Working in social work.

(Sourcebooks for improving human services; v. 6)
Includes bibliographies.
1. Social service—United States. 2. Social work administration—United States. 3. Social workers—Professional ethics—United States.
I. Title. II. Series.
HV91.L35 1987 361.3'0973 86-29700
ISBN 0-8039-2041-5

CONTENTS

To Tohar and Elisheva,
born eighteen years after reunification.
Chai v'kayam.

INTRODUCTION

Don't let the title mislead you. This book is not about how to be a social worker. It may, however, help you be a more effective social worker or employee in a social agency at any level—direct practice, community organization, training, supervision, or management. It may do so by helping you to understand the dynamics at play in a work environment, any work environment, but with a specific focus on the kinds of issues that are addressed on a day-to-day basis by social workers and other human services professionals. I've tried to address these issues by focusing on the personal and professional concerns of practitioners within the context of the work environment and the profession's missions to provide services to clients while remaining accountable to the public.

Roughly half the material appears in an earlier volume, *Careers, Colleagues, and Conflicts: Understanding Gender, Race, and Ethnicity in the Workplace* (Sage, 1985). Why a second book so soon, you might ask? What was wrong with the first? Well, I'd like to think that not too much was wrong with it. But it was relatively short, and didn't give me the opportunity to deal with a number of issues that I think might be important to you. I must tell you that the first book was not the one I had intended to write.

I set out to do a fairly straightforward demystification of agency personnel practices and procedures. About halfway into the first chapter, two students stopped by for a talk. I was amazed to hear myself accused of racist and gender biases because of some remarks made in class. One does not take such accusations lightly when one teaches in a school of social work. I certainly didn't.

None of us is free of prejudices, and I did some inner searching to bring to the surface whatever it might have been that I had conveyed.

It was not a painless process. Nor was it without pain that the two students had approached me. How much of what they had perceived was in me, I wondered, and how much in them?

The next few weeks led me to begin exploration of a wide variety of related issues. These are all reflected in the pages that follow. They deal with culture, ethnicity, personality and conflict in the workplace. They also deal with careers and professionalization, with collegial relationships and with roles and role-conflicts. Writing this book was a struggle. I think reading it will be as well.

In order to write it I had to dig deep inside. I also dug into the literature. And I interviewed dozens of students and practitioners, some of whom you will meet in the book. Their identities are disguised, of course, but perhaps only partially. If you recognize anyone, I hope it will be yourself. In Chapter 1 you will meet Yolanda, Sam, Ali, Millicent, Carl, and Harvey. Don't let yourself be put off by their genders, racial and ethnic backgrounds, social class characteristics or the work they perform at the All-Families Service Center. The place is mythical. The characters are real. They are you and me, and many of the other people you have met at school and at work.

Each chapter focuses on several issues that probe the relationships between people in the workplace. One of the issues we examine is the fit between individual capacities and aspirations and the demands (expectations) placed on them by others on the job or by fellow professionals. Although each chapter is distinct, the issues presented blend into each other and are often dealt with again and again from a different conceptual point of view. Each chapter also includes a set of exercises and rather extensive bibliography.

The exercises are designed to bring *you* into the book, in effect interacting with Yolanda, Harvey, and the others. They are a guide to self-study and analysis. The suggested readings are intended to provide you with a guide for further intellectual inquiry. They include both classic and contemporary sources. You may be conversant with the classic sources from earlier undergraduate and graduate study. You may be familiar with some of the more contemporary materials from your work in a social agency or from your perusal of the professional literature on occupations, personnel practices, management, burn-out and job stress, gender and ethnicity studies, and so on. But juxtaposed the way they are, these materials should lead you to new understandings and to more effective work-related practices.

Chapters 1 through 5, and 7, appear in slightly abbreviated form in *Careers, Colleagues, and Conflicts.* As you'll see from the Table of Contents, I've added four new chapters, which will permit us to explore together, you and me, a number of related issues: the making of ethical decisions, the management of conflict and change, the restructuring and redesign of jobs, and the effective uses of the supervisory process.

Used properly, the book—with its exercises and readings—may help you make more intelligent career decisions. It should also be useful in helping others whom you may counsel or supervise at work.

Feel free to photocopy the exercises for use in your work with colleagues in the agency or the classroom. You might find some that lend themselves directly to work with people you supervise, or with your own supervisor. Modify them to articulate as closely as possible the issues you need to address. But don't ignore them. I learned a great deal as I worked on this book. The exercises are intended to involve you as a partner in the analysis and thought processes. In fact, if you complete a reasonable number—say, two-thirds of them, and then compare your notes with a colleague who has completed a similar percentage, you may find that you each read a different book.

That is as it should be. The book was designed for analysis and problem solving and is intended to set the stage for personal, collective, and organizational decision making. In many of the chapters, I've suggested how and where to use an exercise in practice. You may have additional ideas. Pursue them, please!

—*Armand Lauffer*
Jerusalem and Ann Arbor

Chapter 1

GETTING TURNED ON TO WORK
Satisfaction, Motivation, and Effort on the Job

Yolanda Stephenson turned off her favorite Motown station just before reaching the freeway exit. Straightening up, she squared her shoulders and shook off the rhythms that had filled her head and energized her body since leaving home. By the time she pulled into the lot behind the All-Families Service Center, she was ready to assume the quiet and professional demeanor she was known by and that she expected of herself in the position of clinical supervisor. The switch in mind-set was not unfamiliar. It was a price Yolanda had long been willing to pay for success in social work, her chosen career, for the esteem and respect she received from her (White) colleagues, and for the security that came with a well-paid, tenured position. As the first member of her family to earn a university degree, she felt some other obligations as well.

* * * * *

Samich Fouad Mansouri met Yolanda in the parking lot. They nodded to each other pleasantly but without commitment. "Sam" runs the agency's New Americans Project. As a 19-year-old, Sam had left his native Lebanon because of civil strife but never waivered in his commitment to its victims. He decided early to seek a career opportunity that would enable him to be of service to his countrymen and others in the Chaldean community. To be of service had always been expected of Sam. His father and grandfather before him had both been physicians, tending to Beirut's poor.

Shortly after beginning his undergraduate work, Sam switched from premed to a social work major. An encounter with a counselor at the university, herself an MSW, was the deciding factor. He found in her a dedicated, empathic and helpful professional—a role model for his own career. He has never regretted the choice of social work as the profession through which he would seek to achieve his personal and community-related objectives. On completion of his MSW, Sam began employment at the Center. He continued to study, earning a law degree on a part-time basis. Although the clients he serves are not well understood by many of his colleagues at work, he is respected as a competent practitioner, good administrator and effective advocate.

Eventually Sam hopes to establish a nonprofit organization advocating for immigrant rights. But he is in no hurry. His initial sense of urgency has diminished somewhat (not incidentally) following his marriage and the successive arrival of two daughters on whom he dotes.

* * * * *

Alberta Schmid was already sitting behind her desk in the receptionist's office when Yolanda and Sam walked in. Ali always arrived early in order to get the day's work organized, enjoying the interaction with other staff as they come in. Feeling wanted, knowing she does her job well, and being appreciated mean a lot to Ali. "Ali knows her job. I don't know where we would be without her," Bill Clapman, the agency's director, has told other staff members more than once. And the word gets back to Ali. She also enjoys the give and take with clients, feeling a sense of deep satisfaction when she routes them properly to Center staff. The job does not pay terribly well, but then Ali's education has not gone beyond two years of junior college. Still, the position is secure, and last year when she unexpectedly needed surgery, the agency's extensive health benefits covered all her expenses. Staff members visited her regularly while she recuperated, letting her know how much she was missed.

* * * * *

A moment or two later, Millicent arrived. Millicent Kapinski likes to call herself a "retread." After 20 years of teaching in a Catholic parochial school, she came to the conclusion that life within her order was too restrictive. She also found herself in increasing conflict with Church policy. Now, as a family life education specialist, she has discovered a newfound freedom with full opportunity to express her commitments to others. Her age—Millicent at 53 is one of the older staff members at the agency—and her warmth lead others to seek her out as a confidant. "I've become," Millicent admits with a smile, "everybody's 'Polish mother' around here."

* * * * *

Carl Farrell arrived late. "It really doesn't matter," he thought to himself. "Hardly anyone in this place is interested in the things I care about." As the agency's accountant, he is somewhat of an outsider in an organization dominated by social workers and allied human service professionals. It's not that Carl's tardiness signifies poor performance. On the contrary, Carl does his work competently, but without enthusiasm. He discovered early that excessive zeal, especially when you deal with budgets, sometimes leads to conflict.

And Carl doesn't like to fight. Using a wry humor to keep people at a distance, he does his best to avoid conflict. But all this leaves Carl isolated socially, and this in turn leads to feelings of depression and of being unproductive, misplaced, and unloved. His energy is low and he often feels that life has somehow begun to pass him by. He just can't seem to connect with the upbeat attitude of other staff at the agency.

People at the Center might be surprised to hear of it, but Carl is a jazz enthusiast, playing one or two nights a week at a club in a nearby suburb. It's not something he shares about himself with the others. Although Carl feels something in common with Millicent, whom he respects for her seriousness, and senses a kinship in spirit with Yolanda . . . both the male-female and Black-White thing, and his own normal reticence to become too close to anyone, lead to his isolation from them as well.

* * * * *

Harvey Marcus chose not to come to the agency that morning. He was on his way to the state capital, where he was scheduled to meet with public welfare officials to go over his latest proposal for a series of innovative community treatment facilities. The juices were flowing. Harv always felt this way when starting the negotiations process of putting together a new package of services. "It's the primitive hunting urge," he once confided to his wife. And it paid off, not only for his agency and its clients, but also in terms of his own career. He had moved rapidly in the five years since completing his MSW—a lot faster than he might have by playing it safe on a clinical assignment within the agency. Harvey thought of himself as being on the "cutting edge" of practice.

He was, in fact, on another sort of cutting edge, operating on the boundary, so to speak, between his agency and the community. One nice thing about being on the boundary was the opportunity it provided to expand the programs for which he was responsible. There was a price to pay, of course. One could get too far ahead, cutting oneself off from one's colleagues as one's programs became severed from the agency's core. But it was a risk worth taking, and the rewards, including rapid advancement in responsibility and income, were great.

* * * * *

You've undoubtedly met Yolanda, Sam, Ali, Millicent, Carl, and Harvey—or others like them—at work or at school. You'll meet them again as you read on. We'll explore why they and others choose to work at the jobs they do, why they've selected careers in the human services and the benefits they derive (or hope to derive) from such work. We'll examine the conditions that contribute to job satisfaction and productivity, personal and professional advancement and the achievement of agency missions. As you read each chapter and complete the exercises within them, you will be able to assess your own situation with all its attendant risks and opportunities. You'll be better able to define what turns you on (and off) about work and your relationship with others. You'll be able to define your career objectives more clearly, and to anticipate pressure and tension points to avoid. Let's begin by examining work and working.

THE MEANING OF WORK AND WORKING FOR MEANING

The French word for work is *travail.* In English, travail means "trouble," "suffering" or "exhausting labor." The Hebrew word for work is *avodah,* but its translation into English is "service," and the connotation of service is to render one's duty, to give aid, and to be helpful. Somewhere between these two definitions lies the reality of your situation and mine.

When something is working, it is functional and in good order. When people are working, their activities may or may not be functional or in good order. Unlike things, people have reasons for working and feelings about what they do, how they do it and how others respond to it. Those feelings have much to do with whether they consider work to lead to suffering or service. People work in lots of places and at many tasks. They may work at being good parents, at improving their golf games, at beating the stock market, or at their jobs. For our purposes, we're going to focus on *job-related* work—those activities in which people engage in order to gain material necessities and luxuries. But the benefits they derive, or hope to derive, from work are not only material. They are also social and personal—benefits not limited to the workplace but that, if absent or difficult to achieve, may render the place where you work less than satisfying, and the work you do less than meaningful.

People work to meet their security, social and personal objectives. These might be summarized as follows:

(1) Security objectives
  (a) Earning sufficient income, now or in the future.
(2) Social objectives
  (a) Meeting the expectations of others—family members, friends, the society at large (that its "productive" members will be gainfully employed or involved in the service of others).
  (b) Belonging, being accepted, receiving affection, establishing friendships.
  (c) Being appreciated, esteemed for one's contributions, achieving recognition and status with its attendant impact on self-esteem.
(3) Personal objectives
  (a) Self-actualization, achieving one's own potential, growing and developing in response to challenge.

(b) Engaging in service to others, helping people.
(c) Taking responsibility for social or community change, making a difference.

These objectives are not always so clearly stated, nor are they mutually exclusive. Much of the time we pursue several objectives simultaneously without being fully aware of them or of how they serve either as motivators or as criteria by which we assess our satisfaction at work. For each of us, in fact, several of these objectives interact in tandem so that they are not easy to distinguish, one from the other. Moreover, at different stages in our careers or personal lives, one or some combination of these objectives may be dominant. Even the level of intensity with which they affect our behavior and our feelings about our circumstances is likely to change over time. Nevertheless, it is possible to clarify how these objectives affect us and the work we do, just as it is possible to become more sensitive to how they affect others.

Think a moment about what you already know about Yolanda, Sam, Ali, Millicent, Carl, and Harvey. Take a moment to make an educated guess about each of their motivator-satisfiers.

In making your assessments, you probably took into consideration what you know of each person's background, current work responsibilities, and relationships to colleagues at work. Admittedly, your knowledge about others is limited. You probably know a good deal more about yourself and your own situation. Consider **Exercise 1.1** as a warm-up for a somewhat more difficult assessment. In the second exercise,[1] you are asked to take a look both at yourself and your situation, and to make some determinations about what the future may hold.

That exercise may have given you a chance to think. If you are like most people, chances are that the fit between what you are looking for in a position and what a particular job has to offer you is not all that close on all items. Moreover, as you discovered in completing the first exercise, different people have different motivator-satisfiers. It is not likely that any work setting is going to meet everyone's needs or expectations. This doesn't mean that either you or they should settle for something less than satisfactory. On the contrary, the fact that things at work are not fully satisfactory is often the motivator to make them better. Reality factors, of course, sometimes lead us to accept a

Exercise 1.1

Staff Motivator-Satisfier Assessment

Based on what you know or think you know about them, check those items that you think act as important motivator-satisfiers for each of the agency staff members you were introduced to at the beginning of the chapter. Take a moment to reread the vignettes if you need to refresh your memory.

Motivator-Satisfiers	Yolanda	Sam	Ali	Millicent	Carl	Harvey	1	2	3
1. Security									
a. Income (present or future)									
b. Protection									
2. Social									
a. Meeting others' expectations									
b. Belonging, friendship									
c. Esteem, recognition									
3. Personal									
a. Self-actualization, growth									
b. Serving, helping									
c. Changing things									

Now think of colleagues at work or school. Put their names over Columns 1, 2 and 3 and complete the same assessment for them.

situation that may be less than satisfactory. Sometimes the cost of changing something on the job may be greater than the hoped-for benefit, especially if that something to be changed is you—your sense of self, your skills or the tasks you may be required to perform or your aspirations and those of others who are important to you.

USING CONCEPTS TO UNDERSTAND MOTIVATION

We'll explore a number of these issues when we examine the meaning of careers (Chapter 3), your relationship to colleagues, subordinates and superiors (Chapters 2 and 5), job restructuring (Chapter 8), and the meaning of professional practice (Chapter 4). First, however, it may be helpful to examine what others have discovered about job satisfaction, motivation and meeting needs on the job. In doing so, we'll examine some of the findings of the researchers and the ideas of the theorists who are most often referred to in the literature on personnel practices and human resources management.

Exercise 1.2

Personal Motivator-Satisfier Assessment

1. Begin by determining what you are looking for in a job, any job (Column 1). Rate each of the motivator-satisfiers in terms of importance to you at this stage in your career or worklife. Three stars (***) = very important; two stars (**) = important; one star (*) = somewhat important. A blank indicates that this factor is not important to you at all.
2. Now complete the second column. Here you will be assessing the extent to which your current job meets those expectations. Again, use a three-star rating system, with the stars indicating the extent to which the job provides you with each of the motivator-satisfiers (i.e., *** = very much, blank = not at all).
3. In the third column write "OK" where you feel that no adjustment is necessary because columns 1 and 2 match, or because the degree of congruence is acceptable to you. Put a plus (+) in those rows where the fit is not close but where you think some change in your favor is possible, and a minus (−) if you think there is little likelihood that what you are seeking and what the job has to offer can be reconciled.

Motivator-Satisfiers*	(1) What you are looking for in a job	(2) What your** current job has to offer	(3) Adjustment possibilities
1. Security			
a. Income (present or future)			
b. Protection			
2. Social			
a. Meeting others' expectations			
b. Belonging, friendship			
c. Esteem, recognition			
3. Personal			
a. Self-actualization, growth			
b. Serving, helping			
c. Changing things			

*This juxtaposition of terms is taken from Herberg, discussed later in this chapter.

**If you are not currently employed, think of a job you recently left, or one you are considering as a future possibility.

I want to begin with a warning. There is some danger in limiting our exploration to these theorists. First of all, their ideas are still only tentative and not fully borne out by empirical research. Second, most of what they have written has tended to be accepted uncritically by people responsible for developing and managing personnel practices in many organizations, often with unproductive results. But there are some advantages as well.

Because these are the theorists most often quoted in the literature (and by personnel directors), it is important for you to be familiar with them so as to understand the rationales often used for an agency's employment policies and practices. Such understanding may help you in negotiating more satisfactory working conditions and job benefits. It will help you understand where persons responsible for those policies and practices are coming from, assuming that they are familiar with the same theorists. This is not to suggest that the concepts and theories described in the following pages have neither validity nor potency. On the contrary, they are powerful ideas that can and have been used to create more satisfying work environments based on increased understanding of human behavior at work and the motivations behind that behavior.

Concepts and theories can be used in a pro-active way, leading you to take action on the basis of ideas that have some empirical validity. They can also be used defensively, protecting you from the abuse of others who may be using them incorrectly or selectively against your best interests.

In this chapter we'll examine a number of "need" theories, one at a time, and then explore an expectancy-motivation model that shows some promise of being especially helpful to workers and managers alike. This model draws, to some extent, on the theories discussed earlier.

NEED THEORIES

If you've taken an undergraduate psychology course or delved into any of the personnel literature, you are undoubtedly familiar with the works of the late Abraham Maslow of Brandeis University. In the early 1940s, Maslow, a psychoanalyst and psychotherapist with a penchant for anthropology, attempted to integrate into a single conceptual structure much of what he had learned from analysts like Freud, Adler and Jung, with the work of Carl Rogers, Gordon Allport, Henry Murray, Eric Fromm, and others. He postulated that all persons have a hierarchy of needs. These can be described as follows:

5. **Self-Actualization:** growth, achieving one's potential, self-fulfillment.

4. **Esteem:** self-respect, autonomy, sense of competence and a sense of achievement (internal factors); recognition, status, attention, prestige (external factors).

3. **Belonging and Affection:** acceptance, love, friendship, working cooperatively with others.

2. **Security and Safety:** protection from emotional and physical harm; shelter, warmth, health and mental health protection.

1. **Physiological:** drives to satisfy fulfillment of hunger, thirst and reproductive and other bodily needs.

You probably recognize in this hierarchy all of the motivator-satisfiers we included in the two preceding exercises. Maslow further postulated a notion of "prepotency" which suggests that once a person's lower order needs (physiological and security) are satisfied with some degree of consistency, he or she is freed to pursue higher order needs for love, esteem, and self-actualization. Unfortunately, Maslow did not support his ideas with a great deal of empirical research of his own. Nevertheless, his schema had an enormous impact on psychologists and others concerned with motivation in the workplace. There is an almost intuitive logic to his ideas that makes them easy to understand and accept. But some social scientists are skeptical of the intuitive, while others are too easily captivated by it.

For this reason, the 1950s, 1960s, and early 1970s witnessed a spate of research efforts aimed at validating or disproving Maslow's ideas. In a now classic review of those studies, Porter, Lawler and Hackman found that although there is evidence that the activation of higher order needs depends in part on the satisfaction of lower level needs. the needs for belonging, esteem and self-actualization do not operate in a hierarchical manner. Most people are motivated by and can pursue each of the higher order needs simultaneously. The need for money and security may reduce the readiness to pursue higher order needs, but they too can act as motivators, though they tend to do so only temporarily. Once satisfied, lower level needs no longer motivate. Higher order needs, on the other hand, especially the drive for self-actualization, seem to be insatiable once activated.

In 1972, Clayton Alderfer published research findings that led to consolidating Maslow's hierarchy into three basic needs. His ERG theory combines the two lower level needs into one: *E*xistence. *R*elatedness needs include both esteem and belonging, while *G*rowth needs refer to the search to be most fully what one can become. Although all of these can be pursued simultaneously, frustration of one's existence or relatedness needs can lead to at least a temporary reduction in the pursuit of growth needs. Where there is much opportunity for growth and personal development, existence needs may take on less importance. Conversely, where growth needs cannot be satisfied, greater attention may be directed at securing better pay, working conditions and other existence-related benefits.

At about the time of Alderfer's publication, David McClelland was engaged in using the TAT (Thematic Apperception Test), along with follow-up interviews, to study how people project their needs in response to work-related stimuli. The most commonly verbalized themes were the needs for achievement, affiliation and power—needs expressed with different degrees of intensity and frequency by different people. In some cases these were expressions of personality, in others they reflected the challenges and opportunities available at work, and in still others they seemed to be a function of a respondent's life-stage or place on the career ladder.

For example, *n* Ach (need to achieve) might be high for a young manager whose career is at an early stage and for whom many opportunities to demonstrate competence and receive rewards for achievement are available. For those moving up the administrative ladder, *n* Pow (need for power) might take precedence over the need for achievement at the point where a person finds himself or herself in a position of command or with opportunities to affect the direction of the organization or to influence others within it. Those whose opportunities are blocked might redirect their needs toward affiliation and the establishment of good working relationships with colleagues (*n* Aff—need for affiliation).

In subsequent studies, McClelland and his associates found *n* Ach to be a prime motivator for those entrepreneurs involved in starting up small businesses, while the desire to have an impact on others (*n* Pow) was a strong motivator for those moving up in larger and more complex organizations. Some critics of these studies have characterized the use of quasi-mathematical symbols like *n* Ach and *n* Aff as *n* Bam—*the need to bamboozle*. There may be some justification for this observation, since some researchers tend to believe that their findings reflect more than partial truths. This weakness can be detected among those practitioners who latch onto a theory and ride it for all it's worth, and more.

They follow what philosopher Abe Kaplan has called "the Law of the Instrument." In plain English, this law can be stated as follows: "Give a small boy a hammer and he'll find that everything in sight needs pounding."

It would be good to take note of this observation before proceeding. Maslow, Alderfer, and McClelland's contributions to our understanding have been substantial, but they should not be accepted uncritically. Like other concepts from the social sciences, they should be used by practitioners to the extent that they are found helpful as guides to interpretation and understanding but only sometimes as guides to action. They are too tentative and imprecise to direct our practice behaviors in all instances. We are still, most of us, much like the blind man trying to describe the elephant. Each of our observations should be recorded and used where helpful, but we should not fool ourselves into thinking that any one observer's contribution is enough to comprehend the whole.

This caution notwithstanding, it may be useful to examine one more researcher's efforts to identify satisfiers and motivators. Even before Alderfer began his work, Frederick Herzberg conducted a set of interviews with 200 engineers and accountants in the Pittsburgh area in order to test the relationship between lower order needs and the need to grow and develop psychologically. Interviewees were asked to pinpoint those events on the job that led to increased feelings of job satisfaction, and those others that led to increased dissatisfaction.

Herzberg found that the factors leading to satisfaction were associated with the work itself. They included achievement, recognition, responsibility and advancement. These he called "motivators" because when present they seemed to lead to better performance and increased effort. To the extent that these were absent, there was "no satisfaction," and respondents reported lower motivation to achieve.

The second group of factors tended to be focused more on the work *situation* rather than on the work itself.

If people complained about work, they tended to cite problems in the work context or environment. These "dissatisfiers" included pay and benefits, relationships with colleagues or supervisors, company policies or rules, job security and tenure. Such items were rarely cited as "satisfiers." Herzberg concluded that these "dissatisfiers" (which he later called hygiene and maintenance factors), when improved, tended to lead only to temporary increases in satisfaction (with the elimination of some dissatisfaction). Thus they cannot be considered to be motivators. A major finding of this two-factor approach is that the many people who are motivated by the satisfaction they derive from their work may have considerable tolerance for poor working conditions—in other words, they can live with some dissatisfaction without it detracting from their satisfaction.

Herzberg's "two-factor" theory has spawned hundreds of similar studies in efforts by researchers and personnel directors to determine what might lead to increased motivation in specific workplaces or within specific occupational groupings. Not everyone can be expected to respond the same way as the engineers and accountants in the 11 Pittsburgh firms studied. For example, many human service workers are likely to include "supervision" and "relationships with colleagues" among their satisfaction factors rather than among their hygiene or dissatisfaction factors. In contrast, studies of blue collar workers indicate that some hygiene factors such as better pay are indeed motivators, especially when the work itself is dull and unrewarding.

You may find the two-factor theory intriguing. I do. But I also find it somewhat limiting. First of all, grouping satisfiers and dissatisfiers into a two-dimensional theory of work satisfaction seems to be a grand oversimplification. Second, it tends to ignore any other theories that might be used to interpret or explain findings. The most telling criticism of Herzberg's work is that he made no effort to relate motivators to actual job performance. In fact, his translation of the word *satisfier* into "motivator" has been critized by some as naive at best or as sleight of hand at worst. In conducting his interviews, Herzberg asked respondents whether job satisfaction increased their motivation to put greater effort into their work. Most responded affirmatively. But how else could they have answered? Ask most people if they are satisfied at work, and you are not likely to hear them tell you "yes" but that they are also unmotivated!

USING NEED THEORIES ON THE JOB

Clearly, need theories are flawed, yet they can be used heuristically to comprehend our own motivations and to assess the extent to which outcomes we value are achievable on the job. They can also be used in developing greater sensitivity to our colleagues and their motivations, to the needs and interests of those we supervise, those who supervise us, and to the volunteers whom we may recruit and assign to various tasks.

Let's list the theories we've examined:

—Maslow's hierarchy includes the following needs: physiological, security, belonging, esteem and self-actualization.

—Alderfer regrouped these needs into his ERG theory of Existence, Relationships, and Growth.

—McClelland identified the need to achieve (*n* Ach), the need for affiliation (*n* Aff) and the need for power (*n* Pow).

—Herzberg found that satisfiers (which he later called motivators) were of a different order than dissatisfiers (which he called hygiene factors).

Think about what you already know or have surmised about Yolanda, Sam, Ali, Millicent, Carl, and Harvey, and then go on to **Exercise 1.3.**

As your answers to the questions in **Exercise 1.3** may have suggested to you, motivation is explained by a combination of factors that include the work itself, the need for achievement discussed by McClelland and the combination of extrinsic and intrinsic rewards that may be possible within the workplace. The meaning of those rewards, and the extent to which they are likely to serve as motivators, are explored more fully in what has come to be known as the "expectancy model."

THE EXPECTANCY MODEL

Unlike the work of Maslow, Alderfer, McClelland, and Herzberg, the expectancy model does not limit examination of what motivates people (needs or satisfactions). Rather, it places emphasis on the conscious and semiconscious thought processes that lead people to act in certain ways in the workplace. The underlying assumptions of the model are as follows:

Exercise 1.3

Application of Need Theories to Agency Practice

1. Using either Maslow's or Alderfer's formulation, generate as many questions as you can to help you uncover what motivates each of the six staff members to behave as they do on the job.
2. Are there identifiable prices that the staff members must pay to achieve satisfactions and that may serve as de-motivators? What questions would you ask in an effort to find out?
3. How would you get the answer to those questions—by asking the staff members directly, through observation, by asking others (e.g., colleagues and supervisors)? Why did you answer as you did?
4. Does McClelland's addition of *n* Pow add substantially to the questions you would ask? How?
5. Would you ask the questions differently if you were following the approach used by Herzberg? If so, how? If not, why not?
6. Of the four approaches, which do you find most useful? Why?
7. Assume for a moment that you were the agency's personnel director or the person responsible for employing and assigning the six staff members. How would you use this information in your decisions about whom to employ and for what jobs?
8. Think about your own job. To what extent were these questions asked of you? Should they have been asked? To what extent did you seek answers to these questions in determining whether or not you were interested in the job? If you did not, or did so only partially, how might your decision have been affected by more thorough exploration of these issues?

We, each of us, desire particular benefits and rewards for the things we do, and we may have preferences among them.

We also have expectations about whether, in any given situation, the things we do will lead to a particular outcome, including achieving those rewards we value mostly highly.

The model, which I'll describe more fully in a moment, was first articulated by Victor Vroom. It has since been refined and studied extensively by Edward Lawler III. Vroom uses three key concepts in his model: valence, expectancy, and instrumentality. *Valence* is the extent to which a person values a particular outcome or reward. When you starred the items in Column 1 of **Exercise 1.2** ("What you are looking for in a job"), you were indicating the valence of each of the eight motivator-satisfiers listed.

Expectancy refers to the perceptions a person may have about the probability that a particular circumstance, effort, or action will lead to a particular outcome or result. For example, in Column 2 of the exercise, you indicated your expectations about the extent to which your current job can offer you the rewards you seek. In the context of Vroom's expectancy model, you would want to get even more specific. You would indicate your expectations that certain actions or efforts on your part will yield specific outcomes.

The third concept, *instrumentality*, is what gives the expectancy model its unique character. It refers to the extent to which we believe that a first-level outcome will yield a second-level outcome. For example, you might, as Harvey Marcus does, believe that by "operating on the boundary" you can increase the opportunity to expand programs you are responsible for. Negotiating a contract will enable you to expand the agency's services to a particular client population. By the same token, achieving that outcome may lead to a second-level outcome, thus increasing your personal satisfaction through helping others or changing things. It may also yield rapid advancement and increased income (security needs) and may heighten the esteem with which you are regarded by others in the organization (social needs).

Vroom depicted the model schematically as shown in Figure 1.1. To a large extent, motivation is directly related to *expectancy* × *valence*. Both are in part the result of an individual's earlier experiences, his or her sense of self (ability, capacity to achieve) and trust (expectancy) that rewards will follow accomplishment. These can be tempered by reality—the capacity of the organization or the job to provide desired rewards (refer again to your work on **Exercise 1.2,** but this time look at Column 3).

Researchers have found considerable empirical support for this model. In general, the higher the predicted motivation (based on valence, expectancy and instrumentality scores), the greater the effort. Unfortunately, no single model can be used to explain or predict with total accuracy. We are all complex individuals with multiple objectives, varying abilities to predict outcomes, and limited informa-

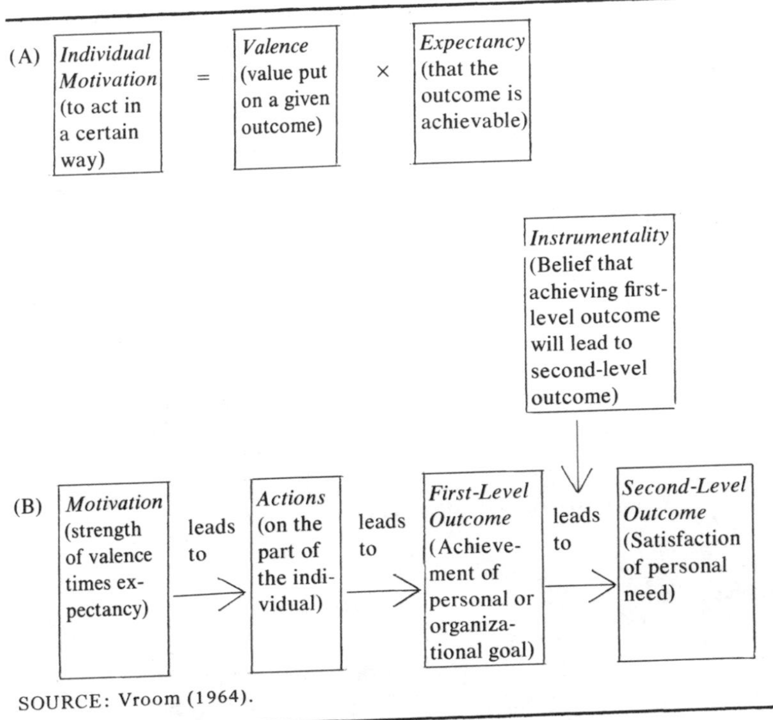

Figure 1.1 Schematic version of expectancy model (modified).

tion about what is truly possible in a given situation. Lawler suggests that these variations can be accommodated somewhat by expanding the diagram to include different expectations and valences. You may find my rendering of Lawler's schematization helpful in examining your own work-related behavior and that of colleagues (see Figure 1.2).

Using this model, let's make some educated guesses about Harvey Marcus's thought processes. The amount of effort Harvey puts into seeking support for new projects and setting up a negotiations process is based on his perceptions of his own abilities and capabilities (expectancy 1-2). He further expects (expectancy 2-3) that his performance has a good probability of leading to a grant or contract to set up a complex of innovative community treatment facilities (first-level outcome 3). That performance and the effort that goes into it will be further enhanced by the importance (valence 3) that this outcome has

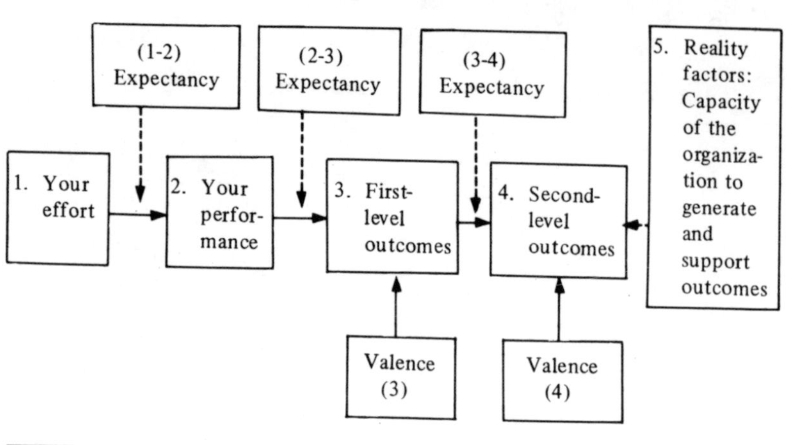

Figure 1.2 Alternate version of Lawler's (1973) schematization.

for him. In turn, getting the grant or contract may have import (valence 3) to the extent that he expects (expectancy 3-4) that it will lead to a better service, important changes and recognition for his efforts (second-level outcome 4). To the extent that he puts a great deal of value on each of these possible outcomes (valence 4) and believes that they are achievable (expectancy 3-4), his efforts are likely to be considerable.

Over time, Harvey's efforts are likely to continue to be high wherever he puts a lot of store (valence) in the outcome and is reasonably certain of its achievability (expectancy). But this is dependent to a large extent on reality factors that may be outside his control. Other agencies may compete effectively for the same contracts or awards; downturns in the economy or changes in public policy may result in priority shifts; a reshuffling of state-level personnel may require returning to ground one and establishing his (and his agency's) credentials all over again. Thus the costs and likelihood of success may outweigh the potential benefits, especially when equal effort might be invested elsewhere—someplace that might yield a greater likelihood (expectancy) of success.

Moreover, Harvey's circumstances and his own motives may change. Having arrived at a relatively secure and respected position within his agency and in the broader human service community,

Exercise 1.4

Application of the Expectancy Model to Your Practice

1. Using the same schematization we found helpful in analyzing Harvey Marcus's thought processes, analyze your own. Begin by spelling out your desired second-level outcomes. You may find that you've already identified them in **Exercise 1.2.** Then spell out your desired first-level outcomes. How much importance do you place on each? Rate each high, medium or low.
2. Now indicate what you will have to do to get to your first-level outcome (your performance). To what extent do you have the requisite skills, knowledge or other capacities to perform adequately (expectancy 1-2)? Again, give yourself a high, medium or low rating.
3. If you perform well, what is the likelihood (expectancy 2-3) of achieving your first-level objective (high, medium, or low)? What is the likelihood that this achievement will lead to your desired second-level outcome (high, medium or low; expectancy 3-4)? What are some of the reality factors (5) that can support your expectations? Consider agency policies, work climate, availability of resources and any other factors you think may be significant.
4. Based on these considerations, is the effort worth making? What changes in reality factors or in your own capacities are necessary to increase the likelihood of achieving both of the desired (first- and second-level) outcomes?
5. With whom should these thoughts be shared?
   —your supervisor
   —your colleagues at work
   —your spouse or significant other
   —others (specify)____________________
6. How might such sharing improve
   —your practice
   —the practices of your supervisors or colleagues
   —your relationship to a significant other
   —your satisfaction on the job
   —your motivation to increase your efforts
   —the ways in which planning and work assignments are made at the agency
   —the ways in which rewards for effort and success are allocated in the agency?

Harvey may be ready to consolidate his gains and protect his investments. With age and experience, he may become more interested in service than in change. This may be expressed by a reduced "hunting urge" and greater commitment to protecting home and property (those programs already established and those clients served by them).

REVIEW AND TENTATIVE CONCLUSIONS

We have explored the contributions of a number of researchers and theorists to our understanding of jobs, job satisfaction and work motivation. And we have completed a number of exercises aimed at increasing our understanding of our own situations. You may have found one or more of the approaches useful and generated a number of insights into your own behavior. I'm going to list some general conclusions I've come to based on my understanding of the concepts discussed. I'll then leave you with room to add your own.

(1) Lower level needs, when unsatisfied, can motivate us to seek changes and improvements, including greater efforts on the job. But lower level needs, once substantially satisfied, no longer act as motivators.

(2) In contrast, higher order needs, when satisfied, lead to greater striving, especially when there are no unmet lower level needs. This is most true of the need to grow and to self-actualize—needs that, once activated, are difficult to turn off. Moreover, higher order needs can be acted on simultaneously. Thus we can work on our social needs (fulfilling expectations of belonging and friendship, esteem and recognition) and our personal needs (being of service, changing things, growing professionally and personally) at the same time.

(3) There is no evidence that being happy at work and feeling satisfied with one's circumstances lead to greater effort or increased motivation (productivity). In fact, there is more evidence to the contrary—that being or feeling productive can be rewarding in its own right or can lead to other rewards.

(4) For some people, job satisfaction is not a means to achieving other ends. It may be an end in itself and should be so considered.

(5) All of us have preferences among the various outcomes that are potentially the result of our efforts. Our expectations that certain actions will lead to desired outcomes will lead to greater efforts on our parts, especially if those outcomes are important to us, and if experience suggests that they are likely.

(6) Clarification of these factors can lead to more effective behavior on our part and on the part of others in the workplace, as well as those outside of work whose respect and esteem we value.

YOUR ADDITIONS

(7)

(8)

(9)

(10)

(11)

(12)

Exercise 1.5

Motivation/Satisfier

Read over the 15 items below. Put an X in each box that applies. Don't take too much time. Just X the items that most strongly reflect your concerns.

If I were looking for a job today, the things I would be most concerned about are:

____ 1. The extent to which I can be myself on the job.
____ 2. How well I fit in, whether I will feel accepted or as a stranger.
____ 3. Opportunities for teamwork and collaborative efforts.
____ 4. The salary being offered.
____ 5. Opportunities for advancement, assuming good performance.
____ 6. The extent to which the work I do will be really meaningful.
____ 7. Opportunities for growth and development.
____ 8. The kinds of health and other benefits available to employees.
____ 9. The relationship I will have with my supervisor.
____ 10. Whether by taking this job I can be of help to others.
____ 11. Whether by taking this job I can contribute to the kinds of social change I think important.
____ 12. How safe the workplace is, and how safe its location.
____ 13. What others might expect of me.
____ 14. Whether I will be recognized for my contributions.
____ 15. The extent to which this is likely to be a stressful place.

(Exercise 1.5 continued next page)

Now circle the number of statements you Xed in the grid below.

A	B	C
4	2	1
5	3	6
8	9	7
12	13	10
15	14	11

If your responses resulted in a preponderance of circles in Column A, you are security-oriented, concerned about income, advancement, benefits and safety. If your responses resulted in a preponderance of circles in Column B, you tend to be social in your orientation, putting emphasis on relationships with others and recognition of your efforts. If your responses resulted in a preponderance of circles in Column C, you tend to be concerned about self-fulfulling accomplishments, doing things that are worthwhile and helpful.

NOTE

1. If you are having difficulty making this assessment, do **Exercise 1.5** first.

REFERENCES

Alderfer, Clayton P. (1972). *Existence, relatedness and growth: Human needs in organizational settings*. New York: Free Press.

Aronson, Edward, & Carlsmith, J. M. (1962). Performance expectancy as a determinant of actual performance. *Journal of Abnormal and Social Psychology*, Spring.

D'Arcy, Carl, Syrotuik, John, & Siddique, C. (1984). Perceived job attributes, job satisfaction and psychological distress: A comparison of working men and women. *Human Relations, 37*(8).

Davett, Cynthia. (1983). Evaluation of the impact of feedback and performance and motivation. *Human Relations, 36*(7).

Farrell, Daniel, & Rusbult, Caryl E. (1981). Exchange variables as predictors of job satisfaction, job commitment, and turnover. The impact of reward, costs, alternatives, and investments. *Organizational Behavior and Human Performance, 28*(1).

Garland, Howard, & Berwick Smith, Gail. (1981). Occupational achievement motivation as a function of biological sex, sex-linked personality and occupational stereotypes. *Psychology of Women*, Summer.

Glicken, Virginia. (1980). Enhancing work for professional social workers. *Administration in Social Work*, Fall.

Herzberg, Fredrick. (1976). *The managerial choice: To be efficient or to be human*. Homewood, IL: Dow-Jones Irwin.

Herzberg, Fredrick, Mauser, Bernard, & Snyderman, Barbara. (1959). *The motivation to work* (2nd ed.). New York: John Wiley.

Kaplan, Abraham. (1964). *The conduct of inquiry*. San Francisco: Chandler.

Lawler, Edward E., III. (1973). *Motivation in work organizations*. Monterey, CA: Brooks/Cole.

Lawler, Edward E., III. (1977). Developing a motivating work climate. *Management Review*, July.

Lawler, Edward E., III, & Porter, Lyman W. (1967). The effect of performance on job satisfaction. *Industrial Relations*, October.

Maslow, Abraham H. (1954). *Motivation and personality*. New York: Harper & Row.

McClelland, David C. (1961). *The achieving society*. New York: D. Van Nostrand.

Pierce, Jone L. (1983). Job attitudes and motivation differences between volunteers and employees from comparable organizations. *Journal of Applied Psychology, 28*(4).

Porter, Lyman M., Lawler, Edward E., III, & Hackman, Richard. (1975). *Behavior in organizations*. New York: McGraw-Hill.

Quick, Thomas L. (1982). *Understanding people at work*. Englewood Cliffs, NJ: Prentice-Hall.

Richardson, Mary, & West, Peggy. (1982). Motivational management: Coping with burnout. *Hospital and Community Psychology*, October.

Schoderbeck, P. P., Schoderbeck, C. G., & Plambeck, D. L. (1982). A comparative analysis of job satisfaction. *Administration in Social Work, 3*(2).

Seybolt, John. (1976). Work satisfaction as a function of person-environment interaction. *Organizational Behavior and Human Performance*, January.

Tziner, Sharon. (1983). Correspondence between occupational rewards and occupational needs and work satisfaction. *Journal of Occupational Psychology, 57*, Summer.

Voydanoff, Patricia. (1980). Perceived job characteristics and job satisfaction among men and women. *Psychology of Women Quarterly, 5*, Winter.

Vroom, Victor H. (1964). *Work and motivation*. New York: John Wiley.

Chapter 2

RUBBING SHOULDERS AND RUBBING WOUNDS
Gender, Class, Culture, and Identity in the Workplace

Millicent Kapinski was perplexed; disturbed going on devastated might be a better description for how she was feeling. Friday night Yolanda Stephenson and her husband Reggie had been at her home with other members of the staff. It had been a quiet evening, full of good conversation and friendly bantering, marred only by occasional references to budget cuts resulting from shifts in government priority. Millicent had gone out of her way to make Reggie feel comfortable, sensitive to the fact that unlike the others present, he was not a professional and might find some of the discussions outside his interests.

Before leaving, Yolanda had taken Millicent by the hand and expressed how much she enjoyed the evening, how comfortable she had felt, and how much she appreciated the tasteful furnishings and especially the Polish rugs and craftwork that adorned the apartment's walls. "It's so good to be with someone who appreciates her own ethnic heritage, and I wish you would tell more about the artwork from Chile." Yolanda referred to the many artifacts Millicent had brought back from her five years in Latin America.

But here it was Tuesday, and Yolanda had barely said a word to her. In fact, when Millicent had invited Yolanda to brown bag it together, she had replied icily: "I don't have to *brown* bag anything, and I don't eat in the office," and turned away. "What's going on?" Millicent wondered.

Ali was wondering the same thing. "Hey," Ali called as Yolanda was going out the door. "If you're eating out today, mind if I join you?" "Not eating today," Yolanda tossed back with a tinge of irritation in her voice. But later at the Sandwiche Shoppe, there was Yolanda sitting in a booth with three other Black social workers from the agency. Yolanda had made it a point, Ali was certain, not to see her come in or acknowledge her presence. What *was* going on?

That afternoon, Sam dropped into Yolanda's office for a chat. He had been feeling isolated. His New Americans project was not all that well understood by others at the All-Families Center. Establishing outreach programs for the Southeast Asians—Thais and Vietnamese—who had recently begun to move into the south side, and for Arabs from Iraq, Lebanon and other parts of the Middle East, was new for the agency. Although given considerable latitude in developing the program, this freedom left him feeling insecure, sometimes "as alone and without anchor," he thought, as the people for whom he was trying to develop services. He had decided to seek out Yolanda for advice because he sensed her to be a person committed to the oppressed, and capable of empathy for others.

As he was sketching out some ideas, Yolanda suddenly interrupted, although erupted was more like it: "What's all this garbage about new Americans? You give the Vietnamese a thousand dollars each, and you help the *Ay*-rabs start businesses in Black neighborhoods throwing Blacks out of work. *We're* not new Americans. My family has been slaving away in this country for six generations. Nobody's giving *us* hand-outs. They're keeping us on the dole. Don't talk to me about no new Americans. We got to deal with *old* Americans first. We built this country and we're still on the outside!"

* * * * *

BLACK MAY BE BEAUTIFUL, BUT NOT WHEN YOU GOT TO BE WHITE TO SURVIVE

Clearly, Yolanda's behavior had shocked her White colleagues, but no more than it shocked Yolanda herself. For several weeks now, Yolanda had been lunching on Tuesdays with the other members of what they called the "BIB-Club" (for Black Is Beautiful). At first she'd hesitated to join. "Don't want to scare off my White colleagues," Yolanda exlained to one of the members. "They might think we're into some kind of plot." Over the years she had carefully built a work identity based on professional competence. She'd been dispassionate in her treatment of clients, both Black and White, and had cultivated pleasant and correct relationships with her co-workers at the agency and in other human service organizations. But her professionalism and success on the job were increasingly giving her trouble.

Like many others from racial or cultural minorities, she had been aware of how her integration into agency and professional life had required compromising her cultural self. And like many other Black women, she had consciously chosen to dress and behave in ways that her White colleagues would not find uncomfortable. She'd long ago given up her Afro for a more conservative, straightened hairstyle. Her dress-for-success "uniform" (generally a two-piece dark colored suit and a leather-bound attaché case) was accompanied by a controlled way of walking, and even of laughing and sharing intimacies. But there were no real intimacies. "Being Black is *intimate*," Yolanda was aware. Being White, for her, was being *distant*.

That is why she had finally begun to join her Black colleagues in the Tuesday Bib-Club sessions. It was a way of "letting my hair up," she joked to others at the table. Had Ali sat in the next booth, she might have overheard the following snatches of conversation:

> "You know, I boogie all the way to work. Got the radio on full force listening to Lionel Richie and any good soul or rock I can find. But I shut it off just before I get into the parking lot. Got to put on the mask. Some of my staff members know I'm into music and like to talk about jazz to me. But it's all that intellectual White "appreciation." Like talking about Fats Waller and Billie Holiday. I mean it's not *today*. Then they talk to me about Alvin Ailey and the Harlem Dance Company. It's condescending, you know? Know what I mean?"

> "There's no way I can be *me* at work. It's like my whole chain of Black identity is broken when I walk in the door. It's survival, but it's survival without vitality. Sure, we've overcome the barriers of being Black and being women, but we're still outsiders."

> "It's worse when I go home. My Joe wants me to be cookin' up his chitlins 'n greens and talks about the studs at the garage. I'm taking tranquilizers and he's into booze. It's no life."

"Least you got you a man! My man up and split. Couldn't take it that I was earning more than him and that folks were calling me 'Mrs.' while they was calling him 'Jim.' "

" 'Boy,' you mean."

The feelings expressed in these snatches of conversation are not atypical. Blacks and other minorities in many areas of professional employment find themselves caught between competing identities. As they enter new worlds they face a collision of values, contradictions in life-styles, pulls away from their cultural or ethnic identities. For some, the pressures can become so great as to generate despair that is no less painful than that of the most poverty-stricken ghetto dweller. It can result in a loss of creative vitality, a severing of the Black or other "sinew" that provides the strength to cope with an often hostile or uncaring environment. Similar conclusions can be made about people from other ethnic or cultural backgrounds. Yolanda's responses to Millicent's party, to Ali's invitation to go to lunch together, and to Sam's ideas about immigrant absorption can be understood against this background.

It wasn't until Yolanda had returned home from Millicent's that she realized how different their lives were. She had allowed herself to relax that evening, to enjoy the surroundings, to appreciate a White woman's furnishings and artwork, another person's cultural heritage. And despite her own position at the agency and her own good taste—she had decorated her home on the northwest side of town with the same meticulous care she had lavished on her own grooming—she felt that her own home would never be as natural and without artificiality as Millicent's. The only thing missing, short of an artifact or photograph here or there, was any evidence of her Blackness. "What would I do with African masks?" she wondered, thinking with some jealousy of the tapestries and pottery Millicent had brought back from South America. And yet, despite the absence of artifacts, Yolanda was certain that her White colleagues would have felt uncomfortable in her home.

What had made things worse was Reggie's response to the evening. "Next time we go to your friends' place, we go in *my* car." Reggie drove a Cadillac that he had carefully and lovingly reconditioned. Yolanda, wary of the stereotype, had purchased a small Datsun for going to work and to use on agency business. "I'm not puttin' my Black ass in your car," she had retorted. "Want me to act like a "nigger?" "You *is* a nigger, a *house* nigger. You ain't got no Black ass."

The fight that followed lasted most of the night. The aftermath lasted longer. Through it all, Yolanda was aware that she was undergoing a profound process of reevaluation. She was lucky—lucky that she was a professional social worker and aware of the many reasons for her reactions. But until now these were reasons she had kept carefully tucked away, applying her knowledge to clients but rarely to herself.

The most recent U.S. Census data report that about 300 Black women were divorced for every 1000 marriages—twice the number as for Whites. Yolanda knew that for Black women with post-B.A. professional training, the figure was 20% higher. She also knew that twice as many Black women were getting professional degrees today as ten years earlier. But for Black men, the percentages had declined by between 10% and 15%. The opportunities that had been opened up for Blacks with the civil rights movement of the 1960s and the Affirmative Action programs of the 1970s had had differential effects for men and women. Yolanda and Reggie were in danger of allowing societal forces to pull them apart.

But Yolanda needed Reggie. She needed the intimacy, the directness of their relationship, the sensuousness in his mannerisms and his movements. Yet she knew that Reggie didn't fit in her predominantly middle-class life-style, a life-style she had never become comfortable with but to which she had clung with the same tenacity with which she had completed school and strived to represent her race and gender at work without ever pushing either. She would break the stereotypes by being good, better than most of her White counterparts at the work she did. But the strains were finally catching up, creating stress that was threatening to unravel everything she had so carefully built, both at home and at work.

By compromising her cultural self, Yolanda had found herself alone, separated from her Black friends no less than from her White colleagues, and from her own husband and his friends. She was certain that the migraines that were beginning to reappear, migraines she had not suffered since college, were symptoms of her isolation. Members of the BIB-Club reported similar psychosomatic symptoms, including menstrual cramps and backaches. Hypertension, diabetes and strokes—common killers of Black women in America—might not be far behind. Tranquilizers, alcohol abuse and cocaine—remedies sought by some of her friends—were not for her.

"Black may be beautiful," she thought, "but not when you got to be White to survive."

* * * * *

OBJECTIFYING OTHERS AT WORK

How White does Yolanda have to be? Harvey Marcus had once objected to her reference to him as White. She had shrugged off his comment without fully understanding the depth from which his remark had come. Yolanda had told him how much she respected his aggressiveness and creativity in seeking new funds and expanding programs for those whom he called "oppressed minorities." "It's easier for you White radical liberals," she had remarked, thinking of how much of an activist Reggie had been when they first met, and how into his car and beer he had become.

"I'm not White," Harvey had responded. "You must be foolin', Harv, you don't look to me like a man of color." "I'm not, but I'm not White either," Harvey had explained with a seriousness that was not normally a part of his demeanor. "I'm Jewish. After the Holocaust, there's no way I could consider myself anything else. You know, it's pretty easy to mistake someone's identity. I was in here one evening in my jeans and a blue workshirt cleaning out some papers, and a new staff member of the children's department asked me to help him move some shelves. He just assumed I was the janitor."[1]

Yolanda had not been ready to deal with Harvey's self-revelation at the time, passing it off with some "dumb remark" she did not remember. But she wondered at it now. And she wondered about Millicent, about Ali and about Sam. Who were they really? Who was she? What were the many pieces that made her into who she was? And why could she not integrate those pieces into a whole personality? Who, besides herself, would she offend in doing so? Who else would she offend if she could not?

A competent professional, Yolanda was aware of the injunction, "Physician, heal thyself." She set out to do so, painful and risky as the process might be. She began by looking at how she perceived others at work, rather than the ways in which she might imagine they perceived her. "I know me," she reasoned. "I don't know them."

In fact, she had painted them, she realized, monochromatically. But Harvey objected to being painted white. Did he also object to her defining him as a "radical liberal," even if the labeling was done in jest? How much fun was there in her remark; how much resentment? She recalled having difficulty with his name when they first got to know each other. "This is Harvey Shapiro," she had once introduced him to a friend. But Harvey's last name was Marcus. Why the confusion in names? Was she also stereotyping him? Name confusion, she realized, often occurs when we are objectifying others, defining them in stereotypic ways, or treating them as part of a "class" in an effort to assign to them certain categories of thought and behavior. As a Black and a woman, she had been the victim of similar slips of the tongue more than once.

Although she had met Millicent long after the older woman had left the Church, Yolanda still thought of her as "the nun," visualizing her in a black habit. Perhaps that was why she had been so shocked to find Millicent's home so warm, and so tastefully and ethnically furnished. Somehow her image of a nun had been different. She had expected a more stark environment.

And what about Sam? His middle name, Fauod, added to his round shape and Mediterranean complexion, brought to mind images of King Farouk, the deposed monarch of Egypt she had first learned about in high school. Sometimes she even thought of him as a monarch, smiling to herself at the designation, and resenting the fact that he was becoming "king" of all those new immigrants. Objectification again? For sure. In truth, Sam had none of the mannerisms associated with the real Farouk. He was a decent, hard-working man, as committed, perhaps more so, to his constituents as she was to her people. No wonder she felt resentment. It wasn't Sam she was resenting as much herself and the centuries of isolation, racism and persecution her own people had suffered. Why take it out on Sam and his new Americans?

Her feelings about Ali were more complex, more difficult to come to terms with. "Why was I so damned irritated when she invited me to lunch? It wasn't just that I was sneaking off to a meeting of the BIB-Club; it was something more. By the grace of God, and my own hard work," Yolanda realized, "I could have been in Ali's job, nothing more than a receptionist. '*Nothing more* than a receptionist!' " Had she absorbed society's sexist and racist definitions? Was she saying that Blacks should be receptionists and had no right to be administrators in an agency? Was she resenting the respect Ali received for the way she did her work, even though she had no professional qualifications? Was she downgrading Ali's contributions to the agency because of a class bias? She would have to work on this one, she realized. It's no easy thing to confront your own bias and your own pain!

Perhaps it's time now to confront some of *your* pain—as a man or woman, member of a racial or ethnic minority, native born or foreign born, new or experienced staff member, heterosexual or gay, young in age or older.

* * * * *

WOMEN'S WORK

Perhaps it is time to find out a bit more about Ali and Millicent. If Ali were to be asked, she would tell everyone she loves her job. "I don't know if I was made for this kind of work or if the job was made for me," she told her mother a few weeks after beginning work at the agency. That was eight years ago.

Ali likes to manage. She always has. As the eldest of five siblings, she had helped her mother with chores around the house, caring for the younger children. After her mother had taken ill—Ali was 11 at the time—she took over the household until her mother regained her strength and was able to return home. No one spoke much about the hospital[2] where Mrs. Schultz had been confined for two years, but Ali knew it had something to do with her mother's depression. Ali's mother had never been a strong person. Even when she returned home, she seemed content, even relieved that Ali was able to take such good care of her three school-aged brothers and her baby sister.

Ali and her father, a foreman at the Stroh's brewery, had grown closer after her mother had been hospitalized, but it had seemed to Ali that as she grew older, that closeness was built on her father's dependence—a dependence that did not disappear when her mother returned. "I'm not cut out for housework and bringing up kids," her father had once told her. "Thank God I have you." Ali liked being needed.

Although she did not do particularly well at school—there was never enough time to do school-related homework with so much "real" homework to do—her teachers liked Ali and gave her good marks on her report cards, more perhaps for her pleasant manner than her intellectual contributions. But Ali's school work was always neat and turned in on time. "Competent" and "a contributor" were adjectives nearly always handwritten on the "work habits" and "citizen-

Exercise 2.1

Confronting the Pain

Think back on instances in which you were treated as a member of a class with the expectation that you would think or behave in some stereotypic manner—a manner that was more than painful.

1. How did you feel about it?

2. How did you respond?

3. What was the response to your response?

4. How should you have responded?

Now that you've examined how others look at you and your responses, take a look at how you view them.

Exercise 2.2

Objectification Assessment

Look over your assessments of Yolanda and the others in **Exercise 1.1** of the first chapter. Because information on each of the six staff members was so brief, you were forced to make some assumptions about each. You may not know much more at this point about the other three names you yourself added.

1. Begin by checking whether your assessment was in some way based on objectification by gender, race/ethnicity or class.
2. Jot down some of your thoughts about why you responded as you did. Follow as thoroughly honest a process as Yolanda did. It won't be easy.

OBJECTIFIED BY:

	Gender	Race/ Ethnicity	Class	Your Thoughts
Yolanda				
Sam				
Ali				
Millicent				
Carl				
Harvey				
1.				
2.				
3.				

ship" columns. The only negative comment she remembered was from her fifth-grade teacher, who wrote "bites her nails too much." This had embarrassed Ali.

Ali was a good citizen. She had to be. It was expected of her. And if she was not competent, who would be? Now with her youngest sister still in high school, Ali continued to live at home, getting up early to fix breakfast for her father, who had to be at the plant by 7:00 a.m., and Martha, who had a 7:15 a.m. Driver's Ed class. This gave her plenty of time to get to the office early, turn on the lights, plug in the coffee, and put the day's schedule in order.

When Yolanda had run out in a huff and then ignored her at the Sandwiche Shoppe, Ali had been thrown into a near panic. She sat at a table alone, unable to touch her food. It felt almost like the day they had taken her mother to the hospital. Ali bought a pack of cigarettes, the first she had opened in three months. Back at work, Ali had pushed any disquieting and depressing thoughts to the back of her mind and reasserted her outward pleasantness. But something seemed empty inside. It felt only a slight bit better at the end of the day when Yolanda stopped by to say she was sorry about being so gruff, that she'd had something on her mind and needed to talk it over with some friends. "But I'm your friend, too," Ali thought, resentful of Yolanda's preference for being with other Black women.

For Yolanda, the apology was not without effort. "She seems so comfortable in her work, like a busy housewife. She's all things I can't seem to be. All the things I've been running away from. Maybe that's what irritates me so," she thought as she inched out of the driveway and reached absentmindedly for the car radio.

* * * * *

Millicent Kapinski was the seventh of eight children and the only girl. Not much had been expected of her as she grew up. A quiet child, the only one in the family without a Polish or Catholic name, Millicent never felt that she quite fit in the family. Given to daydreaming and drawing pictures in her schoolbooks, Mili (she never liked the nickname either) did not have very many friends. She cried bitterly when Mary, her best friend, moved out of the neighborhood.

The first two years of high school were a nightmare for Millicent. She thanked God that her parents had seen fit to send her to parochial school. But even there, the talk among her girlfriends was always about boys and sex. She just did not want to think about boys that way and was equally disgusted by her brothers' talk at home and the innuendos and often overt sexual approaches by John and Stash. She remembered with shame how they had once made her "pee" standing up. She had never confessed this to a priest, and the shame of it was something she could not rid herself of. Priests were men, like her brothers. How could they be trusted?

Her first sense of being someone came when one of the sisters at school approached her to ask that she tutor younger children for their catechism. She loved tutoring younger children and soon volunteered to help out in the Sunday morning day care center in her parish. Later she joined the Latin and Spanish clubs at school, and to her surprise was elected president of the latter. Here, for the first time, she found herself expressing ideas and taking responsibility for special projects. And she liked the feel of it.

No one was surprised when Millicent decided to join Sacred Heart and become a teacher. For Millicent, it had seemed the natural thing to do. She was good with children, cared about them and wanted to reach out to others who, like herself, felt isolated and alone as they were growing up.

Sister Peter Claver, as she was now known, was a fine teacher, creative and caring, well liked by parents, children and colleagues. Her Mother Superior, a warm and supportive woman, saw in the young nun an imaginative educator. She would probably still be teaching today if it had not been for the civil rights movement of the late 1960s and early 1970s. Increasing numbers of Black children were enrolling in the school as White Catholics moved out of the neighborhood and the Church reached out to those less fortunate. She sensed in herself a prejudice about many of the children and had a difficult time understanding their English. "Am I being racist in the way I feel about them?" she wondered.

Sister Peter did a lot of reading about the Black community. She read *Malcolm X Speaks,* Frantz Fanon and others who spoke with a radical and angry voice. And then she found her way to Paolo Friere's *Pedagogy of the Oppressed,* and other writings by liberationalist theologians. She was not alone in her discovery of new and challenging ideologies. There were others in her order, as well as Jesuits at the nearby seminary, who were exploring the same ideas. It was not long before she found herself in the company of Catholic men and women, some of whom had "gone over the wall," who were as questioning of both the Church and their own beliefs as she was. Finding herself increasingly in conflict with Church policy over birth control and abortion, she finally came to the conclusion that there were too many pregnant teenagers, "too much despair, delinquency and substance abuse" around her that others refused to see. If her way was blocked within the Church, she would find a way of dealing with these issues outside it.

After 20 years of teaching, Millicent quietly resigned from her job and her order, took off her habit and returned to the university where she earned a master's degree in adult and continuing education. "That first semester I could hardly concentrate on my studies. I didn't know who I was. I was grieving, grieving for a lost identity and I had to find a new one. Crazy, isn't it? Here I was, 42 years old and I didn't know who I was. Life as I had experienced it had gone sour. Doing my rosaries was no solace." The company and support of other former clerics (she shared a house near the campus with two former nuns and two ex-priests) gave her strength to pass through months of crisis. "I came out of it all the stronger, my own woman for the first time."

On completing her MA, Millicent and another former nun traveled to South America, where they worked at first in small villages in Argentina. In the beginning she felt helpless, as helpless as the Indian villagers with whom she worked. "Are they really capable of change?" she asked herself. The more she worked with the poor, the more she realized that the problem was not in them but in herself. She began to probe her own childhood, her biases, her own racist feelings. All her readings and all her teaching skill, she came to understand, were of no use unless she could understand her own responses to the situation in which she found herself. If these self-confrontations were so difficult for her, she realized, how much more difficult must they be for the villagers? Yet simple people as they were, she found them open to change and growth. She must grow with them.

It was the only way she could deal with her own malignancy—the same class and ethnic biases that led to the oppression (and acceptance of oppression) of those she had set out to help. When the political climate made further educational and community development efforts unsafe, she went first to Chile and then decided to return home. By that time she had developed a critical consciousness—*conscienizacion*, as it was called in Latin America. And she had learned to use *conscienizacion* as a training tool for helping others understand themselves in their situations. It was as much a political as an educational process.

Teachers like herself, in interaction with local people acting collectively, could make a difference. The difference emerged from relationships that led people to "name the world"—that is, to reperceive their personal and social realities, recognizing that neither were fixed, that through critical awareness and action one could synthesize one's values and take responsibility for both self- and communal development. The unity she had once sought in the Trinity she now found in a dialectic of thought and action that led to a renewed commitment to becoming.

Now, six years later, Millicent had integrated both her philosophy and her skills and applied them to the family education programs conducted under the agency's auspices. Her current situation was not without strain, but Millicent was not a flaming militant. She was too old for that. "It might have been different if I had matured earlier," she thought. The best thing a "retread" can do is provide a safe and comfortable ride. And that is how she saw herself—as a support to both clients and staff in their efforts to become and to arrive at destinations of their own choosing.

Others on the staff sought Millicent out on their off hours. She accepted them with whatever they brought—not seeking their confessions but careful not to set up barriers to communication or to engender guilt and fearful emotions. She still recalled her early experience in the confessional booth. "I listen and I probe a bit, trying to get others to reach a little beyond themselves. Maybe I'm a little too pushy sometimes. Guess that's why I've become everyone's Polish mother, with a bit of Mother Superior thrown in."

That is also why she did not take offense at Yolanda's "brown bag" remark. "She's feeling some pain," Millicent thought. "Women understand pain, and that's a good start for any dialogue."

UNDERSTANDING PAIN

Like Yolanda, Ali, and Millicent, none of us is free of gender, racial, and class biases. But to recognize those biases, especially if we ourselves have been victimized by them, takes considerable courage. It entails great risk, both to the defenses we have set up and to the definitions of ourselves we have created to support a positive self-image. And if we strip either defenses or definitions away, what will be left?

Millicent learned, albeit late in life, that in order to help others confront the conditions of racism and classism, she had first to confront those feelings in herself. Unless she did, there was no way she could ask her childhood confessional priest, or the Indian villagers with whom she worked, for forgiveness. Asking for such forgiveness required ascribing to them a goodness she did not feel in herself. But asking others to forgive us assumes that they possess qualities that we do not. And since they are likely to be equally crippled by bias and ignorance, we are bound to be disappointed in them as we are in ourselves. Objectifying others by ascribing superior values or capacities to them can be as crippling as ascribing negative values to them. Both are nonstarters. Guilt and self-doubt are feelings, and we are not, Millicent had come to understand, to be blamed for our feelings. Her South American experience had taught her that feelings are to be dealt with for the sake of our own liberation. We are none of us ever quite free of ourselves and our situations.

Yolanda was taking the first steps toward such recognition in confronting her feelings about her husband, her co-workers, and herself. But what of Ali? She seems to have carved out a niche for herself, a comfortable one. If one asked her, she would shrug off with a smile any suggestion that she too suffered from oppression. Yolanda's assessment would seem to confirm Ali's own. Perhaps it is not Ali's apparent satisfaction in her situation that nags at Yolanda so, but rather the budding recognition that beneath Ali's pleasantness and competence is a person just as oppressed by the need to respond to the expectations and praises of others as Yolanda often feels because of her Black skin and the prejudices of a society that has not rid itself of racism and sexism.

Each of the staff members in the agency, as is the case for each of its clients, suffers some pain. We have only touched on Yolanda's, Ali's, and Millicent's, and we have barely scratched the surface of Sam's, Harvey's, and Carl's. It is not likely that these agency workers will resolve the conflicts and contradictions in their lives that we generally refer to in shorthand as "hang-ups." But Millicent and Yolanda have taken major steps to confront theirs.

For Millicent, this required taking on a new identity and redefining her situation in political terms. For Yolanda, the process of reevaluation is taking a psychological and sociological turn, in keeping with the knowledge and skills she has developed as a social worker. For Ali, an awakening, if it is to occur, may stem from the feelings of anxiety she experienced from Yolanda's apparent rejection. For all three, childhood experiences and the process of growing up and entering the world of work were central factors. For Yolanda, being

Exercise 2.3

Confronting Your Own Pain

Jot down some incidents in which relationships with colleagues, supervisors, subordinates or clients at work touched at the core of your identity—incidents that caused real pain.

1.

2.

3.

Now jot down situations in which something you said or did touched an identity nerve in someone else. Was it a gender nerve, class nerve, race or ethnic identity nerve?

1.

2.

3.

Black in America is at the core of her identity. It is perceived by her as the major factor in understanding her behavior and responses to others.

HELP FROM THE BEHAVIORAL SCIENCES

Each of us has a psychosocial-biological developmental history and a racial-gender-cultural history that help shape our behavior. We need not be nonassertive captives of our pasts. To the contrary, these histories give meaning to the present and make it possible to shape the future responsibly.

I will briefly recap the contributions of two men to our understanding of personal development: Freud and Erikson. You are probably already acquainted with their concepts. In fact, I have selected them because of their familiarity. I recognize that the ideas that each man propounded generated some controversy, and that more recent contributions to the scientific literature have both supported and challenged what each of these "stage theorists" has to teach us.

Sigmund Freud, whose theories, according to Jerome Bruner, might better be characterized as "metaphor," or "drama," was the first in modern times to stress that impulses below the level of awareness have an impact on our feelings and behavior. According to Freud, the struggle between instinctive drives (libido) and societal prohibitions is what gives rise to both personality and behavior. Those impulses that are considered antisocial and for which we are punished or threatened are turned inward only to find new expression as hang-ups, neuroses, dreams, slips of the tongue, art and literature, religion and ideology, myth and other cultural and personal expressions.

Freud postulated five libidinal or psychosocial stages through which all human beings pass. Should we be unsuccessful in resolving conflicts at any of these stages, the resulting frustration may lead to inappropriate and even bizarre behavior. For some, the pleasures associated with each stage may result in fixation and a subconscious refusal to move on to the next stage of development. For example, Freud thought that the source of conflict in the *oral* stage (birth to 18 months) is the cessation of breast feeding or a satisfactory substitute. Fixation at this stage may lead to insatiable demands for mothering (which may be sublimated into its opposite, the need to mother others), verbal abuse, excessive oral behaviors like compulsive eating and nail biting, smoking, and alcoholism.

Children passing through the *anal* stage (18 to 36 months) face potential conflict at the point of toilet training, sometimes finding outlets in such later behaviors as superconformity and preoccupation with rules, compulsive neatness, or in defiance of authority and eruptions of hostility. The *phallic* stage (3 to 7 years) can lead to the Oedipal complex in boys and the Electra complex in girls. In adult life these can be expresed as fear of sexual relationships, frigidity or impotence, homosexuality or difficulty in handling competitive relationships.

Although he considered them of lesser importance in shaping adult personality, Freud also postulated two other stages. The *latency* period is associated with the elementary school years in which boys learn to behave like boys and girls like girls. Sexual reawakening at puberty launches a *genital* period in which equilibriums established earlier are upset. Social and political commitments, romantic attachments to people and causes are born here and may significantly influence occupational choice and personal identity.

Freud and his followers described a number of ego defenses that people use to protect themselves from the pain associated with the anxiety and emotional conflict arising from incomplete or unsuccessful coping in earlier stages:

(1) *repression* (driving a threatening thought or impulse from conscious awareness in an effort to avoid anxiety and guilt);

(2) *displacement* (taking out one's frustration or pent-up hostility on someone "safe," usually someone weaker who cannot or will not strike back—instead of at those directly responsible for our discomfort—a process associated with scapegoating);

(3) *projection* (in which persons attribute their own feelings of rage or prejudice to others because the otherwise resultant feelings of guilt and self-blame might be too difficult to bear);

(4) *denial* (refusal to acknowledge an unpleasant reality);

(5) *sublimation* (in which unacceptable behaviors are repressed only to reemerge in a more socially acceptable form, as for example when rage is turned to social activism);

(6) *regression* (in effect, returning to an earlier and less pressured stage when under heavy strain or stress);

(7) *reaction-formation* (behaving in ways that are directly opposite to one's inclinations because those inclinations are for some reason unacceptable to the actor); and

(8) *rationalization* (by which people find convincing reasons for acting in ways they might otherwise find unacceptable).

If you have had analytic training or are working in an agency that employs analytically oriented therapies, these terms will be familiar to you. On the one hand, you will know enough to realize that quick diagnoses can be harmful, leading to the same process of objectification that we discussed with regard to race, class, ethnicity, and gender. Besides, what good would it do to define Ali's personality as oral, Yolanda's as anal, or Millicent's as compounded by an Electra complex? On the other hand, awareness of ego defenses can be helpful.

Clearly, Millicent understood Yolanda's anger as *displacement*. Will she be equally aware of the extent to which her professional choices have been a *sublimation* of other less (to her) acceptable behaviors? Yolanda, as she pursues her own efforts to understand the reactions she has to other staff members, will recognize that her desire not to offend Whites through unacceptable dress and mannerisms is at least partially related to projective mechanisms, an expression of her own racial and cultural biases. On the surface of things, Ali seems to have it pretty well together. But the anxiety, almost a feeling of panic, she experienced following Yolanda's rejection—her nervous nail biting and return to smoking—suggest that she is a prisoner of a variety of repressions.

Helpful as these constructs are in understanding behavior, you may find Erikson's expanded stages of development even more useful. Erik Erikson, a trained psychoanalyst, possessed a deep sense of history and an appreciation for the methods and concepts derived from anthropology. Much of his research focused on the development of personality and identity. Unlike Freud, he put considerable emphasis on the later stages of development.

According to Erikson, healthy psychosocial development occurs only with the successful resolution of crises at each of eight stages. These stages are labeled (1) infancy; (2) early childhood; (3) fourth to sixth year; (4) sixth year to onset of puberty; (5) adolescence; (6) young adulthood; (7) adulthood; and (8) old age. Although Erikson's work has also been criticized for being too global (especially with regard to the latter two stages, which might be subdivided into more segments that reflect additional crises), we can learn a great deal from it. Keep in mind that a number of researchers have accepted the eight stages described by Erikson but have concluded that personality and identity continue to develop in adulthood as people cope with new challenges and situations.

Infancy (birth to one year) is that stage in which a person learns trust or mistrust. Those who experience consistent and genuine affection, cuddling and responsive care come to view the world as safe and dependable. In contrast, those whose infancy is unpredictable, chaotic or characterized by rejection are likely to perceive the world with fear and suspicion. In early childhood (second and third years), the child explores and develops motor skills. Those who are allowed freedom without overprotection are likely to mature into autonomous individuals, freed of the shame and fear that might otherwise accompany attempting new tasks without sufficient competence or skill.

The theme of freedom is again central to the fourth and fifth years. Those overly confined or restricted are not likely to assume initiative in later life. To the contrary, they are more likely to experience the impulse to be different and creative with a sense of guilt and foreboding. As the child enters and progresses through elementary school, he or she develops either a sense of industry, of mastery over self and environment, or of inferiority and the inability to compete successfully. It is often at this stage that differences in expectations for boys and girls may shape their self-concepts. In some communities, the expectations may be different for Whites or Blacks, Hispanics or Anglos, or for children from middle-class or working-class families. Children may be tracked into different careers and may perceive their life chances according to how they are perceived by others.

Adolescence is that stage when young people try on different identities, shedding uncomfortable ones for others they think might fit better. But the turbulence in this period can also result in role confusion, an inability to develop a centered, positive identity. This is also a period when identity can be shaped by taking on a calling, an ideology, a commitment to people by means of a faith or ideology. The capacity to develop intimacy, to identify with others, to share, care and empathize may occur in young adulthood. The fear of rejection, however, may generate shallow relationships, withdrawal and isolation.

Adults, according to Erikson, if they have dealt successfully with earlier challenges, can reach out beyond their immediate concerns to embrace the well-being of their children and the welfare of others—the society, a particular subgroup or even future generations. He calls this *generativity.* In contrast, some adults become self-centered, concerned only with their own physical well-being and the accumulation of possessions. These Erikson describes as boxed into a process of stagnation. All adults, according to him, strive for some unity, for the integration of their many selves and many experiences. But some see no unity and feel no satisfaction for what they are or for what they have accomplished. Thus, as they approach old age, some may become overwhelmed by a sense of despair, a feeling that there is just insufficient time left to right the many wrongs, to take another path or to try out an alternative road to integrity.

Bernice Neugarten, a sociologist who has concentrated much of her research on the elderly, concludes that age alone is not a decisive factor in personality development—that given the right environment and encouragement, people at any age can grow in their capacities to trust, become more autonomous, assume guilt-free initiative, achieve, take on new roles and assume more positive identities, establish intimacy, assume responsibility for others, and arrive at a sense of wholeness and integrity.

To what extent does your workplace provide the context for such development? To what extent are the agency's environment, its procedures and rules more likely to generate distrust, doubt, guilt, inferiority, role-confusion, isolation, stagnation and even despair? What accounts for your answers: the personalities involved, the agency's rules and procedures, or the expectations imposed on it by forces outside the agency (e.g., accountability mechanisms, funder's requirements, relationships to other agencies, expectations of clients)?

There are two other major schools of psychology, both of which take exception to the developmental psychologists represented by Freud and Erikson. Each may contribute some additional insights into the behavior of the staff member we have been observing and that of individuals in your own workplace. One school is generally associated with the label of "behaviorism" and the other with "humanistic" psychology.

The behaviorist paradigm or model of reality is considerably different from the developmental approach. In most ways, the two models are irreconcilable. Yet we can learn much from each. Behaviorists begin with the assumption that scientists must restrict themselves to observations of behavior. According to them, assumptions about hidden meanings or inferences about cause made from the examination of symptoms is art, not science. Although most behaviorists no longer believe, as did John Watson, a pioneer in American psychology, that all behavior is learned and that none of it is the result of heredity or biology, the influences and stimuli of the environment continue to be of paramount importance in their analysis.

As early behavioral experimentation by B. F. Skinner and others has demonstrated, people (and animals) learn both to generalize and to discriminate in response to stimuli. *Stimulus generalization* refers to the learned ability to match new sensory inputs (sights, sounds, tastes, smells, or touches) with previously absorbed and similar information. The greater the perceived resemblance between the original stimulus and the new situation, the greater the likelihood of a similar (and strong) response. This makes it possible to assimilate earlier experiences, to learn from them, and to apply our learning to new situations. For example, Yolanda's rush out of the agency was perceived by Ali as a form of personal rejection (perhaps related to the sudden hospitalization of Ali's mother). Yolanda's hypersensitivity to hints of racism is a similar example of stimulus generalization.

In contrast, *stimulus discrimination* refers to the ability to discriminate between relevant information and irrelevant information by responding to the former and ignoring the latter. Thus Millicent was able to discriminate between Yolanda's apparent rage and the causes of that rage, which had little to do with Millicent herself. In fact, her work in Latin America and her embracing of *conscienizacion* gave her a strategic tool for helping others reexamine how they respond to and understand the situations in which they find themselves. But Yolanda was trapped in confusion between generalization and discrimination in her responses to the stimuli of the evening at Millicent's. Inappropriate (mistaken) stimulus generalization leads to objectivation, while inappropriate stimulus discrimination can lead to missing important cues.

Appropriate behavioral responses can be reinforced positively, negatively or reciprocally. *Positive reinforcers,* when applied following a behavior, tend to be rewarding. If we want a particular reward and believe that it will be forthcoming—say, pleasant behavior on the part of colleagues or an increase of responsibility on the job (recall Vroom's and Porter's work on expectancy theory discussed in Chapter 1)—we are likely to act (put in the effort) in such a way as to gain the reward. By contrast, *negative reinforcers* may include the removal of a reward or the addition of a penalty or threat of punishment. Finally, *reciprocal reinforcers* are characteristic of much social interaction. Thus Ali's ready smile and her arrangement of the office early in the morning (including the preparation of coffee) lead others to respond to her pleasantly and with some affection. Their responses, in turn, reinforce Ali's desire to please and strengthen her expectation that she will be appreciated (rewarded) for her actions.

You may find these conceptions helpful or limiting. There is still another approach.

Humanistic psychology has sometimes been called a "third force." It is a reaction to the limitations of the traditions of behaviorism and psychoanalysis. Motivation psychologists such as Maslow and others, discussed earlier, maintain that people are different from other organisms in that they actively intervene in the course of events and shape the environments in which they live and work. Their concern is with optimizing the human potential for self-direction and self-actualization.

Carl Rogers, who was a leading figure in the "human potentials" movement, drew his notion of an environmental "field" from earlier work by Kurt Lewin. Boiling it all down into a nutshell, Rogers suggested the following: Short of pathological behavior, people share a basic desire to maintain and enhance themselves. Their behavior is essentially goal-directed, consisting of efforts to satisfy needs as they are experienced. Experience occurs in a social and material field—the environment. The way in which that environment is perceived is different for each person and constitutes his or her reality.

Such perceptions are accompanied by affect, emotions that support (facilitate) or detract from goal-directed behavior. So far, we have some additional support for what we already know about Ali, Millicent, and Yolanda. Clearly, the experience of becoming the substitute mother for one's younger siblings, or of being the only girl in a large family where girls were not much cared about, or growing up Black in a society where occupational success for a Black woman was perceived to be more the exception than the norm, had its effects on the three women as they were growing up. But what of the forces that might lead to growth and change, in contrast with rigidifying their current perceptions and behaviors?

Here, Rogers may be of some further help. He suggested that experiences that are inconsistent with our understanding of ourselves and of the organization of the self may be perceived as a threat. The greater the threat and the more of these perceptions there are, the more likely we are to organize our lives and ourselves so as to hold rigidly to what we are (in contrast to what we can become). The principle is one of self-defense. But removal of objective threats or changes in perception so that we no longer feel a threat to self-structure frees us to examine inconsistent experiences, assimilate these experiences and, in so doing, revise or expand ourselves. Thus human potential is relatively unlimited, and freedom comes with self-actualization.

We have already noted that Millicent and Yolanda are well into this process. Are there conditions in the work environment at the agency that contribute to such a reconstruction of self and reality? We may not have enough information on the agency to make such judgments yet. But what about *your* agency, the setting in which *you* work?

Before moving on, let's take a few moments to discuss still another perspective, one that has to a large extent shaped Millicent's awareness and that may help us to comprehend the French term *travail.* I am referring to the Marxian analysis of work and the forces that shape human behavior. The key concept in Marx's critique of civilization is that of alienation and estrangement. The division of labor in modern life, Marx argued, has led to man's becoming a cog in a wheel. Work, rather than encouraging integration, has led to fragmentation. Only parts of the person are valued at work; only parts of the person are treated when he or she becomes a patient, client, student, member, voter, and so on.

Through a process Marx called "thingification" *(Verdinglichung),* we have become commodities to be shaped and processed and used or sold by the very institutions we have created. In effect, these institutions repress the very life that brought them into being. The development of critical consciousness, *concienizacion,* is the first step in movement from alienation to a sense of belonging and commitment. Marx's idea of a classless society is not so different from Millicent's search for unity, wholeness, and integration.

For the individual, alienation can be reduced by taking on responsibility, by assuming ownership for one's actions. For the organization or for society, alienation can be reduced by a process of shared decision making, collective action and responsibility. To what extent do these concepts help you to better understand Yolanda's estrangement? Harvey's? Carl's?

GENDER-STEREOTYPING AT WORK: THE PINK-COLLAR SYNDROME

When it comes to gender studies, anthropologists and sociologists have tended to be as concerned with the differences (in contrast with

Exercise 2.4

Using Psychological Theories

Take a moment or two to reflect on what you know about behavior. We have briefly reviewed the major contributions of

—Sigmund Freud and Erik Erikson (psychoanalytic stage theorists)
—John Watson and B. F. Skinner (behaviorists)
—Abraham Maslow and Carl Rogers (humanistic psychologists)
and in the human potentials movement.

1. Which of these approaches do you find most useful; least useful? Why?

2. Now take the approach you find most compatible with your own world view (i.e., the one you find most useful) and apply it to a more comprehensive analysis of one of the staff members discussed in this chapter. What else do you need to know? What would you do with this information?

3. Finally, apply the same approach to examining yourself, your response to work-related stimuli and your relations to others on the job. What have you learned? What can you do with what you've learned?

the similarities) between men and women as have the psychologists. All three groups of social scientists are, in their own ways, embroiled in the arguments on the relative weight of hereditary versus environmental causes of gender-differential behavior. Sex-role stereotypes are almost as pervasive in the scientific literature as they are in other cultural expressions. This in itself is evidence of the impact of culture on gender-related roles and on how each of us deals with the expectations of others as we attempt to fulfill our expectations for ourselves.

We are all aware of the media-supported stereotypes of women as mothering and caring, child-focused, expert at reconciling conflict, concerned with attracting men and often using their sex to do so, capricious and emotional, supportive of their men on the one hand, and subtly outsmarting them on the other, scheming and succoring at the same time—stereotypes as contradictory and old as those associated with Eve. Stereotypes perform a number of interesting functions, regardless of whether they are contradictory or complementary and consistent.

First, they reduce the complexity of social reality into shortcuts to understanding, or at least explaining. Thus behaviors that are both assertive or submissive, clever or childlike, are likely to be found "typical of women." But when they are defined as atypical, the woman in question may be found wanting in femininity or aberrant in her behavior. Stereotypes also enable us to respond to behavioral cues in standard ways (generalization in contrast with differentiation). Standardized responses, while limiting, are often comfortable.

The comfort found in sex-stereotyping is as important to women as it is to men. It provides a woman with a sort of touched-up photograph, a treated mirror that enables her to see herself as others (both men and women) do. This looking-glass self becomes the model with which to conform, against which to judge one's own behavior and that of others. Deviation from this image of what one is or ought to be is fraught with danger. It can lead to social ostracism, condemnation, a loss of bearing when one steps "out of place." It can also lead to self-assessment as wicked or inferior, and to feelings of guilt that are associated with the rivalry between women and men.

What has only recently come to be realized is that the new rivalry with men, associated with women's emancipation, or "liberation" if you will, tends to be fought out in two arenas. The first is the general work arena in which women compete with men in occupations that have traditionally been closed to women: business and finance, politics, engineering, and so on. Here women and men have pushed for equal opportunity, equal pay, and other rewards.

The second arena is to be found in specialized occupations in which it has been assumed that women, because of their distinctive qualities, have a special contribution to make. I don't mean secretarial or receptionist work like Ali's. Arguments that women are better suited than men for such jobs can easily be disposed of despite the fact (or perhaps because of it) that they articulate with the biases that relegate women to supportive or secondary positions at work as well as at home.

I am referring instead to the preponderance of women in what have come to be known as the "pink-collar" occupations: nursing, teaching, social work and other human services. Thus even occupations have been dichotomized according to presumed male and female characteristics. The impact that this can have on both career choice and job satisfaction, and on one's personal life, can be illustrated by some of Yolanda's earlier experiences in school and at work.

* * * * *

As an undergraduate, Yolanda had considered majoring either in communications or business—careers, she reasoned, that would pull her forever out of poverty and permit her to put many of her skills to good use. She was discouraged, however, by the anticipated pressures of having to prove herself in work settings where neither women nor Blacks had made any major headway. Volunteer work as a tutor in her sophomore year had given her so much personal satisfaction that she decided social work was both more accessible and more likely to be rewarding—perhaps not in dollars earned, but in terms of acceptance both within the profession itself and within her own family. Her parents would understand social work, and so would her brothers and her friends. But Yolanda still had other dreams.

The first job she took on completing her MSW was as counselor in a GM plant. "If I make it there," she confided to a friend, "maybe I can move into other areas of management." It was at the plant that she had met Reggie, a line foreman whose "style" she felt comfortable with. Yolanda worked hard; she had to. "I felt that if I was successful, I would do something not only for myself, but for women and Blacks too. It was a real motivator.

"I did my work and I did it well, got promoted twice. Then one day I realized the secure structure I'd constructed for myself wasn't built out of bricks at all. It was a flimsy house made of cards and it all came tumbling down." Yolanda had been asked to prepare a proposal for creating an employee assistance program. A concept paper had to be ready in one week. It was, competently and professionally prepared. But it was turned down on review by executives higher up. That in itself did not upset Yolanda.

"What the hell, you can't win on every score. But it's the way my boss handled it that really got to me. 'Sorry, kid, don't sweat it. I guess it was too much pressure to put on a woman.' The bastard really had me in a bind. Here he was trying to be nice, showing me he 'respected' women, but all the time assuming that we couldn't deal with pressures. What did he think, that a man could have done better?"

When Yolanda did well, she had come to realize, she was considered the exception—both as a woman and as a Black. But when she did not succeed, her failures were branded as "collective." Small comfort!

It was about this time that her relationship with Reggie was also coming under some strain. "He just couldn't hack the fact that I was in management, talking to the higher-ups. The guys on the line would razz him about being married to one of the bosses. His being a line foreman didn't make any difference. He still was coming to work in his blues while I wore a black suit and carried an attaché case. 'You don't belong there,' he told me when I told him about the 'pressure on women' remark. He was right.

"That's when I decided to look for a job in a social work agency where I really did belong."

* * * * *

Yolanda's experiences are not atypical. How has sex-stereotyping affected you at work? How did it affect the kind of work you decided to undertake? How would you have reacted to the pressures Yolanda was under? How have you contributed to sex-stereotyping in your agency?

REVIEW AND TENTATIVE CONCLUSIONS

Clearly, rubbing shoulders with others whose histories, psychological reactions, and racial-gender-ethnic-class identities are different from ours can open up scars that we thought long healed. Rubbing shoulders at work can rub old wounds sore.

What conclusions can we draw from all this? I'll list a few. You should then review the chapter and your own work experiences and add others.

(1) Men and women, Blacks and Whites, middle-class and working-class people are different, but much less different than they are the same. An appreciation and acceptance of commonalities and differences is essential to effective working relationships on the job.
(2) Each of us bears some pain that is the result of historical and cultural forces and the ways we have perceived and interacted with those forces. Rubbing shoulders at work is likely to open old sores and may even generate new wounds.
(3) The development of critical consciousness is related to our capacity and willingness to confront the confusion that arises out of inappropriate stimulus generalization, when stimulus discrimination would be more appropriate. This requires freeing ourselves to confront consistent experiences and to integrate inconsistent ones in the emergence of self and identity.
(4) Our work-related identities are not distinct from our personal identities. Identity, once established, is not fixed. Although it is shaped by the ways in which we have confronted crises at various stages of development, conditions at work and our perceptions of those conditions can either reinforce current identities or lead us to change (both positively and negatively).
(5) The relationships we establish with others on the job are to a certain extent shaped by our stereotypes of people and positions. These can lead to objectification, when in fact a comprehension of how people deal with difficulties (e.g., displacement, repression, denial, sublimation and so on) might yield understandings that lead to more satisfying, fair and productive working relationships.

YOUR ADDITIONS

(6)

(7)

(8)

(9)

(10)

NOTES

1. Steve Burghardt describes a similar situation, only this time the worker mistaken for a janitor was Black. He was devastated by his own response to the incident. It was as if he had never excelled in school, never earned his MSW. He was thrown into a panic by the experience, feeling that he did not "deserve to be a professional," that beneath it all, he was still what he and others expected him to be—a "hewer of wood." I am also indebted to Burghardt for much of the discussion in this chapter of becoming in tune with one's own pain and for the vignette in which Yolanda responds to her supervisor's sexism.

2. You will recall from Chapter 1 how important Ali's hospitalization and other benefits are to her.

REFERENCES

Allport, Gordon W. (1960). *Personality and social encounter.* Boston: Beacon Press.

Arguello, David. (1984). Minorities in administration: A review of ethnicity's influence in management. *Administration in Social Work,* Fall.

Arsenault, Andre, & Dolan, Shimon. (1983). The role of personality, occupation and organization in understanding the relationship between job stress, performance and absenteeism. *Journal of Occupational Psychology,* Winter.

Babab, Elisha, Birnbaum, Max, & Benne, Kenneth D. (1983). *The social self: Group influences on personal identity.* Newbury Park, CA: Sage.

Belle, Deborah. (1982). *Lives in stress: Women and depression.* Newbury Park, CA: Sage.

Bourne, Bonnie. (1982). Effects of aging on work satisfaction, performance and motivation. *Aging and Work,* Winter.

Bronfenbrenner, Uri. (1958). Socialization and social class through time and space. In E. E. Maccoby, T. M. Newcomb, & E. L. Hartley (Eds.), *Readings in social psychology.* New York: Holt, Rinehart & Winston.

Brousseau, Kenneth R. (1978). Personality and job experience. *Organizational Behavior and Human Performance, 22*(2).

Bruner, Jerome S. (1956). Freud and the image of man. *American Psychologist,* Winter.

Burghardt, Steve. (1982). *The other side of organizing: Resolving personal dilemmas and political demands of daily practice.* Cambridge: Schenkman.

Clark, Kenneth B., & Rainwater, Lee. (1966). Crucible of identity: The negro lower class family. *Daedalus,* Winter.

Cookey, Charles H. (1902). *Human nature and the social order.* New York: Scribner.

Davis, Larry E. (1983). Racial composition in the agency. *Social Casework,* Fall.

Erikson, Erik H. (1963). *Childhood and society.* New York: Norton.

Erikson, Erik H. (1968). *Identity, youth and crisis.* New York: Norton.

Fanon, Frantz. (1966). *The wretched of the earth.* New York: Evergreen Press.

Faver, Catherine A. (1984). *Women in transition: Career, family and life satisfaction.* New York: Praeger.

Freud, Anna. (1936). *The ego and mechanisms of defense.* New York: International Universities Press.

Friere, Paolo. (1972). *Pedagogy of the oppressed.* New York: Seabury Press.

Garland, Howard, & Smith, Gail Berwich. (1981). Occupational achievement motivation as a function of biological sex, sex-linked personality, and occupation stereotype. *Psychology of Women Quarterly, 5*(4).

Gary, Larry. (1984). *Black men.* Newbury Park, CA: Sage.

Goldburg, Leo, & Breznitz, Schlomo. (Eds.). (1984). *Handbook of stress.* New York: Free Press.

Goodman, Paul. (1956). *Growing up absurd.* New York: Knopf.

Grier, William, & Cobbs, Price. (1968). *Black rage.* New York: Basic Books.

Havighurst, Richard J. (1973). Social roles, work, leisure and education. In C. Eisendorfer & M. P. Lawton (Eds.), *The psychology of adult development and aging.* Washington, DC: American Psychological Association.

Heilbrun, Alfred. (1981). *Human sex-role behavior.* New York: Pergamon Press.

Herbot, Theodore, & Yost, Edward. (1978). Women as effective managers—A strategic model for overcoming barriers. *Human Resources Management,* Spring.

Howe, Louise Kapp. (1978). *Pink collar workers.* New York: Avon Books.

Koumm, Abraham K. (1970). Towards a hypothesis of work behavior. *Journal of Applied Psychology,* January.

Krueger, David W. (1985). *Success and the fear of success in women.* New York: Free Press.

Langer, E. J. (1969). *Theories of development.* New York: Holt, Rinehart & Winston.

Lewin, Kurt. (1948). *Resolving social conflicts.* New York: Harper.

Malcolm X. (1965). *Autobiography.* New York: Grove Press.

Masi, Dale A. (1981). *Organizing for women.* Lexington, MA: Lexington Books.

Maslow, Abraham H. (1970). Self actualization and beyond. In *Motivation and personality* (2nd ed.). New York: Harper & Row.

McNeely, Roger L. (1984). Occupation, gender, and work satisfaction in a comprehensive human services department. *Administration in Social Work,* Summer.

Millet, Kate. (1970). *Sexual politics.* New York: Doubleday.

Mossholder, Kevin, Bedeian, Arthur G., & Armenakis, Achilles. (1981). Role perceptions, satisfaction, and performance: Moderating effects of self-esteem and organizational level. *Organizational Behavior and Human Performance, 28*(2), 224-235.

Neugarten, Bernice L. (Ed.). (1968). *Middle age and aging*. Chicago: University of Chicago Press.

O'Reilly, Charles III. (1977). Personality-job fit: Implications for individual attitudes and performance. *Organizational Behavior and Human Performance,* February.

Pazy, Asya. (1985). A developmental approach to variability in experience of self. *Journal of Humanistic Psychology,* Spring.

Pfeiffer, J., & Lawler, J. (1980). Effects of job alternatives, extrinsic rewards, and behavioral commitment on attitude toward the organization: A field test of the insufficient justification paradigm. *Administrative Science Quarterly, 25*(1).

Powell, George, Posner, Barry, & Schmidt, Warren. (1984). Sex effects on managerial value systems. *Human Relations, 37*(1).

Rogers, Carl. (1970). *On becoming a person*. Boston: Houghton Mifflin.

Rogers-Rose, LaFrancis. (1980). *The black woman*. Newbury Park, CA: Sage.

Rossi, Alice. (Ed.). (1974). *The feminist papers*. New York: Bantam Books.

Row, Alan J., Bennis, Warren, & Bovisarides, James. (1984). Desexing decision styles. *Personnel*, January-February.

Seybolt, John W. (1976). Work satisfaction as a function of the person-environment interaction. *Organizational Behavior and Human Performance, 17*(1).

Skinner, B. F. (1971). *Beyond freedom and human dignity.* New York: Knopf.

Unger, Rhoda Kesler, & Denmark, Florence L. (Eds.). (1975). *Woman: Dependent or independent variable?* New York: Psychological Dimensions.

Watson, J. B. (1924). *Behaviorism*. New York: Norton.

Weil, Marie. (1983). Preparing women for administration: A self-directed learning model. *Administration in Social Work,* Fall/Winter.

Williams, William Julius. (1981). The black community in the 1980s: Questions of race, class and social policy. *The Annals,* March.

Chapter 3

CLIMBING THE LADDER AND CROSSING THE BRIDGE
Careers in White, Blue, and Pink

Harvey Marcus was feeling good about things. He often did, these days. Only last week, he had successfully negotiated a contract with the state whereby the All-Families Service Center would take primary responsibility for the establishment of group homes throughout the county. It would be the responsibility of his department to subcontract with other providers, train their staff, and see to it that high standards of service to clients would be met. His own staff, he felt sure, was up to the task.

Harvey had just finished meeting with the staff to discuss the implications of the new contract, and he was pleased with the way things had gone. Like himself, the others were relatively young, energetic and committed to their work. It was a closely knit group. Not that they partied together after work; Harvey never encouraged that. But he did favor the sharing of tasks and collective participation in job-related problem solving. Harvey encouraged others to take risks, just as he was willing to do himself. And he motivated them to try out different ideas, no matter how outlandish they might at first seem. He hated the cliché sound of it, but he really did believe that "nothing ventured, nothing gained."

Harvey didn't demand personal loyalty, but he did expect commitment to the job and concern for those who were the ultimate beneficiaries of the agency's work. And his role modeling paid off; there were no clock watchers on his staff. The others felt that they were co-workers, not subordinates, although they all understood who was the boss. They also felt that what they were doing was worthwhile, and they gained a great deal of satisfaction from knowing that their efforts paid off. There was something special about working with Harvey. He wasn't always the easiest guy to work with—sometimes he was so far ahead that it was hard to catch up—but the faster he moved, the more rapidly his staff did, too. No two days at the office were ever quite the same. If you liked a challenge, you liked working with Harvey Marcus.

If one were to trace Harvey Marcus's personal history, one might find some clues to his effectiveness and his style. In fact, if one were to ask Harvey what had shaped his personality and choice of career, he'd answer without hesitation: "My folks and my teenage and early college experiences." One of his earliest recollections was attending an outdoor Pete Seeger concert with his parents. "I used to go to sleep to Pete Seeger and Woody Guthrie records," he recalls. "My dad was a labor organizer and my mother was a teacher. When my father's friends were over, the discussions were always political. They were always into righting some wrong. My mom was a little more conciliatory. Like when I had friends over, if I was too bossy, she never hestitated telling me to be more understanding and let the other fellow initiate some of the play activities.

"My childhood was pretty normal, I guess. Music lessons, afternoon Hebrew school, sports. I was into just about everything: Little League baseball, hockey, and soccer. When I got to high school, though, sports were beginning to take second place. By this time I was involved in all kinds of social, religious, and political activities of my own. I was active in the synagogue youth group (even went to Israel one summer), the debate team, all kinds of antiwar, civil rights, and ecology movements. The big push in civil rights, of course, was over. The year I started high school, we were celebrating the fifth anniversary of the march from Selma to Montgomery. A cousin of mine had been killed in those years. You might remember Goodman, Chaney, and Schwerner, three civil rights workers, two Whites and a Black, who were murdered and then dumped in a ditch on their way to do volunteer work with the SNCC. Well, Goodman was a distant cousin.

"Anyway, by the time I was a senior, I was president of just about everything. In fact, there was an article on me in the local press almost every other week. And I knew that my dad was proud of the things that I was doing. I think I was getting carried away with myself. The one memory that stands out the strongest was when Mitch Nelson, head of the teen program at the Y, asked me who I thought I was really helping with all the activities I was engaged in.

"I got real defensive. I started telling him about the importance of all the causes I was into, and all the good we were doing. 'What happened to Maggie Pierce?' he asked me. 'Wasn't she supposed to arrange for the bus to take the kids down to the state capitol?' 'Sure,' I replied. 'But I waited three weeks for her to get the information. I had even given her the phone number and the name of the person to call to find out what the costs were in each of two bus companies. So, when she didn't do anything, I did it. Somebody had to.' 'That's just the point, Harv,' he replied. 'You thought the work had to be done and you had to go ahead and do it. But what about Maggie? She hasn't had all the organizing experience you have, and maybe she's not so assertive. Don't you think you might have helped her feel like she accomplished something instead of feeling that she failed, that she let you down? Somebody who really cares about the other person might have gone with Maggie to the telephone and stood there, even helped her dial, supporting her as she made the contact and got the information. You think of yourself as a leader. What do you think real leadership is about: causes, people, or glory?' I was stunned, not sure of what to think.

"But I did think about it, a lot. In fact, I've thought about it ever since. Mitch was the first social worker I ever met. He was a real role model. In retrospect, I suspect that I went into social work because of him. Otherwise I might have gone into labor organizing or even politics. He helped me to realize that if you want to help others, it's not just the big picture but the little guy, your friend, your colleague, the person you work with, that counts too."

When Harvey graduated high school, he took a year off "to find my roots, to find myself. But I wasn't sure where to look. I knew it wasn't in my father's brand of 'secular messianism.' He and his union buddies were still talking about building some kind of just society here on earth, but mostly they were involved in labor negotiations and union contracts. I didn't think the unions were where it was at. I spent about six months working on a kibbutz in Israel, and for a while I thought I had found my place. I was doing something with my own people, and that felt good. But I guess I'm too much a product of 'the fleshpots of Egypt.' "

Harvey wandered about Europe a bit, returned to the States, and enrolled at the university, "like I was supposed to." Majoring in history and journalism, he continued his activism in a number of student organizations. But it wasn't enough. "Reporting on the news wasn't living it." So Harvey spent a year as a VISTA volunteer working in a Chicano community center in south Los Angeles. "I thought a lot about the opportunities that I had had, and the lack of opportunities for the kids with whom I worked. They often expressed an anger that was turned inward, leading to despair and heavy drug use. There was something beautiful and warm in their families and in their tradition, but they just didn't see it. Whenever I found myself unsure about how to intervene, I thought back about how Mitch, at the Y where I grew up, might have acted. And suddenly one day I woke up and I realized that I wanted to be a social worker."

* * * * *

If we were to interview the other workers at the All-Families Service Center, we'd uncover different histories, but we might also uncover similar patterns of personal development and career choice. In this chapter, we'll examine five theories of career development. The discussion will be grouped under various categories: (1) *trait-factor theories* (in which individuals' capabilities and interests are matched with vocational opportunities); (2) *self-concept theories* (which trace the development of more clearly defined self-concepts as individuals grow older, and that match those concepts to the opportunities available); (3) *personality theories* (in which job or career choices are perceived as efforts to satisfy personal needs); (4) *opportunity theory* and career choice (in which circumstances, generally outside the individual's control, contribute to career choices); and (5) *developmental approaches* (which parallel some of the conceptual frameworks described in Chapter 2). We'll look at the first three approaches together, then move on to the fourth and fifth. Finally, we will examine how different individuals act out their career alternatives and pursue alternative life choices within the agency setting.

TRAIT, PERSONALITY, AND SELF-CONCEPT THEORIES

Almost three decades ago, John Holland, a researcher from Johns Hopkins University, proposed that the adequacy of a person's occupational choice (i.e., the closeness of fit between the individual and the occupation) is largely a function of the extent to which the person is knowledgeable about the self as well as about occupational alternatives. Now this may not be startling information, but Holland's subsequent work generated some interesting propositions. It was Holland's contention that people have different traits and that these emerge gradually over time, leading to relatively appropriate or inappropriate educational and experiential decisions that then have implications for occupational choice. Holland speaks about six kinds of orientation:

(1) Those with a *realistic* (motoric) orientation tend to seek concrete rather than abstract problem situations, scoring high on traits such as concreteness, physical strength, and masculinity, and low on social skill and sensitivity. They avoid tasks involving interpersonal and verbal skills. They might be found to predominate in such occupations as engineering and truck driving.
(2) The *investigative* (intellectual) orientation aims at organizing and understanding (thinking) rather than dominating or persuading (acting), and tends to be more asocial than sociable. Scientific researchers and many academics tend to share these characteristics.
(3) The *social* (supportive) orientation, in contrast, tends to characterize people who seek close interpersonal situations (for example, teaching, social work, and therapy).
(4) The *conventional* (conforming) orientation is typified by a concern for rules and regulations, strong identification with power and status and, frequently, subordination of personal needs. Persons with these traits seek work situations where structure is either readily available or where they can participate in the development of rules and procedures that regulate interpersonal interactions. Accountants and systems analysts tend to fit this pattern.
(5) An *enterprising* (and frequently persuasive) orientation tends to characterize persons in the business and corporate world, where power, the domination of others, the manipulation of forces and status are central to success. But there are entrepreneurial types in the human services as well.
(6) The *artistic* (aesthetic) orientation is manifested in strong self-expression and in the establishment of relationships to others

> through artistic endeavors (music, writing, and so on). People with this orientation may share asocial characteristics with the investigatives but tend to be more feminine than masculine, expressing emotion more readily than other people.

Now, you might assume that most social workers tend toward the social and supportive orientation, and you'd be quite correct. Of the six staff persons we've met thus far, only Carl, a non-social worker, doesn't seem to possess much of this trait. You might identify him as conforming and conventional. In Chapter 6, you'll discover that he is also artistic—but not necessarily at work. Reexamine what you know about Harvey Marcus. Clearly he, like most of us, reflects a number of traits. He is enterprising, investigative, and, to a certain extent, realistic. We already know that Millicent is strongly social in her orientation, but that she is also artistic. Ali is both social and conventional. How would you describe Yolanda? Do you know enough about Sam to identify his most characteristic traits? What about yourself? Undoubtedly you possess some of each of these traits.

How would you rank the traits of others with whom you work: your supervisor, subordinates, the agency administrator, other colleagues? You might want to use the test you just devised to find out. To what extent might such ranking help you understand what leads them to behave in the ways they do? What trait differences might lead to some interpersonal conflict between members of the staff? Clearly, no one's traits are carved in stone, and many of us tend to express one or more of these to a lesser or greater extent at different stages in our lives and in our work careers.

Harvey's personal history illustrates this point. Moreover, Harvey has chosen to act out his work life at the agency so as to be able to find expression for a number of different traits. In that he is quite fortunate. Both his occupational choice and the conditions in the agency and its environment permit him to capitalize on a number of different traits simultaneously. Is this true also of the other staff members at the agency? Is it true of you in your work setting? To what extent does the environment in the agency in which you are employed limit your opportunities to express these traits? Has this environment shaped them somewhat differently, so that you have come to change the order of the hierarchy? Has it caused you to emphasize some traits over others in response to the expectations and reward systems in the workplace?

* * * * *

Exercise 3.1

Hierarchy of Traits

1. Take the six traits we have described (*realistic, investigative, social, conventional, enterprising,* and *artistic*) and list them in hierarchical order, reflecting those that you think most strongly characterize *you*. (Top to bottom reflects high to low.)

   (1) ____________________

   (2) ____________________

   (3) ____________________

   (4) ____________________

   (5) ____________________

   (6) ____________________

2. If you are not sure of an order, design an exercise that may help you decide. First, list five work-related responses that reflect each of the six traits. I'll get you started.

   "When I first started to work at the agency, I
   (1) reorganized things in my office to make things more attractive and aesthetic (*artistic*).
   (2) set out to find out how things work, who is responsible for what, and what resources were available to me (*investigative*).
   (3) asked around about rules and norms, read the procedures manual (*conventional*).
   (4) introduced myself and got to know my co-workers informally by meeting with them both in their offices and outside at coffee and lunch, and so on (*social*).
   (5) checked out the pecking order, finding out who makes what decisions and how (*enterprising*).
   (6) walked around, checking on the layout, equipment (computers and filing systems) (*realistic*).

   Now add 24 more items (five per trait). Look over the scoring instructions for **Exercise 1.5.** Create a similar form for this exercise, with six columns. Take the test and score yourself.

Lofquist and Dawis have described the work adjustment process as one in which a person's flexibility reflects the degree to which one can tolerate a lack of correspondence between the work environment and one's own personal character traits. The more one can tolerate a lack of correspondence, the more flexible the individual. On the other hand, some people become active in attempting to alter the work environment so as to increase its correspondence to their personality styles. Clearly, Harvey is among these. Some people change their place of employment when blocked in the expression of one trait or another. Yolanda, you will recall, worked in the GM plant, which had required investigative and enterprising skills with which she had not been comfortable. For Millicent, the conventional and conforming requirements of her earlier life as a nun and a teacher in a parochial school had become stifling. As she matured, she found an increasing need to express herself artistically, persuasively, and intellectually. What changes have you observed in your own behavior over the years?

Davis and others have used questionnaires and statistical methods to generate a "birds of a feather" hypothesis that assumes that members of an occupational group will exhibit increasingly homogeneous personality traits over time. But this is a controversial hypothesis at best. Its major flaw is that it tends to focus on one trait at a time. In fact, Super and Bachrach point out that efforts to define differences in personality traits among members of different occupations is futile because too much overlap exists, and because both occupations and jobs tend to tolerate a wide range of personality differences.

It may, in fact, be more profitable to look for those factors that influence the sequences of career decisions that people make in response to the opportunities that may be offered them. How they deal with those opportunities may, to a large extent, be a factor of the extent to which they are willing to take risks. According to Atkinson, for example, our motivations to achieve and to avoid failure have a great deal to do with the extent to which we are willing to take risks on the job. Those who seek to avoid failure will frequently set either extraordinarily high or extremely low goals for themselves, whereas those who are influenced more by an achievement motive are likely to aspire to more attainable goals. Thus achievement-motivated people are likely to engage in moderate risk-taking activities.

Fear of failure may increase the likelihood that some people will be willing to consider entering less prestigious occupations. What does this say about Harvey and Yolanda? What does this say about Sam, whose father had been a physician and had expected Sam to follow in his footsteps? Might there be some connection between Sam's selection of social work as an occupation and his (risky) move from Lebanon to the United States? Perhaps it might be more appropriate to assume that risk taking has relevance to vocational behavior, if not to vocational preference or choice. This might explain why both Millicent and Harvey are willing to take considerable risks in the work they do, and how the ways in which they perform on the job contrast with the relatively low risk of selecting a professional occupation that is fairly well suited to their personality traits and that is not particularly high on the ladder of occupational status.

There is yet another theoretical approach that you might find useful in comprehending career development. It is frequently referred to as "social learning theory" and is associated with the work of John Krumboltz. Like the approaches already explored, it also tends to identify the personal and environmental events that shape individual career decisions. It begins by examining inherent attributes like race, gender, physical type and the traits we discussed earlier. But it focuses more heavily on the environment of the workplace (rules, reward procedures, social and technological environment and so on). In addition, social learning theory concerns itself with the individual's learning history.

Many people tend to learn in an "associative" manner, observing the relationships between events and thereby developing a capacity to predict alternative outcomes (contingencies) as the consequences of alternative actions. Others are more "instrumental" in that they've learned that specific actions are likely to lead to specific outcomes. Some social learning theorists suggest that a person's interests, or the ways he or she acts out career decisions, may be more the outcome of experience than of personality traits. Because outcomes are specific (getting a job, being rewarded for effective performance, moving up the ladder), one learns to adjust one's traits in those directions from which reinforcement is likely to come.

People who are realistic about themselves and the world around them are not likely to act in ways that generate costs that exceed their perceptions of current or future gains. For Yolanda, earning an MSW degree was not particularly risky and was clearly worth the investment, whereas working at GM, despite her earlier expectations, required paying too high a price for the rewards available.

Anne Roe, a clinical psychologist whose early research interests focused on factors that lead to artistic creativity, has also directed investigations toward uncovering the ways in which developmental patterns affected by earlier childhood experiences lead to both career choices and the particular ways in which people act out those choices. Like many of the researchers described in Chapter 1, she also concludes that needs that are routinely satisfied do not become motivators, and that higher order needs, in the sense of Maslow's self-actualization propositions, will disappear entirely if they are only rarely satisfied. Lower order needs will become dominating motivators if they are only rarely satisfied, and this may block the appearance of higher order needs. She also concludes, however, that needs that are satisfied after an unusual delay will become motivators when both the strength of the need is great and the amount of delay between arousal and satisfaction is prolonged. This may help to explain the rather radical shift in perspective and behavior on Millicent's part, after some 20 years as a teacher and a nun.

Roe's research also focused on specific child-rearing techniques, particularly the ways in which parents interact with children. She analyzed overdemanding, overprotecting, and accepting parental behaviors. *Overprotective* parents tend to make excessive demands on their children, yet they will fulfill and satisfy their physiological needs. However, they may be somewhat less prompt in gratifying demands for love and esteem. Children of overprotective parents learn to place emphasis on the speed with which needs are gratified. Thus, although lower level needs tend to be gratified quickly, higher order needs become more connected to dependency on others and, later in life, to conformity. By definition, *overdemanding* parents make excessive demands on their children, but they also impose conditions on the love offered the child. ("I'll love you if you do this or that.") Thus both overprotective and overdemanding parents are to some extent rejecting their children. In contrast, *accepting* parents tend to gratify their children's needs at most levels.

Roe concludes that children who grow up in an accepting atmosphere are more likely to select one of the helping professions, whereas scientists, engineers, accountants, and others who are not heavily person-oriented in their work tend to come from a home atmosphere where they may have experienced both the coldness and rejection sometimes associated with overdemanding parents. Nevertheless, even these people may choose helping professions if the need for esteem, love and belonging is intense, and if some opportunity for its gratification exists.

Ervin Staub, a psychologist from the University of Massachusetts, has published an interesting book on the biological and social origins of good and evil. Based on extensive interviews, he concludes that there exists a pattern of child rearing that seems to encourage altruism in later years. It requires a warm and nutrient relationship between parent and child in which parents not only espouse altruistic values but also exert firm control over their children. These parents use a combination of firmness, warmth and reasoning, pointing out to children the consequences of misbehavior, as well as of good behavior. They actively guide the child to do good, to share and to be helpful. Staub concludes that children who have been coached to be helpful tend later to be more altruistic when a situation arises in which they can help others.

These are the same children who are likely to select occupations in which they can be helpful to others on a regular basis. Both their self-concept and their social needs are actualized through and in the helping process. Altruistic adults tend to have mothers or other significant caretakers who explained to them the consequences of being hurtful, and who did so with a great deal of feeling. Calm and unemotional admonitions do not seem to produce altruists. On the other hand, children of chronically depressed mothers seem to be particularly sensitive to the distress of other children, and are often preoccupied by it. This preoccupation may also affect occupational choices.

Have we discovered something more about Ali, Harvey, and the others at the agency? About yourself?

BOYS AND GIRLS ARE NOT THE SAME. NEITHER ARE MEN AND WOMEN

Much of what we've discussed so far has been gender-neutral; that is, we've assumed similar factors to hold true for both boys and girls, men and women. In point of fact, however, boys and girls do grow up differently in our society. The way in which they are socialized leads to differences in adult perception about the self, about one's career and about the best ways to pursue that career. There are, of course, hazards in generalizing from the experiences of a few. Nevertheless, I think the benefits of sharing some of the All-Family Service Center staff's recollections of the childhood experiences that shaped their work-related identities may be worth the risk.

* * * * *

Ali speaks: "I suppose if I had my druthers, I would have gone to college. Two years at the J.C. (junior college) weren't enough. I might still do it when the kids (her brothers and sisters) are all out of the house and don't need me anymore. But if I were to tell you what I really wanted, it was a normal mom and a normal family life.

"You know, I never had what I thought was normal. For sure, not the TV idea of normal. Like on those family shows they used to have on TV. You know, the mom fixes breakfast for the kids in the morning, the father goes off to work, and the kids go off with clean clothes to school, and the parents are there when the kids need 'em, when they've got a problem. When my mom first was hospitalized, my aunt came over, and she was like that. She came from Cleveland, and she was warm, and she was caring, and she straightened out the house for us. All the rooms were clean and neat for the first time that I could remember. I helped her the way I used to help my mom when she was sick, but Aunt Flora, she was something else.

"She knew just how to get things organized, how to put them in the right places, and how to make everybody feel good about themselves, not only because they had clean clothes, but because they were clean inside.

"My mom had sometimes tried to make us feel important, but we were important only if we didn't make life more miserable for her. I knew I was important because I took care of her. But when Auntie Flora came, I began to feel important 'cause I was me. I realized we could be a family even if my mom wasn't there. My Aunt Flora made me feel I was a good person, and I decided that I would be good.

"That's my main goal in life, to be a good person, to be decent, to be helpful to others. I didn't want my brothers and sisters to feel the pain of my mother's loss. I made sure they always had clean clothes and breakfast on the table. Sure, I'd like to have a college degree, but I don't think a college education is all so important. What's important is to do your work well, to make other people feel good about themselves and to feel good about your own self. I know all this talk about women being as good as men. Sure they are. But we don't have to be off and doing the same as men. What I like most about working in this agency is that women can be women here, I mean the way they should be.

"They're helpful to others. They make them learn about themselves and deal with their own problems. Social work is really all about mothering in the best possible way. That's why I respect Millicent and Yolanda so much. They're good at what they do, and they really care about people. And in my own way I'm good at what I do, too. And people know I care about them."

* * * * *

Yolanda explains: "I used to think I was different, but as I get older I realize how much I've been shaped by the system. I don't mean just because of my black skin. That may be the biggest part, but it's still only part of it. The other part is that I'm a woman. When I was in high school, I was determined not to turn out like some of the others in my neighborhood. My dad worked hard. Too hard. And my momma was a secretary. When she wasn't doing somebody else's work in the office, she was helping us kids grow up to be somebody. My parents always taught me to be the best that I can. They tried to teach my brothers the same thing, but they were defeated by the system, mostly because they were Black. But Black girls didn't have so hard a time of it. Maybe it's because White teachers weren't so scared of us. We didn't have to act macho.

"I tried to excel at everything when I was at high school. I even became a cheerleader. We were known as the T 'n' A squad. That's for 'Tits and Ass' (she laughs). We were supposed to make sure that everybody cheered in support of the team. The boys, after all, were taking the falls, and they were the ones who were going to win and lose for all of us. But we weren't above generating some attention for ourselves. It was our job to get everybody behind the team so that the boys would succeed. That's how it was, and I guess that's how it still is.

"My momma wasn't just a secretary; she organized and kept track of things so that her boss would succeed. And he did. Sure, he moved up and he brought her along with him, but it was always his moves, even if she had been the one to make it possible. You know that old saw: 'Behind every successful man there stands a woman.' Well, that was my momma. My daddy may not have been so successful, but Momma was always there anyway.

"One thing I learned from my momma . . . if you're going to succeed, you'd better work your darnedest at it. If you're good, people will know it. Not that I don't care about my husband. Reggie gets a lot of support from me, and I know it's tough on him, being a Black man and all. But I was determined to make it on my own. When it was fashionable, I wore a dashiki. But I'm no African. And if you're going to make it in America, you got to do it as an American. So after I traded my T 'n' A uniform for a dashiki, I turned my dashiki in for a dark suit. But you know, it wasn't enough. That crack about putting pressure on a woman at GM, that wouldn't have happened to a man. I worked hard on that report, and I worked on it all alone. I think it was really a good piece of work. I wish that I could have discussed it with someone else before turning it in. I'll never know, because I never really got any feedback on it."

* * * * *

Millicent speaks of the influences on her development: "You know, it's funny. It wasn't until I became a "sister" that I was exposed to some of the lessons that boys learn as they're growing up. When I became a nun, I learned that you didn't have to like everybody else that you interacted with. There were important things to do, and you could do it together with other women. It wasn't easy for us to learn to share responsibilities with people who were so different from us. We were fortunate in having a strong ideology, a religious belief that sustained us. We were also told what to do and how to do it. Boys learn some of these lessons earlier.

"I think back about my brothers. When I was in school, we had one *team* sport—volleyball. Our other sports were all *individual*—swimming, track and tennis. But my brothers played football and baseball. They learned how to be team members early. You didn't have to like the other members of the team, you only had to play with them. If it took five to play basketball, you didn't have to like the other four. And if you needed nine to play baseball, you learned how to get along for the benefit of the team. And if you needed eleven for football, it didn't matter whether they were Catholic or not, smart or not so smart, from one side of the tracks or another. What counted was that the team won. I didn't learn much about winning as a little girl, and I didn't learn much about counting on others or getting along with them even if I didn't like them."

* * * * *

Harvey explains: "When I decided to take this job, it was clear to me that I was either going to be successful—that is, that I was going to be able to make a difference in terms of placement opportunities for people in real need—or I would have to move on to another job, perhaps even another agency. And when I look for other staff for my department, I look for people with similar kinds of concerns. It's only recently that I've begun to realize that some of my attitudes may be sexist. It even feels sexist to be saying this. So let me explain.

"When Mel Stanford applied, what I liked about him was that I saw him as a 'comer.' He knew the kinds of questions to ask, and those questions weren't only about the job itself. He wanted to know what kinds of opportunities there might be for advancement. He was loaded with ideas, and I liked that. And I wasn't kidding myself that he'd stay here forever. But I knew that with people like him aboard, we'd expand the department's functions, and as long as we grew, there'd be opportunities for him to expand his own areas of responsibility as he showed capability and initiative. That's the kind of person I am, and that's the kind of staff I want around me.

"When Billie Jean Elving applied for a job, she came with superb recommendations. She asked good questions, too, but they tended to be about the job as it was currently defined. I think she liked what I had to tell her, because clearly she wanted to make a contribution to others. Billie Jean was looking for self-fulfillment on the job, for an opportunity to do important things and to do them well. I was sure she would. But I was equally certain that without a great deal of support, I couldn't expect her to take initiative for expanding the department's functions. When I asked her what she wanted out of her career, she looked blank. And then she responded: 'We're not talking about my career, are we? I can tell you what I want out of this job: an opportunity to do something worthwhile.'"

* * * * *

Harvey Marcus may have hit on a difference in the way in which men and women approach their careers, a difference that he was not quite ready to put into words. This difference is discussed more fully in a study by Margaret Hennig and Anne Jardim. In it, they describe their interviews with 100 successful women managers. Their conclusions are worth summarizing, as they may help to provide some insight into the comments made by Ali, Yolanda, Millicent and Harvey.

Hennig and Jardim conclude that men and women respond to both jobs and careers in ways that reflect different habits of thought. For example, women tend to respond in the present, describing their jobs in terms of the activities they perform and as a means of support, or a contribution to the family's earnings. They tend to see their careers as reflecting an opportunity for personal growth and self-fulfillment, and as a way of achieving personal satisfaction while making a contribution to others.

Men, on the other hand, see jobs in the context of *now* and *later,* simultaneously. Men tend to visualize a career as a series of jobs, a progression leading to greater recognition and reward. For men, jobs seem to be part of a career, whereas women separate the two issues completely, with the job being viewed as something that exists in the here and now, and a career being perceived in an intensely personal light.

Perhaps this has to do with early socialization in which girls learn to separate personal from career goals. In attempting to satisfy their own and society's perceptions of a woman's role, there is for some an intense pressure to succeed so well at the woman's role that no one might question their mastery of it. Only when they are secure in this role are they free to pursue occupational goals. But when they are free, they attempt to do it all. This has sometimes been referred to as the "supermom" syndrome. It also results in women switching off and on different persons, with one person on the job and another at home. Such an approach may explain the complex of feelings that Yolanda is experiencing (see Chapter 2). It may also help to explain why Ali has, in effect, turned the office into a home in which she clearly fulfills what she perceives to be an appropriate female role. We might suspect that Yolanda knows a great deal more about Reggie's job than he does about hers, and that she may even think about her own work as a job, and about his work as a career, limited as it may be within the context of the opportunities available to him at the plant.

Hennig and Jardim also talk about differences in the personal strategies pursued by men and women. Men tend to ask, "What's in it for me?" thus bringing the future into current consideration. In contrast, women tend to think more about how they will be judged in relation to their current work. The personal skills drawn upon for that work will also be different for men and women. Boys' sports are team sports, as Millicent observed, in which winning is important and in which individuals suppress feelings in order to make their contributions to the team. Boys learn this on the playground, on the street and in team activities at school.

Girls, in contrast, have few parallel experiences. The prestigious sports for them tend to be tennis, swimming, golf, gymnastics and skating—one-on-one sports in which winning and losing may be less important than how one plays the game. Technique becomes important, while strategy takes second place. For adult women, this may lead to an inordinate emphasis on performing well in the here and now, based on the assumption that promotion, if it comes, will be a recognition for competence. This is essentially a passive approach.

For men, on the other hand, getting ahead may depend on how well one works as a team member. Promotions may depend as much or more on how one gets along with others as on the extent to which one performs competently. The "old boy network" continues to be important. It is probably exploited by knowing how to relate effectively to others, to make important contacts, to be recognized for one's contributions and to use such recognition for being delegated additional responsibility.

CAREER FROM A DEVELOPMENTAL PERSPECTIVE

These notions are supported by the work of Donald Super, who proposed that vocational self-concepts develop on the basis of children's observations of and identification with adults. He concludes that a person's mode of adjustment in one period of life is likely to be predictive of techniques used to adjust in later periods.

While it is possible for an adolescent's identification with a significant other to lead directly to an educational or vocational decision,[1] it is more likely that this identification will lead to a chain of events that might not have occurred otherwise, and that may have significant vocational implications. Harvey reflected this in his recollection of the influence of a social worker at the Y.

Super's life-stage theory of vocational and career development suggests that people progress from an exploratory stage in which they test various alternatives and even undergo trial work experiences (like Sunday school teaching, volunteering, working in VISTA or testing out an alternative career like newspaper reporting), and then make a commitment. These experiences lead people to seek training, which in turn leads to the emergence of a new identity. The nature of that identity may be different for women than for men because of both different societal perceptions and differences in one's own self-perception.

Super's work is complemented by that of Ginzberg and his associates. They perceive vocational choice as an irreversible process characterized by a series of compromises between wishes and possibilities. It begins with a fantasy period in which the individual (generally a child) thinks of himself or herself as a movie star, a millionaire or a fireman. This leads to a tentative period in which interests, capacities and values are explored in the context of life chances and opportunities.

Having reached the point of understanding personal likes and dislikes, the young adult achieves some understanding of his or her capacities. Tempering these with personal and social values, each person begins to explore ways to implement tentative choices. This is the beginning of the realistic period in career choice. It leads to a crystallization based on the exploration of a number of alternatives. Ginzberg assumes that this realistic stage occurs at the age of 18-22, but as we have seen, as new opportunities present themselves, even mature adults can continue their explorations, often changing their perceptions of both self and opportunities.

Murphy and Burck have suggested that a midlife developmental period should be added to Super's stages. They argue that when as many as one out of five physicians express dissatisfaction with their careers, when so many women are entering income-producing careers after having raised families and when more and more people are exploring alternatives in their 30s, 40s, and even 50s, a new notion of development may be necessary.

Regardless of earlier successes, they suggest, it is not uncommon for people in mid-adulthood to experience a decrease in self-esteem, to question the meaning of their own lives and to reexamine their personal values as a part of an overall process of stock taking. The attainment of a certain amount of economic success may be accompanied by the realization that even achieving one's earlier career objectives is no longer fully satisfying. Moreover, once children have left the home and are no longer dependent, the availability of new opportunities leads to a reactivation of one's search for a close fit between values, interests and capabilities. Golumbiewski observes that midlife career transitions increasingly occur between the ages of 35 and 45. Some people at this point experience a great deal of torment as they examine from whence they have come and conclude that they have not arrived at any place worth being. A colleague of mine has a sign on his door saying, "I got there, but I don't know where I'm at."

There are some significant differences in the way in which researchers and theorists have defined the midcareer period over the past 30 years. For example, in 1951, Miller and Form described it as a trial work period, leading to a more stable period in the mid-40s and on to retirement. A few years later, Super described the ages between 30 and 40 as the period in which a career is established, moving into a period of maintenance around 50 or 55. But by 1978, Edgar Schein observed that while many people achieve full membership early in their career stages (around age 30) and enter midcareer at age 35, this does not necessarily lead to a period of stability or establishment. In fact, for many, a midcareer crisis is likely to occur sometime around age 40. And that crisis may lead to a shifting in career, disengagement or reaffirmation.

Although it does not fully reflect the many "ministages" of career development that Americans currently experience, the four-stage process model developed by Van Maanen and Schein summarizes and integrates much of the work done by earlier theorists. It's reproduced with some modifications in Figure 3.1. Look it over. Do you anticipate repeating any of the four stages more than once? Have you already done so? Many women who return to school after a "career" a homemaker and others who shift occupations or specializations have.

In much of today's literature on occupations, including that found in popular magazines and newspapers, one finds increasing reference to initial work periods and even exploration occurring at ages 40 to 50. This is especially true for women who are returning to the workplace after many years of child rearing and homemaking. For others, midcareer changes are perceived less in crisis terms than as an emerging norm. This is increasingly common for those professions and occupations that do not (unlike nuclear engineering or medicine) require an enormous upfront investment of time. There is some evidence that people are selecting initial careers on the basis of their perceptions that their choices are likely to lead to a great deal of flexibility in making subsequent choices. Thus, studying law or social work, or even teaching, may provide opportunities to make contacts that will lead to quite different occupational choices than those for which one was presumably prepared. Nevertheless, for most people who were trained 15 or 20 years ago and who entered their occupations at that time, midlife transitions can still be traumatic.

External Influences and Individual Experiences	*Internalization Processes*
Stage 1: Exploration	
–absorbing occupational images from the media, movies, T.V.	–trying on image, what sort of work would fit, gratify
–looking at examples of models (parents, siblings, teachers)	–identification with role models
–advice from trusted models	–self assessment of own talents, aspirations, self-image
–success or failure in related school, sport or social experiences, other self-tests	
–success or failure in trial work experiences (i.e., summer job, volunteering)	
–constraints or opportunities based on family circumstances, location, history, economics	–clarification of ambitions, goals, personal motivations
–preliminary choice of occupational path: (a) job or (b) school (college major, vocational training, professional school)	–enlarged self-image based on integration of capabilities and opportunities, social and educational accomplishments
–counseling	–continued assessment, reassessment of self, life's options
–letters of recommendation	
–evaluation of aptitude and achievement tests	–anticipatory socialization based on all of the above
Stage 2: Early Career–Finding a Job, Getting Established	
a. Mutual Recruitment	
–organization seeks talent	–individual looks for good job, career opportunity
–labor market tight or open	–heightened expectations or reality shock
–job market tight or open	
–testing, screening, selection	–preparing to be evaluated by others, feelings of confusion and insecurity
	–dealing with possibility of acceptance or rejection
	–developing image of job or occupation based on application process
b. Acceptance and Entry	
–job is offered with given conditions	–making the job choice, major work-related commitment

Figure 3.1 Career stages and processes.

- assignment to further training or to specific assignment.
- formal and informal initiation rites, orientation
- conferring of organizational status (i.d. cards, parking stickers, org. manual, etc.)

- self-testing, activation of need for achievement, avoidance of failure
- feeling of acceptance, readjustment of self-image
- beginning identification as "member"
- beginning development of personal occupational identity, separation from earlier work or student identities

c. First Job Assignment

- meeting with supervisor, co-workers
- learning period, indoctrination
- movement from partial or tentative to full performance (doing the job like everyone else)
- opening up for new or expended opportunities, responsibilities

- gearing self up to being tested in the "real world"
- feelings of playing for keeps
- socialization by supervisor, co-workers, subordinates, clients, i.e., "learning the ropes"
- reality shock with discovery of what work is really like, including "scut work" and "dirty work"
- testing commitment to the job, occupation
- considering new opportunities, career themes

d. Leveling off, Transfer, Advancement

- feedback, performance review, career counseling, salary action (usually more frequent but has special meaning here)
- if transferred or promoted, repeat of the five steps under 2c
- if individual fails, "does not fit in," or has to be laid off, the process goes back to 2a)
- if individual is suceeding, goes on to develop a speciality or special areas of competence leading to a period of real contribution in that area of competence and that area of competence is needed in the organization, the individual is given actual or *de facto* tenure

- feeling of success or failure
- reassessment of self-image and how it matches perceived opportunities in occupation/organization—"Is there a career here?"
- sorting out family/work issues and finding a comfortable level of accommodation
- forming a career strategy, how "to make it"—working hard, finding mentors, conforming to organization, making a contribution
- decision to leave organization if things do not look positive
- adjusting to failure, reassessment of self, occupation and organization—effort to avoid losing self-esteem, elaboration or revision of theme

Figure 3.1 Continued *(continued)*

	–turning to unions or other sources of strength if feeling unfairly treated or threatened –growing feeling of success and competence, commitment to organization and occupation –period of maximum insecurity if organization has formal tenure review–"Will I make it or not?"

e. Achieving Permanence

–the granting of tenure or –not getting tenure (losing job, reassignment to lesser status or responsibility, or probationary status)	–feeling of achievement, of acceptance, of having made it; move to Stage 3 –personal crisis leading to reassessment of self, competence and career choice; testing of prior assumptions –examination of alternative possibilities leading back to 2a or on to Stage 4.

Stage 3: Midcareer–Stabilization and Maintenance

–more crucial, responsible work is assigned	–new confidence may lead to reassessment, more assertive relationships, modification in career timetable
–expectation of maximum productivity transmitted	–expectation of self regarding productivity may waver between responding to work expectations and relaxing a bit
–induction into organizational secrets –new problem: dealing with person who may have "plateaued out" on productivity	–problem of keeping motivated to learn, expand, innovate; avoiding complacency, burnout or fatigue
–finding room for new workers	–dealing with threat from younger, better trained or more energetic newcomers

Stage 4: Late or Second Career: Maintenance or New Horizons

Alternative a. Maintenance

–jobs assigned and responsibilities draw primarily on wisdom and perspective and maturity of judgment –more community and society oriented jobs –more jobs involving teaching others,	–possible thoughts of "new pastures," second careers, new challenges, etc., in relation to biosocial "midlife" crisis –working through midlife crisis toward greater acceptance of oneself and others –more concern with teaching others,

Figure 3.1 Continued

less likely to be on the "firing line" unless contacts and experience dictate	passing on one's wisdom both at home and at work –psychological preparation for retirement –deceleration in momentum –finding new sources of self-improvement off the job

Alternative b. New or Transformed Career

–new job or career opportunities are presented, in same occupation or different ones –more informal, network-based exploration, similar to Stage 1, goes on	–personal re-imaging and assessment, similar to Stage 1, but based on expanded life experience
–reentry into Stage 2 but with more rapid likelihood of advancement to Stage 3	–Stages 2, 3 and 4 assessments, skill and responsibility expansion –possibility of 3rd or 4th career shifts

Stage 5: Decline and Withdrawal

–formal preparation for retirement	–acceptance of reduced role or responsibilities –defining unique and innovative role or
–retirement ceremonies, rituals –possible emeritus status with continued opportunities to contribute as advisor, part-time worker, volunteer, etc.	–acceptance and withdrawal –learning to perform in new role or –learning to manage less structured life –deciding whether to cut oneself off from former occupation, colleagues, or "keeping up" –creating new patterns of family and community relationships, in effect, creating a new "retirement career" through informal and volunteer associations (requiring similar rites of passage as those described in earlier stages)

SOURCE: This listing is based loosely on the work of John Van Maanen and Edgar H. Schein (1977), but has been expanded to include new understandings of 2nd and 3rd career opportunities, expanded retirement and continued developmental processes. You might wish to use the chart to assess the career stages of several of the people you met in this book—Yolanda, Harvey, Carl, Millicent, and others . . . or to review your own career and work experiences. Are you or any of the others on a "fast track," a "slow but steady" course?

Figure 3.1 Continued

Midlife transition often involves a disparity between one's achievements and one's aspirations. "I'm tired of being owned," another colleague of mine recently admitted. "I want to be my own person." And this from a university professor, who presumably has more "academic freedom" to pursue his own interests than might be the case for most people in our society! For those who are successful in becoming their own man or their own woman, a career change in midlife may result in a horizontal rather than a vertical move. Fortunately, this does not necessarily require starting out all over again. After all, how often can one scale Mt. Everest?

Both Yolanda and Millicent made lateral (horizontal) career shifts. Of the two, Millicent's was clearly the more radical. For Yolanda it entailed moving from the private sector to the voluntary sector, but she remained in social work. Millicent continued in her role as an educator, but the shift from working with children in a parochial school to counseling adults in a family services agency required a radical transformation in her identity and her perceptions of the world. For her, the Church no longer provided clear guidelines for occupational progress or personal identity. She expressed and acted on a need to reassert control over her own self-development. She chose not to follow passively a course of action set in motion years earlier. Although age tends to be negatively correlated with risk taking, for her, dissatisfaction with life as she had come to know it required a new process of self-testing, a new period of training and a new set of responsibilities in a different institutional environment.

All three women quoted in this chapter expressed different responses to the occupational stereotypes developed as children. Although all three continue in sex-stereotyped occupations, personality factors and self-perceptions have influenced the way in which they act out their career decisions. All three not only desire to work, but need to. And all chose occupations in which the opportunity for achievement was clearly present.

OPPORTUNITY AND CAREER CHOICE

Throughout this chapter we have accepted the likelihood that external circumstances, including chance and opportunity, have a significant impact on both occupational choice and the outcomes related to such choices. In contrast with the psychologists whose work we have examined in some detail, it is probably fair to suggest that most sociologists would argue that being at the right place at the right time may have a greater impact than character traits, personality or other developmental factors. Osipow concludes that to many psychologists, "chance" represents an irritant to be minimized so that better decisions might be made and events brought under the control of the individual.

In contrast, sociologists are more likely to focus their attention on external variables, those forces that are generally outside of the individual's control or over which the individual may have only minimal control. Thus social forces like the economy, societal attitudes and prejudices, and chance meetings or acquaintances—in effect, "the throw of the dice"—may have more to do with where one ends up occupationally than many of the variables discussed here.

In the mid-1950s, Theodore Caplow documented the rigid limits on the variety of career choices available to some members of society, leading him to conclude that for some, occupation is hereditary. Hollingshead's famous study of *Elmtown's Youth* provided an earlier foundation for the conclusion that social class and occupational aspirations were closely connected. So far, we haven't said much that would suggest any major disagreement with the conclusions arrived at by the psychologists discussed above.

However, Peter Blau and his associates have provided a conceptual framework that places the occupation and its position in society more centrally in the line of vision. Blau suggests four characteristics of occupations and individuals that should be considered as key factors in career choice:

(1) the individual's occupational information and the available information on that occupation;
(2) the individual's technical qualifications and the functional or technical task requirements of the job or occupation;
(3) the individual's social role characteristics and the nonfunctional social and institutional requirements of the occupation; and
(4) the individual's reward-value hierarchy and the amounts and types of status, financial, or intrinsic rewards offered by the occupation.

Let's take the first item. The amount of information an individual may have about a particular occupation, job or career choice may be less dependent on his or her innate abilities or developmental history than on the extent to which society provides information about the occupation or career, and the extent to which the occupation or profession in question is successful in making itself known to potential recruits. Second, jobs change, occupations grow technically and professions expand in their knowledge and technological bases. As they do so, they require members with specific competencies and capacities.

These requirements may not always be as technical as they seem. For example, the rapid growth of programs aimed at minority groups and the poor in the 1960s and 1970s required social workers who were not only sensitive to the needs of the oppressed but whose own experiences were similar. Social work undertook an intensive effort to recruit minorities to graduate schools, and when this was not possible indigenous personnel were recruited and trained as paraprofessionals. Many went on to earn Associate of Art degrees in the human services. The civil rights movement and Affirmative Action programs likewise increased occupational and career opportunities that were directly linked to "protected" minority status.

The political activism characteristic of that period made social work a particularly attractive profession for those who were themselves politically active. It provided them with career opportunities in community organizing, social planning, policy development and politics itself.

Nevertheless, activism is not the major draw to social work. We've already said a good deal about the current identification of social work in the public eye as a female occupation. Thus those whose social role characteristics tend toward the helping and the nurturing are more likely to select an occupation that not only supports but requires such behavior. Finally, occupations such as social work may be limited in the financial rewards and the social status or prestige that they can confer on their membership. However, they are high in other rewards: belonging, self-actualization and self-fulfillment. This is particularly true for those who possess the appropriate trait hierarchy (refer to your own self-assessment in **Exercise 3.1**). Nevertheless, the extent to which social work and other careers in the human services provide you with the opportunity to actualize and fulfill yourself may be more a factor of the occupation itself than of those traits.

CAREER STYLE AS A FUNCTION OF ORGANIZATIONAL STYLE

Clearly, work and careers are integrally related. The place where you work is the arena within which career decisions and moves are often made. If *careers* refers to the stages and levels of occupational growth and development, the *arena* refers to the place where the action takes place. That action can be within a social agency, where most social workers are employed, or in the larger community or field-of-practice arena (for example, community mental health, substance abuse or aging). In each of those arenas there may be opportunities for upward or horizontal mobility. Upward mobility generally refers to movement either into managerial or specialist levels within an organization or else out of the organization into a more responsible job. Such moves are frequently accompanied by an increase in responsibility and autonomy, better pay and working conditions and more prestige. They may also be accompanied by more pressure and job stress. Large agencies, particularly those with tall hierarchies in which there are many levels of management, or those in which there is a high ratio between managers and subordinates, afford the greatest opportunity for upward mobility.

For many professionals, however, upward mobility is not a goal. Among my own colleagues at the university, for example, I would find few professors aspiring to become deans or university presidents. Most of us, in fact, shy away from becoming department heads because it would take us away from our direct relationships to students and from our cherished free time to do scholarly work. Most schoolteachers do not aspire to become principals, and most social workers value direct practice, moving only reluctantly, sometimes with more than a few protesting kicks, up the occupational ladder. Many, in fact, might define upward mobility in terms of increased skill and competence. The job title may not change, but recognition of such competence by colleagues, both within the agency and outside, is perceived as advancement. For many, movement into a managerial role would be diverting at best and would more likely be perceived as requiring considerable sacrifice.

For many human service professionals, lateral mobility might be much more appropriate. As we noted earlier, this was the case for both Millicent and Yolanda. For some social workers it might mean a shift from treating individuals to working in family treatment, or from community work to protective services. Such shifts may entail some retraining but rarely require downgrading in terms of salary and benefits.

Large agencies that provide a wide variety of services or that serve many populations and cover multiple geographic locales also provide considerable opportunities for lateral moves, as do smaller agencies that are in a growth or expansionary phase of development or that shift their programs and services in response to new needs and opportunities. Examples include women's crisis centers and home health care services for the disabled. In some of these settings, in fact, workers may be expected to shift jobs or perform multiple jobs at a moment's notice. Such agencies generally have flat structures, with few or no levels of hierarchy between practitioners and top management.

In a study of the performance of professionals in a variety of different occupations, Dalton and his colleagues identified four career stages for professionals. Unlike the Van Maanen and Schein model presented above, Dalton focused only on the process of becoming established once one has entered an occupation. You may recognize your own experience in the model. In stage 1, the central activity is helping others while learning and following directions. The professional's primary relationships to others are those of apprentice and colleague-in-the-making, a set of relationships in which he or she is often dependent. In stage 2, the professional moves to greater independence, and he or she performs as a co-colleague, interdependent with others. In the third stage, the central activity may shift to training, supervision, and liaison work with other professionals and organizations. Frequency, the professional is now a mentor, adviser, and helper to others, often assuming responsibility for their performance and assignments. In the final stage, the professional is involved in shaping the direction of the organization, sometimes sponsoring others in their growth and development, exercising increasing power and authority over both others and programs.

On the surface of it, these four stages seem self-evident. In practice, however, there are sufficient individual variations to suggest that this formulation is more ideal than real. Entering professionals on the "fast track" frequently shift to stage 4 without moving through the previous three stages. Many people whose personal styles and aspirations so dictate prefer to remain in stage 2 throughout their careers. There is another formulation, that perceives career style as a function of bureaucracy, that you may find more insightful. Certainly it is provocative.

Anthony Downs,[2] a social scientist with the Urban Institute, describes five career styles common to most complex organizations, each of which is a different response to change (Downs, 1967). I think you will find his analysis instructive and recognize both yourself and many of your colleagues and supervisors within it. He refers to "climbers," "zealots," "advocates," and "statesmen." Before we examine each of these, one at a time, I want to point out that these categories tend to deal primarily with upward mobility within an organizational setting and thus are too limited to serve as a framework for analysis of all aspects of occupational careers. Nevertheless, they do provide some important insights into why people behave as they do in social agencies and other work settings.

The "climber" is on the move up, hopefully, to the top. There are a number of ways in which he or she can get there. The most direct is promotion. One way to improve the odds for promotion is to be recognized as competent at carrying out one's official tasks. Another is to get involved in as many committees and subgroups as possible.

If the chances for promotion are relatively small, the climber may resort to aggrandizing his or her area of responsibility. This strategy is often perceived by others as empire building. The more resources under the climber's control, the more influence he or she has within the organization and the more indispensable the climber becomes. The surest way to build an empire is to increase the number of personnel directly under one's control. As the number of subordinates increases, added staff must be justified by absorbing more programs and responsibilities. These may come either from areas previously controlled by other people or from new programs generated by the climber.

When the path to promotion is blocked and when empire building is not feasible, the only route left for a climber may be to jump to another agency, selling personal skill, expertise, and confidence. The only real constraint here is the job market. If there are no jobs available for the climber and all possible contacts made during the empire building process have been tried, then the climber's path may be blocked. The response is often frustration that may be expressed in interpersonal conflict.

In terms of leadership style, the climber tends to control subordinates closely to ensure nobody else is seen as a rising star. This style of leadership often suppresses innovation from below. Nevertheless, the climber believes, rightfully so, that the more change there is, the greater opportunity for advancement of subordinates as well as himself or herself.

The second type is the "conserver," who in many ways is the opposite of the climber. Like climbers, however, conservers tend to be concerned mainly with themselves. Unlike climbers, conservers strive to maintain the status quo. They are very much against any change that would threaten the relatively secure position they presently occupy. They prefer to be told exactly what to do so that they will not be blamed for any possible mix-up. Conservers supervise their subordinates closely in order to prevent innovation that might upset standardized and tried procedures and policies. In short, you may recognize the conserver as the typical bureaucrat.

The "zealot" is very stubborn and believes he or she knows what is wrong with, or what is best for, the agency or one of its client populations. Win or lose, zealots fight the good fight, always on the side of right. Typically, they have a high energy level. The ability to fight all odds continuously and still maintain enthusiasm is precisely their strength. For these reasons, zealots become excellent change agents. They are often effective in the start-up of a new program or a new agency. Unfortunately, the same degree of innovation is not expected of subordinates. Loyalty to the zealot is.

The "advocate" is a person who has exceptionally high commitment to the goals of the organization or department of which she or he is a member, or to a client population serviced by the agency. Great pride is taken in the accomplishment of the agency's or department's service goals. The organization advocate has two major skills: the ability to protect his or her part of the organization against all external threats—hence in a budget meeting, for example, he or she will fight to get the most for her or his agency; and the ability to mediate conflict within his or her department or organization. The combination of these two skills makes the agency advocate the person likely to be promoted to the head of an organization. The client or consumer advocate does the same for those with whom he or she is concerned. In doing so, consumer or client advocates are more likely to be in conflict with others in the agency. Consumer advocates are not as likely to head a service agency as are agency advocates.

All advocates use what can be called a situational approach to leadership. Hence, innovation is encouraged when appropriate and discouraged when superfluous.

The "statesman" tends to be more concerned with the welfare of society as a whole than with the agency or a particular client population. Regardless of the impact on the organization, the statesman will do what he or she *perceives* to be in the best interests of society. Unlikely to devote much time to performing detailed, day-to-day activities, the statesman spends a good deal of time developing overall plans and objectives. Statesmen do well in public relations type situations or any area that interfaces with clients or the public at large. When backed up by managerial staff who are zealots or advocates, they make good agency administrators, but not when left on their own.

* * * * *

REVIEW AND TENTATIVE CONCLUSIONS

Blue-collar, white-collar and pink-collar careers are different. So are the factors that lead people to making career choices and that lead to career opportunities.

(1) Trait theory postulates that a combination of innate and developmental factors leads to different personality traits that, in turn, correlate closely with occupational choice and with the ways in which people perform on the job. Single traits by themselves may not be a determining factor, but combinations of traits, when perceived in hierarchical order, are very often decisive.

(2) Learning theorists suggest that career choices may be more the outcome of experiences than of personality traits. Learning is associative and instrumental, and what people make of what they have learned is likely to have a significant impact on who they try to imitate and on their selection of work-related alternatives.

(3) Child-rearing practices and early socialization lead to self-perceptions, which in turn lead to career choices.

(4) Boys and girls do not grow up in the same society, and not all siblings grow up in the same families. What they learn about teamwork and how they come to evaluate themselves may not only lead to specific career choices but may also affect the ways in which they perceive both jobs and careers. For men, the two seem to be closely interrelated. For women, jobs and careers may be perceived separately; the latter taking on a distinctly personal character.

(5) Recent findings by those relating life-stage approaches to career development suggest that people move through a process that includes fantasy, testing and trial work, training and commitment. But commitment may not be a forever thing. Increasingly, people take stock at midlife, and this reevaluation may lead to significant career

Exercise 3.2

Career Patterns

Downs writes of five career styles: climbers, conservatives, zealots, advocates, and statesmen. Next to each of the staff persons listed below, indicate the designation(s) you think most clearly characterizes their styles.

Yolanda Stephenson	________________	________________
Samich Mansouri	________________	________________
Alberta Schmid	________________	________________
Millicent Kapinski	________________	________________
Carl Farrell	________________	________________
Harvey Marcus	________________	________________
Yourself	________________	________________

1. None of us are limited to a single style. Moreover, our styles may change at different stages in our occupational careers. What would it take to shift Carl from his current style to that of a climber or statesman?

2. If you've identified any of the staff members as zealots, under what circumstances might they become climbers, advocates, conservatives or statespersons?

3. If you've identified any of the staff members as advocates, are there circumstances in which their behavior might shift to that of climber, zealot, conservative or statesperson?

4. It's no secret that you identified Harvey as a climber. Do you think he'll be so identified throughout his career? Why? Why not? Substantiate your answer on the basis of what you already know about Harvey and what you know about career and occupational development from having read this chapter.

and occupational shifts, particularly when new opportunities present themselves.

(6) "Closeness of fit" between the individual and the occupation or job may be related to characteristics of both, including knowledge and information, skills and technical requirements, social role characteristics and reward-value hierarchies.

(7) Within any organization, people develop career styles, some of which may change as the individual becomes older or as the length of service increases. Typical styles include climbing, conserving, zealotry, advocacy and statesmanship.

YOUR ADDITIONS

(8)

(9)

(10)

(11)

(12)

NOTES

1. Recall that both Sam and Harvey decided on social work at least in part on the basis of certain experiences with social workers who served as role models, and

that Ali was much influenced by her aunt, who took over when her mother was hospitalized.

2. The following ten paragraphs are taken from Lauffer (1984).

REFERENCES

Atkinson, J.W. (1957). Motivational determinants of risk-taking behavior. *Psychological Review,* Summer.

Barnet, R. C. (1975). Sex differences and age trends in occupational preferences and occupational prestige. *Journal of Counseling Psychology,* January.

Baruch, R. (1966). *The achievement of motive in women: A study of implications for career development.* Unpublished doctoral dissertation, Harvard University, Cambridge, MA.

Blau, Peter, Guspad, Joseph W., Jessor, Richard, Parnes, Herbert S., & Wilcok, Richard C. (1956). Occupational choice: A conceptual framework. *Industrial Labor Relations Review,* July.

Burlin, F. D. (1976). Locus of control and female occupational aspirations. *Journal of Counseling Psychology,* January.

Caplow, Theodore. (1954). *The sociology of work.* New York: McGraw-Hill.

Chernesky, Rosyn. (1983). The sex dimension of organizational process: Its impact on women managers. *Administration in Social Work,* Fall/Winter.

Clark, E. T. (1967). Influence of sex and social class on occupational preference and perception. *Personnel and Guidance Journal,* Winter.

Collins, Eliza G. (1982). Stepping out of glass slippers. *Harvard Business Review,* March-April.

Dalton, George W., Thompson, P. H., & Price, P. L. (1977). *Organizational dynamics.* Washington, DC: AMACON.

Davidson, Marilyn, & Cooper, Gary. (1983). *Stress and the woman manager.* Oxford: Martin Robertson.

Davis, James A. (1964). *Great aspirations.* Chicago: Aldine.

Dawis, Robert V., & Lofquist, Leonard H. (1976). Close personality style and the process of work adjustment. *Journal of Counseling Psychology,* January.

Doughtie, E.B., et al. (1976). Black/white differences on vocational preference inventory. *Journal of Vocational Behavior,* January.

Downs, Anthony. (1967). *Inside bureaucracy.* Boston: Little, Brown.

Farshan, Barbara L., & Goodman, Barbara H. (Eds.). (1981). *Outsiders on the inside.* Englewood Cliffs, NJ: Prentice-Hall.

Form, William H., & Miller, Delbert C. (1951). *Industrial sociology.* New York: Harper & Row.

Francesco, Anne Marie, & Hakel, Milton D. (1981). Gender and sex as determinants of hireability of applicants for gender-typed jobs. *Psychology of Women Quarterly,* 5(5), Supplement.

Ginzberg, E. (1972). Towards a theory of occupational choice: A restatement. *Vocational Guidance Quarterly,* Spring.

Ginzberg, E., et al. (1951). *Occupational choice: An approach to a general theory.* New York: Columbia University Press.

Golumbiewski, R. T. (1978). Mid life transition and mid career crisis: A special case for individual development. *Public Administration Review,* Summer.

Harmon, L. W. (1970). Anatomy of career commitment in women. *Journal of Counseling Psychology,* January.

Hennig, Margaret, & Jardim, Anne. (1977). *The managerial woman.* New York: Doubleday.

Holland, John L. (1973). *Making vocational choices: A theory of careers.* Englewood Cliffs, NJ: Prentice-Hall.

Hollingshead, A. B. (1949). *Elmtown's youth.* New York: John Wiley.

Holloway, Stephen. (1980). Up the hierarchy: From clinician to administrator. *Administration in Social Work,* Winter.

Kadushin, Alfred. (1958). Determinants of career choice and their implications for social work. *Social Work Education,* April.

Kerson, Toba, & Alexander, Leslie. (1979). Strategies for success: Women in social service administration. *Administration in Social Work, 3*(3), Fall.

Korman, A. K. (1966). Self esteem variable in vocational choice. *Journal of Applied Psychology,* Winter.

Korman, A. K. (1970). Towards a hypothesis of work behavior. *Journal of Applied Psychology,* January.

Kravitz, Diane, & Austin, Carol. (1984). Women's issues in social service administration. *Administration in Social Work,* Winter.

Krumboltz, J. M. (1979). A social learning theory of career decision making. In A. M. Mitchell et al. (Eds.), *Social learning theory and career decision making.* Cranston, RI: Carroll.

Lauffer, Armand. (1969). *Social actionists come to social work.* Ann Arbor, MI: University Microfilms.

Lauffer, Armand. (1984). *Understanding your social agency* (2nd ed.). Newbury Park, CA: Sage.

Leibowitz, Zandy B., Farran, Carla, & Kaye, Beverly. (1980). Will your organization be doing career development in the year 2000? *Training and Development,* February.

Lipsett, L. (1962). Social factors in vocational development. *Personnel and Guidance Journal,* Winter.

Lofquist, Leonard H., & Dawis, Robert V. (1969). *Adjustment to work.* Englewood Cliffs, NJ: Prentice-Hall.

Lyles, Marjorie A. (1983). Strategies for helping women managers. *Personnel,* January.

Miller, Donald C., & Form, William H. (1951). *Industrial sociology.* New York: Harper.

Murphy, P., & Burke, H. (1976). Career development at mid-life. *Jounral of Vocational Behavior, 9*(4).

Osipow, Samuel H. (1983). *Theories of career development* (3rd ed.). Englewood Cliffs, NJ: Prentice-Hall.

Patti, Rino, et al. (1979). From direct service to administration: A study of social workers' transitions from clinical to management roles. *Administration in Social Work, 3*(3), Fall.

Roe, Anne. (1956). *The psychology of occupations.* New York: John Wiley.

Roe, Anne, & Klos, Donald. (1969). Occupational classification. *Counseling Psychologist,* January.

Sarason, A. (1977). *Work, aging and social change.* New York: Free Press.

Schein, Edgar. (1978). *Career dynamics: Making individual and organizational needs.* Reading, MA: Addison-Wesley.

Slocum, William L. (1965). Occupational careers and organizations: A sociological perspective. *Personnel and Guidance Journal,* December.

Staub, Ervin. (1985). *Altruism and aggression.* New York: Columbia University Press.

Super, Donald E. (1957). *The psychology of careers.* New York: Harper & Row.

Super, Donald E., et al. (1963). *Career development: Self concept theory.* New York: CEEB Research Monograph No. 4.

Super, Donald E., & Bachrach, P. B. (1957). *Scientific careers and vocational development theory.* New York: Teachers College, Columbia University.

Van Maanen, John, & Schein, Edgar H. (1977). Career development. In J. Richard Hackman & J. Lloyd Suttle (Eds.), *Improving life at work.* Santa Monica, CA: Goodyear.

Chapter 4

CLAIMING PROFESSIONAL STATUS
Professionalism, Semiprofessionalism, and Deprofessionalization

Sam was in a quandary. The staff meeting had gone all wrong. He knew he was somehow to blame but wasn't sure of what he could or should have done differently. There had always been some misunderstanding about the New Americans Project, but he had just not expected such vituperous opposition to his proposals. At first Sam had felt personally attacked; then he became defensive about both his ideas and his clients.

Sam had proposed expansion of the project in both scope and the number of clients to be served. In a well-documented memorandum distributed before the meeting, he had shown (to his own satisfaction) that the funds available through a federal grant and state support could be used more efficiently by building on the strengths of the family and network structures that existed in both the Arab and Southeast Asian communities. His proposal was straightforward.

By reducing the number of professional social workers and public health nurses assigned to the project, it would be possible to employ a larger number of people from within both communities. These paraprofessionals would perform both outreach and counseling functions. Their involvement, he reasoned, would have several advantages over the current operation of the project: (1) The new Americans, with some training and guidance, would be employed in meaningful tasks, thus facilitating their integration into American society. (2) Because they knew and understood the needs of the populations from which they themselves had come, paraprofessionals would be able to more readily identify people with special needs for which the agency was equipped to provide service. (3) As persons culturally indigenous to these populations, they would provide an effective communication link between the agency and the new Americans.

Sam understood that his proposal would have to be accepted by the department heads at the agency. That's how things operated. Decisions to move into new program areas or to modify long-standing operating procedures were always made consensually, in open dialogue among colleagues. He knew he would have to substantiate whatever claims he made about efficiency or the improvement of services. He was prepared for this. But he was not prepared for the overwhelmingly negative response generated by his paper. "What makes you think that people who have been in this country only for a year or two, perhaps no more than a few months, could possibly take on the professional chores of assessment, treatment and referral?" someone had challenged. But this was not exactly what Sam had proposed.

"We've always prided ourselves in our commitment to confidentiality. If you are right that these people network among themselves, how can you expect them to maintain professional confidences? Wouldn't some of your clients find it difficult sharing personal information with others who are so much like themselves, perhaps no more competent to deal with the problems presented than the clients themselves?" someone else had asked. "These people need all the help they can get and that we can give them," a third had volunteered. "Let's not treat them any differently or with less respect than we would our other clients. They deserve and they need the best professional service."

"Building a volunteer core within each of these communities, yes. But professional help and volunteer involvement are different than turning over responsibility to paraprofessionals. I saw enough of this," another staff member offered, "in the Model Cities[1] program to know that paraprofessionals are likely to organize themselves into a distinct political force. That may have been OK for Model Cities, but this isn't a political agency. We are professionals providing a professional service."

Only Millicent Kapinski had supported his ideas, and even then with some reservation. "Sam's ideas have considerable merit," she had argued. "We should not dismiss them out-of-hand without some further thought and careful analysis. Let's look at what he's really proposing: involving members of the client population in service delivery and needs identification, finding more effective ways of communicating with people whose language skills and lack of familiarity with our institutions make it difficult for them to accept and utilize services, and increasing our outreach and ultimately the numbers of clients served at no cost to the agency. Those are worthwhile goals. But the mechanisms he is suggesting are different from those we employ in our other departments. So let's not reject the goals so quickly, let's examine the mechanisms and the alternatives we might find to them." The meeting had ended on this note of both consensus and disagreement. "OK, so Millicent saved my skin," Sam thought, "but where do I go next?"

THE TRIUMPH OF PROFESSIONALISM

What Sam Mansouri first perceived as an attack on himself, then on the populations for whom he had responsibility and finally on the plan he was proposing was perceived by other staff members as an appropriate defense of professional standards. Professions like social work deliver services, generally advice or action, to individuals, organizations and larger institutions, to groups of people or to the public at large. Professional services, it is generally assumed, are supported by esoteric knowledge systematically developed and applied to client problems. This knowledge may be substantive or theoretic, based on cumulative experience, experimentation and observation. Generally, it is a mixture of all three. Professionals claim that their practice should rest on such knowledge and that they are competent to apply it to problems by virtue of their study and apprenticeship under those who have mastered that knowledge.

When we think of a "real pro," we often have in mind someone who is skilled, competent in the application of knowledge, dedicated and devoted to others, and consistent in his or her professional behavior. To a large extent, this is because professionals, as Everett Hughes[2] has pointed out, *profess* to know better than others the nature of matters within their occupation's domain. Such matters include the causes or consequences of certain behavior and the techniques or technologies that might be used to influence behavior or ameliorate conditions considered negative for certain classes of people. They also profess the right to apply those practices and areas of knowledge to people in need. Sometimes professionals attempt to claim an *exclusive* domain; that is, they demand and often receive the exclusive right to practice in prescribed ways and with certain people. Well-established professions, like medicine and law, have been largely successful in receiving support from the general public for such claims of exclusivity.

People acting in their professional capacities are expected, even required, to think *objectively* about matters that others might deal with on the basis of less systematized knowledge, more limited intellectual exploration, greater sentiment or emotion and often with fixed and rigid points of view. Because professionals do profess to be skilled and qualified, they ask that they be trusted. They may even demand that clients share with them secrets that are related to the problems being dealt with. In turn, they commit themselves to confidentiality and to the use of those secrets only in the best interests of the client. This demand for trust has yet another consequence.

Many professionals claim that only others similarly initiated in knowledge and practice can effectively judge whether a professional's performance is both skilled and ethical. For example, physicians consider it their prerogative not only to define the nature of disease and health but also to determine how medical services ought to be distributed and paid for, and the criteria by which medical practice is to be evaluated. They resist efforts by nonphysicians to define any of these issues. Similarly, social workers not only develop technologies like case work, community work, case management and specially tailored approaches to supervision but also engage in actions aimed at affecting public policy. In turn, policy affects both types of practices and the services available to populations in need. Thus, while professions like social work are themselves products of social change (new knowledge and emergent technologies, and modifications in the ways in which risks are shared and services are provided as a consequence of industrialization and urbanization), they also attempt to shape the forces that lead to their own growth and the expansion of the services they consider essential to the well-being of others.

What this requires is a certain amount of solidarity, a commitment to professional values and norms, an ideology that espouses concern with populations at risk, a willingness to share a common fate and a sense of trust in other members of the profession. While members of some other professions and occupations may be expected to be equally committed or competent, members of the general public, even of the populations served, are not equally deserving of trust. Nor is the expression of commitment by such publics likely to be accepted as a substitute for competence.

Many social workers are at pains to prove that their work cannot be done effectively by amateurs (untrained or even partially trained people involved in interventions on the basis of commitment or good will). This is an understandable defense of professionalism. It took at least two generations of practitioners, trained at universities, before professional social work practice was distinguishable from the volunteer friendly visitor and the social actionist or reformer. Although social work underwent a period of "deprofessionalization" in the mid-1960s and early 1970s, in which paraprofessionals and others were involved as nearly full-fledged social agency team members, and in which the professional degree was downgraded from the MSW to the BSW, in the 1980s social work has begun to focus inward, determined to deepen knowledge and improve skill.

Some professions, social work included, may not be as successful in substantiating their claims or in winning exclusive rights to perform what they profess. Claims of competence from multiple sources may lead to competition between different professions for clients, for the right to perform certain services and for status, prestige and material rewards. But such claims also lead to cooperative endeavors and joint efforts. Because social work is in many ways among the least exclusive of professions, its success is largely dependent on the ability of social workers to establish effective linkages with other occupations and community resources. Moreover, social workers accept the involvement of clients in decision making and other actions as a basic point of philosophy and an essential ingredient in their technology. These characteristics notwithstanding, a strain toward exclusivity in social work remains nevertheless, as it does in all professions.

With this background in mind, let's return now to Sam and his situation.

* * * * *

Harvey Marcus had been sitting quietly throughout the meeting. Part of him had been straining to defend Sam's proposal, but the better part of valor, he felt, was to keep his counsel to himself. "There

Exercise 4.1

Objections to Change on the Basis of Professionalism

Based on the foregoing discussion, identify as many separate reasons for objections to Sam's proposal as you think might have motivated the others at the staff meeting. Describe these briefly, in a sentence or two.

1.

2.

3.

4.

5.

6.

7.

8.

are better ways of handling this," he thought. Based on what you know about Harvey, what do you think he had in mind?

As supervisor of clinical services, Yolanda Stephenson was convinced that Sam's approach was totally in error. You have probably already guessed at some of the reasons and have jotted them down in the exercise. But Yolanda didn't object to Sam's goals as articulated by Millicent. She just didn't think that Sam's approach was appropriate to this agency, and she had made that point clear at the staff meeting. But she felt for Sam. Her earlier, private outburst at the New Americans program was behind her, but her sense of propriety and of professional prerogatives was strong. If she were to meet with Sam privately to discuss her feelings, what are the issues she would raise?

You already have a good idea of where Millicent stands. You know enough about her background and experiences in Chile to have a good sense of how she regards involving people in comprehending their situations and acting on their comprehensions. But Sam's proposals trouble her, too. Look over the list of objections you jotted down in **Exercise 4.1**. On which of these does she base her reservations?

Share your ideas with others who are reading or have read this book. Do they agree with your assessments in **Exercise 4.1** and **Exercise 4.2**? On which points? Where is there disagreement? Now put these ideas aside for the moment, and let's reexamine what else we know about professions and professionalism. We'll then go on to consider the roles of paraprofessionals, volunteers and clients in an agency's "human resource mix."

UNDERSTANDING PROFESSIONS, PROFESSIONALISM, AND PROFESSIONALIZATION

Professionals think of themselves as being different from other occupations, and to a large exent they are. We're not talking here about absolute differences; we're talking about differences of degree. These differences are reflected in

(1) a *general and systematized body of knowledge* that the profession considers exclusively its own;
(2) a commitment to the *communal or public welfare*, in contrast with the more private interests of the individual members of a profession;
(3) a perception that an occupation has not only a right but a duty to be *self-governing and autonomous* in its determination of appropriate practices;

Exercise 4.2

Resolving the Contradictions

Knowing what you know about Harvey, Yolanda and Millicent, consider how each might help Sam reconsider his proposal so as to resolve the contradictions between the dominant staff point of view and the ideas in Sam's proposal.

1. Harvey's ideas:

2. Yolanda's ideas:

3. Millicent's ideas:

(4) a claim to a *jurisdiction of certain problems* (and certain publics or clients) over which it should have *authority*; and
(5) a distinctive *occupational culture* replete with its own folkways and relationships, one that is *recognized* as distinctive by the general public.

Social workers, like other professionals, argue that they have a body of knowledge that has been systematically and rigorously developed through scientific research and practical experience. This body of knowledge, it is further claimed, can be taught and applied to practice, that is, to social intervention with individuals, groups, communities and the larger society. This knowledge base, of course, is not exclusively that of social work. It has, to a large extent, been borrowed from psychology, sociology, political and economic science and the practical experiences of other allied professions (medicine, law, urban planning, education and others). Nevertheless, its organization, the way in which components of the knowledge base are integrated with each other, as the professional claims, is exclusively that of social work.

Like other professionals, those in social work postulate that the transmission of knowledge requires an elaborate and formal system of training. Some of that training, for beginning-level competence and skill, can be conducted within a bachelor's level degree program. More advanced knowledge, however, must be transmitted through a master's (MSW) or a doctoral training program that may lead either to a DSW (doctor of social work) degree or to a more theoretic and research-based Ph.D. The location of these basic educational programs in a university setting is important.

It is argued by most professionals that if such training were to be nonacademic, it would be less than professional. Academia, it is assumed, ensures that the knowledge transmitted to students is both theoretically sound and generalizable. In contrast, the knowledge base of other occupations, where the training may not be university-based, would tend to be more practical and limited. Further, the systematic knowledge of professional training, it is presumed, discourages the inconsistencies and lack of integration in the knowledge base that are found in some nonprofessional occupational groupings. It is no wonder that some professionals might fear that the transmission or transfer of their knowledge to others who are less than fully professionally trained may result in inconsistent, ineffective and perhaps even dangerous practices.

Staff members at the All-Family Services Center have an image of their organization as being highly professional in its orientation. "When we started the adoptions and foster care unit," the agency's director had written in a paper prepared for the regional conference of the Child Welfare League, "we decided to recruit the *best trained staff* available, and then to provide them with additional training opportunities. Besides assigning some of our more experienced workers to the unit, we recruited young MSWs from Columbia, Michigan, and Wisconsin—schools with top-notch reputations as educational institutions and places where faculty members were reputed to be national leaders in child welfare because of their contributions to research and theory development. But even then we weren't satisfied. We sent two of the staff people to intern in the State of Oregon's Permanency Planning Project, where new knowledge and new approaches were being tested to make sure that kids would no longer be bounced around the foster care system without any hope of ever being permanently located with a family that cared about them. And our unit supervisor participated in the Project CRAFT[3] training at Michigan.

"In the long run," he concluded, "this training paid off in the professional quality of our work and in the effectiveness of our staff." It had additional pay-offs as well. The agency's reputation as a "professional place to work," and as an organization with high professional standards, was bolstered by the fact that there were frequent opportunities for staff members to continue their professional education, both through in-service training and through opportunities to attend conferences and participate in university-based courses and workshops.

In addition to their emphasis on a *knowledge base,* professionals also view themselves as being *community-conscious,* performing a public service rather than serving private interests. By contrast, when unions talk about better pay, better working conditions and more worker involvement in setting agency policy, they are reflecting private, not public, interests. Thus members of any profession will tend to distinguish the concerns of their professional associations from those of unions and protest movements, even unions of professional workers. "Professionals have no business unionizing," Millicent had argued at an organizing meeting called by a local affiliate of the American Federation of State, County and Municipal Employees. "Our work should be directed toward the best interests of the child, the best interests of the disabled and the best interests of the isolated elderly."

I don't mean to suggest that all social workers or all members of other human service professions feel the same way. In many places, social workers, nurses, teachers and others *are* unionized. In fact, teachers' unions and the professional association to which teachers belong are often one and the same organization. The National Education Association and its state affiliates often function as professional associations at the state and national levels and as unions at the local or organizational level. Interestingly enough, the demands presented in contract negotiations—for example, more educational leaves for teachers, better pay and working conditions and smaller teacher/student ratios—are almost invariably phrased as being in the public interest, since the education of children is improved by improving the relationship between teachers and children and the quality of teachers' competence and skills.

The differences between professions and other occupations are perhaps more a matter of degree than of substance. The *norm of altruism* exists in varying degrees in all occupational groupings, but professionals justify their claim to altruism in several ways. First, they establish *codes of ethics* that are intended to symbolize their commitments and to serve as the standards against which practitioner behavior is judged. Second, they claim to involve students and initiates in a long socialization process that includes professional training in an academic setting, as well as various forms of internship under experienced and certified practitioners. Finally, they do, on occasion, disbar or decertify their practitioners for unethical practices, generally defined as activities that are clearly aimed at the disadvantage of the populations they are serving while increasing the advantage for the practitioners in question. Agencies are considered to be more "professional" to the extent that they adhere closely to ethical standards and to appropriate norms of behavior.

This *self-regulating behavior* is the justification frequently cited for the claims made by many professionals that they should be relatively free of external control. Many professions demand a license to perform their activities as they see fit. What they attempt to do, in effect, is to carve out areas in which members can only be evaluated by their peers. They do this by engaging in self-study, establishing standards for practice and, frequently, establishing certification programs that are intended to ensure competent practice. Some may even distinguish between levels of practice. Further, they recognize exceptional practice through a variety of awards. Your local NASW (National Association of Social Workers) chapter undoubtedly offers a "social worker of the year" award and may further divide that award into "advocate of the year," "clinician of the year," "administrator of the year" and so on. Each of these represents a cherished professional value or role.

A more objective evaluation of professions and professionalism, however, shows little evidence that professional autonomy contributes to high standards of professional service. There are some who argue that ethical codes are not set up to protect the welfare of the clients, but instead serve to conceal the activities of the profession from public examination by permitting none other than fellow professionals to penalize those who violate the norms.

The growth of the consumer movement in the United States has led to closer scrutiny by the public of the activities of various professions. The increase in both private and public action suits against individual practitioners (as well as the organizations that employ them) for malpractice has forced some professions into stricter self-governance, as well as greater acceptance of limits on their autonomy. Often these limits are imposed through state and local licensure procedures. Nevertheless, professions have had considerable influence in establishing standards that are passed into law. For example, national associations and their state and local chapters frequently design model legislation that serves as the basis for licensure. In many cases, public commissions are set up to review examinations that professionals are required to pass to receive certification. Generally, how-ever, these bodies are composed to a large extent of members in good standing within the profession itself.

Some professions are more successful than others in staking a claim to a particular turf, thus acquiring a mandate to serve a specific client population, deal with defined problem areas and apply technologies for which they are especially suited and their members effectively trained. But they may not be alone in staking those claims. Other occupational groups may make counterclaims. Thus far, no occupational group has successfully challenged the legal profession's access to the courtroom, although individuals may be permitted to act in their own defense.

The medical profession continues to maintain hegemony over health care services, but not without some challenge from nurses and allied medical professionals who claim both the competence and the right to perform certain tasks that have previously been performed only by physicians. Clinical psychologists and social workers have also made significant headway in wresting authority from psychiatrists over certain client populations. For example, whereas at one time only those who treated clients under the direction of a psychiatrist might be eligible for reimbursement through third-party payments (i.e., insurance payments), today social workers may be permitted the same privilege.

Further, what was once referred to as the "medical model" has been challenged as inappropriate to social work and other human service occupations. This model might be stated as follows: The physician, by dint of traning and experience, is both more knowledgeable and more competent to determine appropriate treatment, based on careful and scientific diagnosis. Proponents of the medical model argue that if clients were to be treated as consumers rather than as patients, determining what service or what treatment they wished to buy, they would be likely to receive poorer service, often making the errors inherent in lay versus professional judgments. Perhaps the appropriate word here is not *consumer* but rather *customer*.

Professional services, by definition, are not like the products offered in a department store or cafeteria. Customers are expected to evaluate their own needs and judge whether the investment is worth the outcome. Patients are not. "The customer is always right" may be appropriate to the purchase of consumer goods, but it is totally inappropriate, from the perspective of the medical model, when it comes to making judgments about complex, life and death matters that only a competent professional can decide. Not only has consumer activism led to a challenge to this model, but the very nature of medical practice has produced the need to involve patients in decisions. Indeed, active support of the patient may be necessary in many forms of treatment (especially in areas where mental health or chronic illness are involved).

Social work, in contrast, has always given at least lip service to the involvement of the client in determining his or her needs and in selecting from alternative ways to deal with the problems for which service has been requested. The ethos of a "client's right to self-determination" is central both to the social worker's statement of professional ethics and to many of the technologies involved in enabling people to "help themselves." Nevertheless, elements of the medical model are found throughout social work practice. Remember, we are referring only to models. In the real world of practice, no profession fully reflects the characteristics of a single model.

The pure medical model is not to be found anywhere, since clients always have considerable power over professionals. In hospitals as well as social agencies they may, through their participation in committees and boards (representing the public), even have the power to hire and fire professionals. Those going to private practitioners have the power to cease attending and to select another practitioner if they so desire. If the uncontested authority of the professional ever existed, it clearly does not at the moment, nor is it likely to in the future.

Revelations of professional abuse and malpractice have led to accusations of elitism and of a lack of concern for or commitment to the welfare of clients in favor of the pursuit of financial gain (in contrast with the professions' claims of being community-conscious). Clients have become increasingly sophisticated consumers of professional services, and this sophistication can be traced to the expansion of formal education, the availability of client-focused books that demystify medical and other practices or that assist in individual self-help, the growth of self-help groups that compete with and/or cooperate with professionals, the attention of the mass media, and the growing activism of women's groups, Blacks and other minorities, as well as certain functional categories of consumers (ex-mental patients, parents of the developmentally disabled, adult adoptees, and others).

PROFESSIONS AS COMMUNITIES AND CULTURES

You have undoubtedly heard or run across the term *professional community*. Not all professionals have a sense of themselves as part of a community, but many do. Members are bound by a common identity based on common values, clearly understood role definitions, relatively clear boundaries, the power of reproduction (via the transmission of culture to succeeding generations) through schooling and internships and, to a certain extent, a common language (what we refer to as "professional jargon"). The community includes formal professional organizations like the American Medical Association or the NASW, colleges and training schools, the organizations or agencies in which professionals work (like social agencies or human service organizations), as well as all kinds of informal groupings within the profession. These groups include participants involved in social and legislative action, and others involved in a variety of leadership roles. These leaders are the role models who epitomize in their behavior the competencies and attitudes that the profession values.

Professions, like other communities and cultures, have their own distinctive histories. And like their counterparts, they tend to be selective about what and whom to include in those histories. Social work in the United States traces its roots to the settlement house movement and the progressives of the 1860s and 1880s. Early heroes and heroines include Stanton Coit, who established the University Settlement in New York, and Jane Addams, who established Hull House in Chicago. The Charity Organization Societies of the 1870s were established to coordinate the work of myriad private, mostly voluntary social services for the poor. Theirs was a humanitarian response to the urban poor who were ill, jobless, inadequately housed and/or exploited. Their activities included both legislative and advocacy efforts that led to the establishment of juvenile courts and child welfare reforms. At the same time, the COSs applied "scientific methods" to service coordination and referral.

In the mid-1920s, Mary Follett and Edward Lindemann were leaders in the community movement that pioneered efforts to organize primary groups in communities where people lived. They promoted the establishment of cohesive social units that would assume responsibility for themselves and guide their own destinies, and in so doing ensure the expansion of democracy. In the 1930s and 1940s social workers not only assumed leadership for the growth of America's social welfare programs but developed or adopted new technologies that led to more effective clinical and group practices.

I have mentioned a few of social work's heroes and heroines, its founding mothers and fathers. But professions may also have their villains. In the political climate of the mid-1980s, Ronald Reagan and Reaganomics were pictured as villains. Thus history and folklore combine to help professionals define who they are like (and who they are not like). It can be dangerous for an individual member of a profession to identify with a villain or to agree with many of a presumed villain's notions or policies.

Professional culture has a considerable impact on the growth of a professional community. To a large extent, this stems from the de-

Exercise 4.3

Professionalism and Your Agency

How "professional" is your agency? Based on your observations, to what extent are each of the characteristics of a profession also characteristic of your agency (high, medium or low)? Is this appropriate? How would you change or modify the situation?

	High, medium, or low	Is this appropriate?	What should be changed?
1. Practice is built on a systematic body of *knowledge*.			
2. Practice is oriented toward the community welfare (*altruism*) in contrast to the private interests of staff.			
3. The agency and its staff have considerable *autonomy* over the nature of its programs, the population served and the way it provides these services.			
4. The *authority* of the host profession's culture and professional collegial relationships have precedence over bureaucratic or organizational demands.			

In balance, would you say that the agency is "too professional" or "not professional enough"? Please justify your answer in terms of the norms of knowledge, altruism, autonomy and authority we have been discussing.

velopment of *colleagueship* within each professional group. All occupations establish certain formal and informal criteria for membership inclusion. They also legislate, generally informally, the form and extensiveness of the relationships established between fellow members.

There are rites and obligations of colleagueship, both in theory and in practice. We have already noted that in most professions only one's colleagues are presumed to have the right to judge whether one has practiced ethically and effectively. For this reason, colleagues must be able to take each other's sentiments for granted. They must be able to communicate freely and openly among themselves and to share confidences that could not be repeated to uninitiated ears. Even the rules of confidentiality, those that limit the sharing of information outside "the fraternity" or "the sorority," are frequently waived with one's colleagues.

Colleagues share what Everett Hughes has called "guilty knowledge." This is a private knowledge shared only among colleagues through the subtle use of argot or jargon. For example, a psychiatrist can say shocking things about patients in technical terms to fellow psychiatrists that they would never share in lay terms to lay people. Other physicians will use black humor in the operating room but would never consider sharing the same jokes with a patient's family or even with members of the hospital's board of directors.

Trusting their colleagues, fellow professionals can say things to each other in such ways that they feel confident they will be comprehended and accepted. Their jargon is more than scientific; it is an assurance that what they intend to convey will be properly understood by others.

CLAIMING THE RIGHT TO BE TRULY PROFESSIONAL

You've probably observed that some occupations are "more professional" than others, or at least are so perceived by their members and the public. On what basis are such perceptions founded? One might be defined as "sociological," a second as "historical" and a third as "political." In the sociological approach, different occupations are contrasted on the basis of the extent to which their attributes approximate the norms discussed (altruism, knowledge, autonomy, and authority).

Using the historical, or process, approach, we might say that an occupation has become a profession when the following have occurred: (1) it has a name that is clearly identifiable to its own members and to the public at large; (2) its members are organized into a professional association that sets standards, establishes and maintains a code of ethics and provides advocacy not only for its members but for the welfare of the public at large and the particular populations that the profession serves; (3) it has one or more professional schools, generally university-based, through which knowledge is developed, codified and transmitted; and (4) it is recognized as a profession by law, through processes that include both licensure and certification and the exclusive (although sometimes shared) right to perform certain tasks, serve specified populations or use a designated set of technologies.

The third approach to determining when an occupation has become a profession is more clearly political. From this perspective, professions are distinguished from other occupations in that they are more successful in convincing the general public that their claim to mandates should be honored to the partial or total exclusion of other occupational groups. There seem to be three sources of such political power. The first is *timing*. Some occupations were simply there earlier and have been around for a longer period of time. Thus physicians, the military and the clergy have long-standing claims to professional status.

The second source of power stems from the extent to which a profession deals with high levels of *uncertainty*. By this I mean the issues that they handle that clients feel incompetent to deal with by themselves. In earlier times, when problems seemed to be less complex or when solutions were less technical, it may not have been as necessary to have so many specialized professions. A *shaman* or medicine man could deal with health, mental health, and even political issues. Today, however, we need a wide variety of health and mental health professions, political scientists, economists, legal specialists, and others to deal with the ever-increasing complexity created by uncertainty.

This uncertainty doesn't have to be intrinsic; it can be artificially produced. For example, in the guise of providing clarity, some consultants have mystified organizational processes so as to increase the demand for their services. Attorneys have mystified divorce, thereby artificially creating an area of uncertainty over which they exercise considerable control. Whether by accident or collusion, accountants have created such complexity in the tax laws as to make their services (to some of us, at least) indispensable.

A third source of power is *indeterminacy.* There is an interesting paradox to be found in the fact that many of the things that professionals do are not explicitly defined, and are in fact largely indeterminate. Thus psychiatrists, family therapists, and social work clinicians involved in direct practice with clients are expected to have wide latitude in their choice of action and the judgments they make. The problems presented are so complex, however, that it is not easy to break down the required responses into step-by-step procedures. In contrast, the determination of eligibility for public welfare assistance can easily be broken down, much as one would break down the steps in an assembly line procedure. For this reason it is not necessary to hire professionals to do eligibility determinations.

Family treatment, by being defined as indeterminate, requires the competence of a trained professional who can be expected to behave on the basis of relevant knowledge and with adherence to an ethical code. What makes this so paradoxical is that the very inability to codify information and procedures in certain areas of practice is the basis for claiming authority over those areas. And yet professional knowledge is presumed to be not only transmittable but codifiable.

Does this in some way help to explain the reluctance of the All-Families Service Center staff members to employ paraprofessionals for work with the New Americans Project?

SOCIAL WORK AS A SEMIPROFESSION

Amitai Etzioni, a sociologist from Columbia University, has classified occupations along a continuum based on the extent to which they have been successful in their claims for designation as full professions. His analysis suggests that the internal attributes of professionalism are much less influential in laying claim to professional status than the issues pertaining to political power. Etzioni's continuum looks like this:

(1) Historically *established professions*—physicians, college professors, clergymen, lawyers and engineers;
(2) *New professions*—natural scientists like biologists and chemists, and social scientists like economists and sociologists;
(3) *Semiprofessions*—nurses, social workers, librarians and teachers;
(4) *Would-be professions*—accountants, personnel managers, funeral directors, chiropractors, pharmacists and business executives;
(5) *Marginal professions*—lab technicians, insurance agents, medical technicians and others generally given "paraprofessional" status.

Our concern here will be with the *semiprofessions*, particularly social work.

Social work—like nursing, library science, and teaching (at the secondary and elementary school levels)—is not merely classified as a semiprofession but as a *female* semiprofession. Women make up approximately two-thirds of the social work profession, four-fifths of the library profession, 85% of those involved in teaching elementary school, and virtually 98% of those practicing nursing. This is not the only reason that these occupations have been sex-labeled, however. For a wide variety of reasons, women have been locked into a relatively small number of occupations. Their identification with the semiprofessions is particularly apt in terms of stereotypic gender and sex-role characteristics.

Women are expected to be in occupations in which their performance is to support the role of males (for example, nurses in relation to physicians). They are also presumed to be caring, oriented toward helping and toward providing succor (social work). Moreover, they are expected to provide child care at home and, by extension, in the classroom (teachers). There may even be some similarity between their responsibilities for homemaking (including the storing, categorizing, and dispensing of food) and similar work performed in libraries (where they do much the same to information).

Against this background, it is not difficult to understand why social work and the other female occupations have been designated as semiprofessional rather than as having achieved fully professional status. In our society, women do not share power equally with men. What is particularly ironic is that semiprofessionals tend to have control over large areas that deal both with uncertainty and with practices that are difficult to define (indeterminate). Relationships between social workers and clients, school teachers and students, nurses and patients are often focused on issues that require a great deal of professional competence and skill. And yet this frequently goes unrecognized by the general public.

Parents often feel that they can teach better than teachers. I've never met a social worker who hasn't been told by a family member or friend how to do his or her job better, how to deal with a particular problem, or what policy should be adopted to deal with a particular complex of social problems.

Several years back, when I managed a large and, by all standards, successful continuing education program for professionals in the human services, I was faced with some interesting challenges. Psychiatrists, for example, were loathe to register for family treatment courses and workshops offered under the auspice of the School of Social Work, despite the fact that these programs were of an extraordinarily high quality. Psychiatrists, I was told, were just not going to admit their ignorance before people whom they did not consider to be colleagues and who were members of an occupational group of a lower social status.

Interestingly, I found that many social workers seeking management training were willing to pay three or four times the fees charged by the School of Social Work at management workshops conducted by the Business School. Again, I was convinced that the training programs offered under our auspices were equally as good and often better because they were directly aimed at the practice problems faced by managers in human service organizations. In fact, we frequently used the same instructors, after having worked closely with them to help reshape their presentations to deal with issues of importance to social agency managers.

I have to share one anecdote with you. The director of the state department of mental health in a midwestern state, a psychiatrist with very few biases about other occupations, had asked me to develop a course on consultation for directors of community mental health centers. At the time, state law required directors to be psychiatrists. "Thanks for your confidence," I said, "but it'll never work. Psychiatrists are just not going to come to a School of Social Work to learn about consultation." "Oh yes they will," he replied, pulling a set of new forms from his briefcase. "These are the reporting forms that I'm requiring all community mental health center directors to complete before they get reimbursed by the state for any consultation done by their agency staff members. I know you guys (social workers) know more about consultation than we do, but as far as they're concerned (the psychiatrists), social workers know how to fill out forms. If I tell them they have to come to you to learn how to fill out these forms, they'll be there!"

There may be several ways to cope with semiprofessional status. One is to get the support of professional elites in the male-dominated professions. The anecdote I shared with you worked for a particular workshop, but it may not work for an entire occupational grouping. Nevertheless, the principle may be worth pursuing. In this case social work was perceived to possess technical competence and skill that another occupational group did not. If social workers, nurses, schoolteachers, and librarians possess some competence that is sufficiently in demand, they may very well be able to negotiate for greater power or control over their own work.

As you are probably aware, practitioners in these semiprofessions tend to work in organizations. As such, they are employees and thus subject to all the bureaucratic forms that prevent employees from using discretion and reduce control over their own work. As physicians increasingly become employees in large-scale medical organizations, they too will find themselves in a similar position to that of other employed professionals.

As we noted in Chapter 3, women are less likely to move up in the organizational hierarchy than are men. Management is still heavily male-dominated. Clearly men are overrepresented in the management of social agencies and as principals or administrators in the school system. The women's movement, as it grows in strength, may lead more women into managerial positions. If so, it is likely to have some impact on the status of the female semiprofessions.

There may, however, be another way to cope with semiprofessional status, and that is to opt out of the competition altogether. Some years ago, Willard Richan and Allan Mendelsohn argued that social work's search for professionalism is bankrupt. Efforts to claim professional status, they postulated, were self-aggrandizing. This may be the reason for what Epstein has termed social work's "disengagement from the poor." The intellectual pretensions of seeking professional status lead to an erosion in activism and an effort to emulate other occupations that offer higher status and better-paying clients.

Further, acceptance of worker status (in contrast with professional status) may lead to gains for clients as much as for members of the occupation. Thus the successful efforts of teachers to unionize has led to similar efforts among social workers, nurses, and librarians. And the collective bargaining objectives of these unions has often focused on the improvement of services to client populations. Even members of the more established professions, like college professors and physicians, have begun to unionize. Thus the distinctions between the professions and the semiprofessions may begin to dissolve. Collective action through unionization may do more to right the imbalance in power between occupational groups than any arguments that might be made about technical competence or superior ethics.

DEPROFESSIONALIZATION

Without being explicit about it, we've already examined some of the forces that may lead to a gradual "deprofessionalization" of the professions. They include the revolt of clients, encroachment and competition from other occupational groupings, and unionization related to employee status. We've also discussed another factor—the potential for using paraprofessionals to do things some professionals do, and other things they may not be able to do as well. Michael Austin has documented the blurring of demarcations between the professionally trained worker (with a BA or MSW degree) and nonprofessionals or aides who increasingly assume responsibilities formerly allocated only to those with professional training.

For example, case-aides often follow up on released mental patients, formerly the role of a social worker. Information referral specialists with no formal training (other than that received on the job) may carry out tasks that were at one time reserved for community organizers. Even social work's development of case management and its claim for exclusive competence in this area is under attack as aspects of referral and follow-up are delegated to less trained (and less expensive) personnel. Although the paraprofessional "movement," as it was called in the mid-1960s and early 1970s, is hardly a movement anymore, it has spawned a wide variety of new occupational classifications that include people with less than BA degrees who perform intake, assessment and follow-up functions that were formerly the exclusive domain of professional social workers.

Today, even clients have challenged the exclusive domain of the professional worker. Self-help groups, at first resisted by many professionals, have now come to be seen as full partners in the healing process. There are, at present, more than 10,000 associations of self-help groups dealing with issues as diverse as weight control and the reduction of family violence. In many cases, social workers have initiated, guided and then launched these groups toward growing independence.

REVIEW AND TENTATIVE CONCLUSIONS

It's time again to review what we have learned thus far. I'll start. You add your own conclusions.

(1) Professionals profess to know better what to do and how to do specific tasks in relation to specific populations and specified problems.
(2) Professionals claim to possess a body of general and systematized knowledge that can be codified and transmitted to others, to be committed to the public good in contrast with private concerns, to have the right to be self-governing and to have jurisdiction over certain problems and certain client populations with regard to which they should have sole authority.
(3) Professionals have their own distinctive cultures and share characteristics commonly identified with a community. These include history and folklore, a common language and a shared sense of destiny or purpose.
(4) Some occupations are more successful than others in laying claim to full professionalism. Social work, together with other "female" occupations, tends to be designated as a semiprofession. This may be less a factor of its knowledge and areas of competence than of the general perceptions of society about that knowledge and competence. It is to a large extent based on sex-stereotyping and on what have come to be perceived as "appropriate" female roles in our society.

YOUR ADDITIONS

(5)

(6)

(7)

(8)

(9)

(10)

NOTES

1. An antipoverty program in the early and mid-1970s.
2. Hughes's analysis is substantially encapsuled in the following few paragraphs. For a further explication, see Hughes (1963).
3. Curriculum Resources for Adoption and Foster-Care Training was a national project conducted in the mid- to late 1970s.

REFERENCES

Austin, Michael J. (1978). *Professionals and paraprofessionals.* New York: Human Sciences Press.

Barber, Bernard. (1963). Some problems in the sociology of the professions. *Daedalus,* Fall.

Bucher, Rue, & Strauss, Anselm. (1961). Professions in process. *American Journal of Sociology,* Fall.

Buffrin, William, & Rituo, Roger. (1984). Work autonomy and the mental health professional. *Administration in Social Work,* Winter.

Epstein, Irwin. (1970). Professionalization, professionalism, and social work radicalism. *Journal of Health and Social Behavior,* January.
Etzioni, Amitai. (Ed.). (1969). *The semi-professions and their organization.* New York: Free Press.
Friedson, Elliott (Ed). (1973). *The professions and their prospects.* Newbury Park, CA: Sage.
Froland, Charles, Pancoast, Diane L., Chapman, Nancy J., & Kimboko, Priscilla J. (1981). *Helping networks in human services* (esp. Chap. 8). Newbury Park, CA: Sage.
Goode, William. (1957). Community within a community: The professions. *American Sociological Review,* Spring.
Greenwood, Ernest. (1957). Attributes of a profession. *Social Work,* Spring.
Haug, Marie. (1973). Deprofessionalization: An alternative hypothesis for the future. In Paul Halmos (Ed.), *Professionalization and social change: A sociological review monograph.* Keele, Staffordshire: University of Keele.
Haug, Marie, & Sussman, Marvin. (1969). Professional autonomy and the revolt of the client. *Social Problems,* Spring.
Helfgot, John. (1974). Professional reform organizations and the symbolic representation of the poor. *American Sociological Review,* Fall.
Hughes, Everett C. (Ed.). (1958). *Men and their work.* New York: Free Press.
Hughes, Everett C. (1983). Professions. *Daedalus,* Fall.
Johnson, Terence. (1972). *The professions and power.* London: Macmillan.
Lauffer, Armand. (1970). *Social actionists come to social work.* Ann Arbor, MI: University Microfilms.
Loewenberg, Frank M. (1968). Social workers and indigenous nonprofessionals: Some structural dilemmas. *Social Work,* July.
Richan, Willard C., & Mendelsohn, Allan R. (1973). *Social work: The unloved profession.* New York: New Viewpoints.
Ritzer, George. (1977). *Working: Conflict and change* (2nd ed.). Englewood Cliffs, NJ: Prentice-Hall.
Roth, Julius. (1974). Professionalism: The sociologist's decoy. *Sociology of Work and Occupations,* January.
Toren, Nina. (1972). *Social work: The case of the semiprofession.* Newbury Park, CA: Sage.
Walsh, J. L., & Elling, R. H. (1968). Professionalization and the poor: Structural effects of professional behavior. *Journal of Health and Social Behavior,* January.

Chapter 5

BECOMING A COLLEAGUE AND ENTERING THE AGENCY'S CULTURE

Perspectives, Cultures, and Perceptions

Betsy, Mike, Cyndi, and Mary Jo are graduate social work students assigned to do their field practicum at the agency. They are in their second semester at school but in their first semester of practicum assignment when we first meet them. Although each was assigned to a different supervisor (Betsy works in the clinical services department under Yolanda's supervision, Cyndi works on family life education under Millicent's guidance, Mike is assigned to the New Americans Project under Sam's direction, and Mary Jo is a community placement worker in Harvey's department), the four were encouraged by their school-based faculty adviser to "network" with each other. Schedules permitting, they meet every Tuesday at lunchtime. Early discussions were revealing.

Cyndi: I came here wanting to become the best social worker I can. I feel that this is a really good placement, and I've got a terrific supervisor. But this is such a complicated place to get to know. There's so many things going on and to learn. Sometimes I feel a little lost, but I think they've (the faculty) prepared us pretty well, especially in our practice courses.

Betsy: I feel the same way. After five months of classroom work, this (the agency) really feels like the real world. But there's so much to learn here.

Mary Jo: Yes, but thank goodness for the classroom preparation. I guess I'm lucky that I worked at an agency for a couple of years before coming back to school. It helps me put everything in perspective. I don't mean that I know how to do all my assignments yet, but I've learned enough about practice so that I can talk to Harvey (her supervisor) and the other staff pretty comfortably.

Mike: I don't know. I feel like things that I'm going to be doing are real important, but I feel so inadequate. I'm not used to feeling that way. I guess it's going to take a while, sort of absorbing the atmosphere and learning what's appropriate and what's not. I wanted to work with some Vietnamese families right away, but Sam held me back. Told me to walk around the neighborhood and just observe.

Cyndi: I'm doing some observing too. I agree with Betsy. There's so much to learn.

The conversation then focused on some of the ambiguity that the students were feeling about their roles in the agency. If there was consensus about anything, it was that the agency was a good place to *learn,* that what they were doing or would soon be doing was "real social work," not just classroom theory. That didn't mean denigrating what they were learning in the classroom; if anything, they wanted a chance to see how it could be applied. Two of the students expressed some frustration over having been assigned to different departments. "I know I'm going to have to work hard at it to be a good clinician," Betsy said. "But I'm envious of some of the things you guys are doing. I guess I really want to do everything, learn everything. It's all going to help me when I graduate." "It would have been easier starting out," Mike added, "if we had all been assigned to a single unit at the beginning of our field placements."

* * * * *

The discussion represented a certain diffuseness. Like other students in the early part of their professional training, they wanted to learn everything that would enable them to be good and effective practitioners. They also wanted to apply what they were learning in the classroom, and they were somewhat frustrated at the slowness with which they were assigned responsibilities. "I'm really willing to work hard," Mary Jo had said. "I'd even put in more than the hours that are required if I thought that what I was doing was really being helpful to somebody, and that I was *learning* something from it." "I feel the same way," responded Mike. "But I've got other pressures, too. I've got to watch my time, 'cause I'm working part-time and I don't want my class work to suffer. Getting A's is important to me."

In effect, what was happening was that the students were beginning to define their situation and to establish priorities for themselves. *Learning* clearly was the priority. But they were trying to reconcile what they perceived to be differences between learning in the field and learning in the classroom. The Tuesday lunch conversation two months later, about halfway into their first term in the field, reflected some of the same concerns but was beginning to take a somewhat different turn.

Betsy: I'm still trying to learn everything, but I'm beginning to realize that maybe it's just not possible.

Mary Jo: You can't do it all. Even in my own department where everybody kind of shares the workload, you have to set priorities.

Betsy: The way you and Mike talk about your assignments is so different from mine. Maybe our department is just structured differently. We each (other clinicians) have our own caseloads, and while we sometimes share problems at staff meetings where we case each other's clients, we're each expected to work independently. I get a lot of support from Yolanda. I want to learn all I can from her.

Mike: I feel the same way about Sam. He's got a lot to give, and a lot to teach, stuff that's not in the textbooks and in the coursepacks. I mean, he's really been there, he knows where it's at.

Cyndi: Sometimes I feel my supervisor (Millicent) isn't giving me enough responsibility. But she's really pushing me to get to know myself and how I respond to things. I really want to please her.

* * * * *

At this point, the students' perspectives seemed to be shifting from the diffuse and long-term ("I want to learn everything I can") to the more realistic and short-term ("I want to please my supervisor" and "You can't do it all"). They were also beginning to look to the agency more and to the school less for cues about appropriate practice behavior. While they were still finding their support group helpful in confronting their common plight as student interns in a professional agency, they were also beginning to identify themselves more closely with their supervisors and the departments to which they were assigned. Clearly, getting to know everything was taking second place to performing effectively and appropriately as defined by the supervisor and perhaps by others in the department.

About six weeks later, Betsy, Cyndi, and Mike attended a Tuesday brown bag luncheon.

Mike: Should we wait for Mary Jo?

Betsy: She's not coming today. She's having lunch with my supervisor and some of the other Black social workers. They have something they call the BIB club—BIB, for "Black Is Beautiful," I guess (shrugs her shoulders).

Cyndi: I don't think I can make it next week, either. I mean, there's a lot to do in the family life education program. We've got a big conference coming up. Millicent's expecting a lot from me, and I don't want to disappoint her. I hope you don't mind (raises her eyebrows and wrinkles her nose).

By the middle of the second semester in the field, the students were hardly ever able to make a quorum. "I don't feel so much like a student around here anymore," Cyndi explained to Millicent at one of her weekly supervisory sessions. "I mean, sure, I know I'm a student, but I feel more like a professional worker. Even though I'm here only three days a week (the students were on campus on Thursdays and Fridays), I feel really identified with the agency and especially with the family life education program. I mean, you've given me some real responsibilities, and I feel like I'm part of a team.

"I find myself talking less about school here at the agency, and more about the agency back at school. In fact, the only time Betsy, Mike, Mary Jo, and I ever get together is in our staff development and training class. We talk about the agency a lot. I'm lucky that the assignment I have for that class fits naturally into the kind of things that I'm doing here (at the agency). The others are having a little harder time, but we're each designing programs that we're trying to put into practice here at the center."

* * * * *

DEVELOPING PERSPECTIVE AND ENTERING THE WORK CULTURE

There are a number of concepts through which we might analyze the progression of Cyndi's identity from that of student to that of responsible agency worker and a member of her departmental team. I'm going to use two: "perspective" and "culture." Half a century ago, Karl Mannheim observed that the way in which we conceive things is determined in part by the social or cultural setting in which we find ourselves. George Herbert Mead observed that when people face problematic situations, they attempt to develop coordinated views that guide their actions. He called this the emergence of *perspective*.

In the examples given above, the definition of the problem situation changed for the students over time. Initially the problem was how to cope with the ambiguities and the multiple demands made on them in the agency. Their initial perspectives grew out of collective experiences—the experiences they'd shared at the university, and the experience of being new and unsure at the agency.

Before developing perspectives in common, they relied on those learned elsewhere or borrowed from others. For example, at first they reflected some of the perspectives of their faculty, attempting (or at least hoping) to make a systematic application of classroom knowledge to the work situation. Mary Jo drew in part on her earlier work experiences. Wanting to learn everything at first, they soon limited their aspirations to something more realistic: satisfying one's supervisor and doing one's work well and effectively (limited as that work might be). The changes in perspective were in part the result of facing problems in common with other students, but increasingly they found themselves dealing with work-related problems that they had in common with staff members in the departments to which they were assigned. Eventually, as we shall see, their perspectives became those of colleagues in those work units rather than those of students.

I'm using the term *perspective* much as Howard S. Becker and his associates used it in a study of student culture in the medical school. Drawing on Mead's definition, it refers to a coordinated set of ideas and actions that a person uses in dealing with some problematic situation. It is reflected in a person's ordinary way of thinking and feeling and acting. We all bring different perspectives to our work. Those perspectives are based on earlier experiences and, to a larger extent, on our identification with others whose opinions we value. Robert Merton called this "reference group" behavior. I'm certain you have been in a situation where, in taking action, you asked yourself how someone else whose opinion you respect might respond to what you were doing. In turn, what you were doing and how you were doing it might to a large extent have been influenced by your expectation that this someone might approve or disapprove of certain actions. We all do this as we learn to differentiate between what we perceive to be appropriate and inappropriate in given situations.

This may lead to the emergence of short-term and long-term perspectives. Short-term perspectives include *initial* (I want to learn everything I can), *intermediate* (I want to satisfy my supervisor), and *final* (I want to fit in around here) stages. These may or may not articulate with *long-term* perspectives (I want to be the best social worker I can be).

Although individuals may at first bring different perspectives to bear on a common situation, as they interact with each other they develop group or common perspectives—modes of thought and action that guide their behavior. I'm not talking here about attitudes or values. Values are not necessarily situationally specific. In fact, they tend to be generalized and abstract. They help us evaluate what is good or what is bad, desired or undesired, but not necessarily what is appropriate or inappropriate in a given context. Whereas values may lead to a general predisposition that we may choose to ignore in a given situation, perspectives contain judgments about specific situations and tend to lead to action.

I've always been amazed at how students at the University of Michigan School of Social Work seem to know how long a term paper is supposed to be. I rarely give them guidelines, but by the time they've reached the second semester they know that 10-12 pages will be acceptable, and that somewhere between 15 and 30 footnotes is the norm. How do they learn this if it is never stated explicitly?

Attitudes are personal and also provide some predisposition to act in one way or another, but they don't compel us to act. Perspectives do, however, because they are arrived at collectively by those persons involved in interactive situations and who face a common problem. Harvey Marcus reflects on some learning and unlearning he had to do as a teenager and young adult. "People sometimes call me a workaholic," he says with an ingraciating smile, "but I'm not. Sure, I work hard, but I work to get results. My staff expects me to work hard, and I expect them to. And none of us are afraid of putting in some extra time, evenings or weekends, when needed. Look, I'm not a rate buster. I learned long ago that rate busters get punished.

"When I was a kid, working on a kibbutz in Israel, I worked my *butt* off. Everybody did. As a matter of fact, the harder you worked and the more productive you were, the more status and prestige you had. You were, after all, contributing something to the common good, and hard work was really valued. Then when I returned to the States and got a job on the night shift in a factory while working on my undergraduate degree, I learned that not everybody shared those values. At first, I figured if I worked a little harder then I was required to, I could take an extra long break and crack some of the books for my morning classes. I soon learned that rate busters weren't much appreciated. It wasn't what people said to me, it was the fact that they didn't say anything, that they shunned me at breaktime. At first, I didn't catch on. Finally, one person did say that if I worked my part of the line faster than the others, pretty soon everybody'd have to be working at the same rate. The union wasn't going to like it.

"I don't mean to be saying that as a way of patting myself on the back. People develop certain expectations of themselves and of each other. They figure that everybody who's in the same boat ought to be pulling their oars together. I suppose that's correct. Only on some boats, everybody pulls their oars faster than folks on other boats."

The emergence of perspective leads to a body of collective understandings that influence the behavior of people in specific roles. When the perspectives that people hold are related to the positions they occupy in an organization, we can say that an organizational culture is emerging. As a matter of fact, it may result in two cultures: a "management culture" and a "worker culture."

Agency culture or cultures take on characteristics of their own. The culture informs people subtly about the rights and privileges they possess and the duties and obligations associated with particular positions. While the culture may be influenced by the work situation, it also tends to be influenced by external factors: the norms, values, and ethics inherent in the profession to which the majority or dominant staff members belong, and the larger societal culture. In fact, the various subcultures in the larger society may have considerable influence on agency practice and on the perspectives of agency staff members.

Sometimes these cultures clash. Thus, as we saw in Chapter 4, Sam's efforts to develop a cadre of paraprofessionals who are more reflective of the cultures of the new Americans for whom he has

Exercise 5.1

Identifying Perspectives

1. List the perspectives held by the students whose experiences were described here.
   a. Long-Term

   b. Short-Term
      (1) *inital* (on first entering the agency)

      (2) *intermediate* or provisional (toward the middle or end of the first semester)

      (3) *final* (end of second semester in the field)

2. Which of these perspectives would you define as realistic/unrealistic? Why?

3. Do you think their perspectives complement or conflict with those of their field instructors (supervisor) and of the faculty at the School of Social Work? If so, how? If not, why?

4. Now describe a situation in which your perspective changed over time. How did those changes occur?

responsibility came into conflict with the professional culture that dominates the agency staff's perspectives.

CULTURE SHOCK

"Just before my last semester in school," Betsy recalled, two years after we first met her, "I told Yolanda that I wanted a community organization experience. There wasn't much chance for me to do any kind of outside work in the clinical services department. Yolanda agreed with me that working with Harvey Marcus in the community placement department might give me just the kind of opportunity I was looking for. But she warned me about the 'culture shock' I'd be likely to face. And was she on target!

"It really was like going from one culture to another. In clinical services, we did extensive diagnosis and testing and we provided clinical counseling. It may be true that we (the staff in the department) didn't all use exactly the same approaches to counseling—about half the staff were behaviorists, and the others were analytic in their approaches—but we had a more or less formal organization and everybody did their job in pretty much the same way. What I mean is, it was like a 9 to 5 place. We saw clients, you know, the 50-minute hour bit, and we recorded our notes, and we 'staffed' difficult cases together when necessary. It was all very professional.

"Sure, we did some follow-up and sometimes it was necessary to do home visits or to meet with professionals in some other organizations on behalf of the client—you know, like schools, the courts, the nursing home—and the standards were high. I mean, it's a good department. Very professional. You would expect that with somebody like Yolanda as a supervisor. I mean, people dress for the job. I wouldn't have thought of wearing my student clothes at the agency.

"Now, the community placement department, it was like a different world. A lot of the men wore jeans, and the women wore slacks. I don't think I ever saw Harvey wearing a tie except when he had to go to the state capitol or when he was off to some foundation hunting up a grant. Nobody ever closed their office doors, and there was a lot of working together. Maybe it's because we didn't see so many clients individually. Most of our clients, if we had any, were out in the community, in placement or needing placement. Mostly we worked on finding and licensing group homes, and then supervising or consulting with them. And, of course, a lot of people working in the group homes dress pretty informally.

"I mean, they would have to. You aren't going to be dressed up in a suit if you're working with staff who supervise kids in a group foster home, or with people who run adult group foster homes for senior citizens and ex-mental patients. I guess you could say the way we dressed at the agency was the way in which our clients—the providers of direct services to people needing placement—dressed. Maybe that's the way they expected us to dress. But dress wasn't the only thing.

"It was the way staff were always throwing out and testing new ideas. It wasn't just Harvey's style, although he encouraged it. But it was like, if there was a better way to do it, we should be trying it. No rigid behavioral or Freudian approaches here. I don't mean to say that people were rigid in the clinical services program, but they were tight. Here, everybody hung loose. It didn't matter what theory you used. Any idea, if it worked, was good.

"At first, I was really upset. It wasn't just because I had to move out of the office and into the community, either locating neighborhoods where we could put in a group home, or organizing community groups to support the work of some of those homes. That's what I was looking for, a CO assignment. And I knew that community workers tended to be more informal than some others in the profession. But I really found the style shocking. Maybe it's me, and my own rigid way of looking at things. But I don't think so. It just didn't seem to me that these people were professional, if you know what I mean.

"I don't know, but I think I'd have a hard time going back to Yolanda's department. I've come to respect and appreciate the openness and the give and take of the community placement staff. They're not any less serious, or any less professional than anybody else that I've worked with. Maybe they're more so. They really work hard at what they do. And they're committed. I mean, they really care, and not just from 9 to 5. They're doing real advocacy work. And that's real social work."

* * * * *

Like professions and other occupations, all organizations develop their own cultures, complete with taboos, folkways and mores. Within limits, it is possible for a single organization to develop a number of subcultures, so long as they reflect the general norms and values of the larger system. These cultures reflect the history of the department or the organization, its internal structure and the way in which it deals with its external relationships. It may be influenced by the types of people the organization attracts, its work processes, physical layouts, modes of communication, and the exercise of authority within the system. The culture in turn exerts its own influence.

The organization or the units within it will develop collective feelings and beliefs about the appropriate way to do things and pass these on to group members. Perspectives developed in the past are imposed on those who enter the organization or the unit within it. Thus the culture of each organizational unit provides a frame of reference within which members interpret the appropriateness of certain activities and actions.

Interestingly, while members may be clear about why they do things, they are not likely to be aware of the basic frames of reference that they use in arriving at certain judgments. The differences between one unit and another only become clear when someone like Betsy crosses from one environment into the other. As Betsy pointed out, the nature of the interaction in relationships with the unit's clients may have something to do with the emergence of a certain culture within the unit. This may become even clearer if we examine client influences on the New Americans Project. Recall the discussion in the previous chapter.

* * * * *

Here it was two days after the staff meeting where Sam Mansouri's proposal for a paraprofessional program had been shot down, and Sam was still wondering what had happened and why. At least Harvey should have supported the proposal. After all, Harvey was a friend. They had known each other in graduate school, and while Sam had been in the clinical track while Harvey was a community organization student, they had taken a number of classes together and were immediately drawn to each other.

The fact that one was an Arab from Lebanon and the other an American Jew who had spent time in Israel is what initially attracted them. As Sam explains it: "Because my family are Maronite Christians, we always felt somewhat marginal in the Middle East. When I was younger, I listened to Israeli music on the radio a lot and watched Israeli programs on television. I dreamt for peace between our peoples. When I met Harvey, I found someone who was an American Jew and who also understood marginality. But he had also shared

Exercise 5.2

Describing Organizational Culture

1. Briefly describe the different cultures in two organizations with which you have been affiliated (say two agencies, an agency and a professional school or an agency and a church). Point out what is similar and what is different between them.

2. What are the bases of these similarities and differences?

some Middle Eastern experiences and yearned like I did for peace between our peoples."

Although Harvey was an American, and born in this country, Sam marveled at the ease with which Harvey moved into leadership positions, often taking on liberal political causes, and often challenging conventional wisdom. This is what particularly perplexed him about Harvey's lack of support at the meeting. He decided to drop in on Harvey that afternoon to find out what was going on. Was it him (Sam)? Was it the way he had made the presentation? Was it something in the agency's climate that he had missed?

"Look, old buddy," Harvey explained later that afternoon. "For a guy who's really sensitive to culture and cultural differences, you really missed the boat on this one. My staff and I can get away with all kinds of things that you can't. We're kind of on the periphery of the agency. We don't work directly with individual clients. We work with community groups and other agencies. So because the case worker and educator types on the staff don't quite understand what we do, they don't impose the same standards on our practice as they impose on yours.

"But you're providing direct services to people, and this agency thinks of itself as a direct service agency, and it has high professional standards. You've got three things working against you. First, you're dealing with populations that the rest of the agency staff are not competent to deal with, or at least we know that their methods won't work. Your clients are not Westerners, and the way in which they handle problems is not the way in which we're equipped to help them. So you're already putting demands on us with the New Americans Project that not only require sensitivity to the cultures of Asian and Arab populations, but that may challenge our cherished ways of helping people deal with problems.

"Second, there's a high premium here (at the agency) put on professional standards. It's only natural that people will be afraid that we might dilute those standards by including less than professionally trained people on the staff. I don't think people are worrying about their jobs, but they are worrying that they, *we,* won't be doing our jobs to quite the standards we value. You were saying to us that our methods don't work, and that some other people with less training will be more effective. Well, that's a pretty strong challenge, and we weren't ready to deal with it.

"But the biggest problem is that you violated some pretty important norms around here about the way in which we make decisions. Look, you've been around long enough to know that this is a pretty open agency. We really do make decisions collectively. But we never make them formally until we've already made them informally. You brought in a whole new proposal without properly preparing us. People just weren't ready to deal with your recommendations. You didn't give those ideas a chance to percolate, to kind of bubble up over time. I mean, Yolanda and certainly Millicent would have been more open if they'd had a chance to think about the issues more and had been able to develop a professional rationale for what you were suggesting. You just don't bring new ideas to a staff meeting. We rarely make tough decisions at staff meetings. Can you remember a single incident in which there was as much feeling and anger expressed about a new proposal? I can't. And it had nothing to do with your proposal. It had to do with the fact that we weren't ready for it.

"You may be feeling bad about the way things went, and you've got the biggest stake in it. But they're feeling pretty bad, too. First of all, no one likes to turn down a colleague. But they're also feeling violated because you sprung one on them that they weren't ready for."

* * * * *

Harvey left something out of his analysis. What he was unaware of, because he himself had only been at the agency six years, was that in the early 1970s the All-Families Service Center had built up a fairly extensive paraprofessionals' program as part of its efforts to extend services to a low-income housing complex. While initially the program had met with some success, it had backfired when the paraprofessionals had begun to advocate for clients against the agency itself, defining the agency as the tool of the "White racist establishment." The aftermath had left its residue of bitterness. Even the term *paraprofessional* had become a red flag, *red* in more than one sense. History has a way of influencing norms, attitudes, values, and perspectives. As they become ingrained into agency culture, they are likely to endure over time, even when circumstances change.

HOW MIGHT SAM HAVE BETTER PREPARED THE STAFF?

Sam might have been more successful if he had begun by sensitizing other staff members to both the special needs and the special characteristics of the "new American" populations that his department was serving. This he might have done by participating in case conferences conducted within the clinical services department whenever issues pertaining to the agency's Southeast Asian or Chaldean clients came up.

In doing so, he would have had an opportunity to point out that establishing a working relationship with clients from a particular background depends at least in part on having genuine respect for that background. And such respect requires an understanding of the client's culture. He might also have sought opportunities to work collaboratively with the family life education program that Millicent directs. One cannot expect new Americans to function as old Americans. They bring with them to their new country established concepts of sharing, of familial relationships, of acceptance, of suffering, of optimism, and of self-help that are indigenous to their own cultures.

For some cultures, social work techniques of communication that focus on the individual client may not be appropriate. The social and familial networks through which new Americans seek help must be understood. For people coming from traditional cultures, the help-seeking pattern usually includes going for help to family members first, and that family may include an extended family kinship network—aunts and uncles, cousins, and others from the same village. It may also include seeking help from a religious leader. Only when these networks are incapable of helping will new Americans consider seeking help from institutional providers.

Moreover, help from institutions like the All-Families Service Center is not likely to be productive (whether it is focused on intrapsychic problems, housing, job seeking, and so on) unless such help takes into account the availability of supports in the external network. And those supports are likely to be present only if members of the network perceive them as being appropriate—that is, contributing to the maintenance of the network and in keeping with long-standing values and traditions.

Americanization need not include de-Vietnamization or de-Arabization. However, it does require helping new Americans make use of all their internal resources in connecting with and making use of new resources in the American environment. This may require changes in technique and even in personnel, but it need not require changes in social work's basic value orientations.

Gisella Knopka and others have made this point quite clear. Social work practices are based on two absolute values: a respect for the dignity of the individual, and a commitment to encouraging the responsibility of individuals and communities for the less fortunate. But these values can be applied differently. Americans prize individuality, while other cultures may prize the family and the group culture more highly. In traditional cultures, even significant personal aspirations may be understood best within the context of the larger group from which the individual comes.

Thus responsibility for others in some cultures belongs to the family and the immediate members of a network. Institutions like social agencies may be perceived as distant and foreign, and social work and educational interventions that ignore such cultural patterns are not likely to be successful. Certainly Millicent is aware of this. Her practice experiences in South America were built directly on people's own experiences and their interpretation of their situations. Yolanda's sensitivity to her own cultural heritage includes a deep awareness of what it means to be left out, to be misunderstood and to be defined as deviant or alien.

With these facts in mind, it might have been possible for Sam to bring others to the conclusion that the agency would be more effective if it involved representatives of the two cultures as outreach workers and as case-aides. Further, by using the terminology *outreach worker* and *case-aide* he would have avoided raising the red flag of paraprofessionalism.

If you have suggested approaches that increase the likelihood that decisions and actions will be taken in a collegial manner, you are on the right track. Colleagues are associates, fellows in the same organization or profession. Colleagues, you will recall, must be able to take each other's sentiments for granted. They must be able to communicate freely and openly among themselves and to share confidences that will not be repeated to uninitiated ears. If Sam can't share with others his professional concerns about the populations for whom he's responsible because he's overly defensive of them or because he doesn't feel that the staff will understand or appreciate the uniqueness of their cultures, then he is not fully accepting the other staff members as colleagues.

One's professional colleagues are defined as those who have similar training, similar values and who are engaged in similar core tasks. That may be why the students we looked in on earlier in this chapter felt a collegial bond to each other at the beginning of their work at the agency but soon found themselves pulling apart as they developed stronger collegial relationships to people in the particular units to which they were assigned.

While one might feel closest to those engaged in a similar practice, one also feels close to those performing similar roles in a different department in an agency. Thus supervisors might find much in common with each other and less in common with supervisees doing the same kind of work that the supervisor may have performed only a few months earlier. To a large extent, these changes occur because people perceive themselves as being "in the same boat." You'll recognize in this discussion much of what we said earlier about reference group behavior, and about the development of common perspectives.

PERCEPTIONS

You might think Harvey's comments were perceptive. Actually, they represent a difference in perception between Harvey and Sam. Other differences were reflected in the earlier comments on Sam's proposal by different members of the staff.

Perception is not only a matter of seeing. It's a matter of selecting and organizing what we see or otherwise observe; in effect, a way of understanding the world around us. We are all familiar with the blind men and the elephant story. One, you will recall, walked around a leg and concluded that the elephant was a tree. Another, on the feeling the elephant's tail, concluded it was a snake. And so on. Considering the various sensations the elephant must have experienced, one wonders what he would have concluded about man had he been similarly blindfolded! And that's just the point, about perception.

The features we notice depend on where we stand in relation to an event or phenomenon: as a participant, as an observer, as an initiator, or as a respondent. I'm writing this chapter scarcely a month after what has come to be known as "the space shuttle disaster," in which the lives of all the astronauts on board were lost, and only three days after a terrorist bomb blew a hole in the side of an American airliner flying from Rome to Athens. I'm quite certain that everyone involved directly or indirectly in these—those on board at the time of the incident, those observing it from earth, or via electronic media, those somehow responsible for security or safety, those by intent or by inattention responsible for the damages themselves—each will perceive the incident differently.

Our perceptions are also based, in part, on the ways we learned to interpret certain stimuli and how we think others might interpret them. The ways in which Harvey and Yolanda dress for work (Harvey in cords, a sweater, and sport jacket, and Yolanda in a formal, dark suit) may be as much a response to their perceptions about how others (colleagues and clients) will perceive them as it is a matter of personal style. The ways in which we behave are based not only on our education and experience, but is also a response to how we perceive others will perceive us.

All this may seem so self-evident as to be hardly worth writing about. But what may be less obvious is that perception depends on how we select from among the many stimuli with which we are bombarded, and how we categorize and organize those stimuli so that they make sense to us. To be comprehended, new stimuli must fit into the ways in which we already understand and know the world. Thus, when Yolanda ran past Ali on the same day that she had responded to Millicent's lunch invitation by remarking that she doesn't "brown" bag anything, both Ali and Millicent had perceived Yolanda's actions quite differently. Millicent had sought to understand the source of the pain that Yolanda might be feeling. Ali, in contrast, had been pained by Yolanda's behavior, perceiving it as a personal rejection. In this case, Millicent's perception had been accurate, Ali's distorted. Perceptual distortions can be grouped in the following categories: (1) the halo and horns effect, (2) projection, and (3) stereotyping.

Harvey was frequently subjected to the halo and horns effect. Within his own department, and in his relationships with many of the local city and state offices with which he deals, Harvey is perceived of as innovative, committed, and competent (halo). And most of Harvey's comments and suggestions will be received in that spirit. But elsewhere in the agency, there are some, including other departmental supervisors, who see Harvey as brash and an empire builder (horns), as what Anthony Downs refers to as a "climber."

Psychologists have long known about a related phenomenon, the *pygmalian effect*, in which perceptions can become self-fulfilling prophecies. You may have read of Robert Rosenthal's famous study in which teachers were given names of pupils, randomly selected, and told that the children had been identified by a new test as being on the verge of blooming intellectual development. By the end of the school year, these children were found to have gained in intellectual ability when compared to other children. Teachers also perceived the labeled children as more adjusted, appealing, active, and affectionate. Does this suggest something to you about how colleagues or clients are treated at work, or about how some improve or others deteriorate in performance, growth, or effectiveness?

Projection, you will recall, is a defense mechanism used to transfer blame to another person. We use it to protect ourselves from unacceptable feelings by attributing to others negative attitudes we may hold. Projection biases perceptions. It leads to attributing one's own prejudices against clients, men or women, minorities, supervisors or supervisees, to the other party. Was Yolanda projecting when she became angry at Millicent the day after the party?

Projection often leads to stereotyping, a process in which we attribute behaviors or attitudes to individuals on the basis of our perceptions that they are common to all members of the group or category to which the group belongs. As we learned earlier, Yolanda, who had fought much of her life against being stereotyped, was now devoting as much energy to overcoming her own tendencies to stereotype others. Recall her feelings about Harvey and Sam discussed in Chapter 2.

ATTRIBUTION THEORY

There are a number of behavioral scientists who tend to group themselves, or be grouped by others, under the category of "attribution theorists." Basing their work on Kurt Lewin's discussion of behavior as being a function of both personality and environment, they assume that people's perceptions are the result of either personality characteristics (traits, skills, motivations, effort, charisma) or of external situational characteristics (chance events, external rewards, organizational structure, and so on). Attribution researchers focus their studies on the processes by which people come to attribute behaviors primarily to personality or to situational causes.

One of their more salient findings is that people tend to evaluate the performance of others differently than they would evaluate their own performances. For example, some people, in evaluating the positive performance of others, would attribute the cause to situational factors, but in evaluating their own successes, might attribute the causes to personal factors. Examining the reasons that Sam's proposal was rejected, Harvey focused in part on situational factors. Harvey sees his successes at the agency to a large part the result of his own talent and effort. The opposite is also true.

Edward Jones, a social psychologist, found that when people observe the negative behaviors of others, they tend to underestimate situational influences and overestimate the influence of personality characteristics. But when they try to comprehend their own *un*succesful behaviors, they tend to overestimate the importance of the situation and underestimate the importance of their own personality traits. Apparently, it is too difficult for people to deal with both factors simultaneously, or to give equal weight to both. He explains these binds as follows.

Because we tend to know more about our own behavior than do others who observe it, we're more likely than others to be aware of the different ways that we behave in different situations. Actors and observers tend to notice different aspects of behavior because they observe it from different vantage points. Observers are likely to notice actors' nonverbal cues, whereas actors are more likely to respond to their own feelings and their awareness of their own perceptions. Finally, we all tend to view ourselves as complex and flexible in responses to environmental stimuli, whereas we tend to impute to others personality traits that are more limited.

The tendency to attribute someone else's behavior to their personality traits depends on how well we know them and on our own capacity to be *empathic*. Thus, Millicent was able to take Yolanda's perspective and in this way search for the situational causes of her behavior. Harvey was able to do the same in his analysis of organizational climate, putting himself not only in Sam's shoes but in those of the other participants in the meeting in which the paraprofessionals' issue was discussed.

It might also be interesting to examine why people reacted to Sam as they did. Notice I said "to Sam" rather than "to Sam's suggestions." Sam's actions were considered to be inappropriate by most of the other supervisors. When people act in ways that are not either desirable or acceptable, we tend to attribute their behavior to their personal characteristics (knowledge, insights, awareness, and so on). We don't give equal attention to what may be wrong in the situation itself that may have resulted in appropriate behavior. A more dramatic example might be in an almost universal tendency to blame victim (substance abuser, delinquents, pregnant teenagers) rather than examining the situational causes for their behavior.

We also have a tendency to internalize inappropriately, that is, assume that someone else's behavior was meant to affect us in certain ways, positively or negatively. For example, when Ali was ignored by Yolanda in the Sandwich Shoppe, she internalized her rejection, seeking something wrong in herself. Had she been a more secure person, she might have defined the reasons for Yolanda's behavior as something hurtful or spiteful in Yolanda.

Most of the time, the attributional processes that we employ are not fully thought out; we are only barely aware of them. Nevertheless, our attributions are likely to affect the ways in which we respond to others. Greater awareness may enable us to avoid the traps of self-confirming errors in perception. And in so doing, we may be able to reduce some of the misunderstandings that often exist in agencies and other work settings.

REVIEW AND TENTATIVE CONCLUSIONS

Let's review what we've added to our understanding of work in an organizational setting.

(1) When people work together or face common problems over time, they develop a collective prospective on what to do and how to act.

Exercise 5.3

Perceptions and Attributions

1. Describe a situation in which you incorrectly perceived an incident that involved interaction with a colleague. Was your misperception based on your position as an observer, initiator, or respondent? Did it stem from or result in a halo and horns effect, projection, or stereotyping? Explain.

2. Now do the same for a situation in which you or something you did was perceived incorrectly by others.

3. In either of these incidents, did your explanation take personality or situational factors mostly into account? Which? Why?

This perspective may be mediated by earlier experiences and the role models, but is nevertheless strongly influenced by the current situation.

(2) Perspectives can be long- or short-term. The latter go through initial, intermediate and final (relatively permanent) stages.

(3) Perspectives are related to the emergence of a group or organizational culture. Such culture is shaped by a common history as well as by external environmental or societal forces. The culture finds expression in norms, values, folkways, decision-making processes, dress, and other behaviors. While agencies have overall cultures, alternative expressions of such cultures, and sometimes even different cultures, may be found in different departments. Moving from one department or organization to another may entail a certain amount of culture shock when accustomed patterns are challenged by other ways of viewing and doing things.

(4) Perception is the way in which we understand the world around us. It begins with selecting from among the many stimuli to which we are subject, and then organizing the material we've selected in a way in which it makes sense to us.

(5) The attribution process begins with observation and perception, then moves on to a determination of whether observed behavior was intended and the causes of such behavior. Those causes are generally attributed to situational or personality factors. We tend to oversimplify causes by focusing on either one or the other, often focusing on personality when we observe someone else's behavior (especially if it is perceived as negative), and on situational factors when we evaluate our own (unless it is seen as positive).

YOUR ADDITIONS

(6)

(7)

(8)

REFERENCES

Ayers, Robert, & Nachamkin, Beverly. (1982). Sex and ethnic differences in the use of power. *Journal of Applied Psychology, 67*(4).

Becker, Howard S., Geer, Blanche, Hughes, Everett C., & Strauss, Anselm. (1976). *Boys in white: student culture in medical school.* Chicago: University of Chicago Press.

Cohen, Lynn R. (1982). Minimizing communicative breakdowns between male and female managers. *Personnel Administrator,* October.

Delgado, Melvin. (1979). Hispanic staff in non-Hispanic settings: Issues and recommendations. *Administration in Social Work, 3*(4), Winter.

Gordon, Judith R. (1983). *A diagnostic approach to organizational behavior.* Boston: Allyn & Bacon.

Gudykunst, William, Stewart, Leon P., & Ting-Toomey, Stella. (1985). *Communication, culture ad organizational processes.* Newbury Park, CA: Sage.

Hughes, Everett C. (1958). License and mandate. In E. C. Hughes (Ed.), *Men and their work.* New York: Free Press.

Jayaratne, Srinika, & Chess, Wayne A. (1984). The effects of emotional support on perceived job stress and strain. *Journal of Applied Behavioral Science,* March.

Jones, Edward E., & Davis, Kennedy. (1965). From acts to dispositions. In Lawrence Berkowitz (Ed.), *Advances in experimental social psychology.* New York: Academic Press.

Jones, Edward E., & Nisbett, Richard E. (1971). *The actor and the observer: Divergent perceptions of causes and behavior.* Morristown, NJ: General Learning Press.

Kelly, Harold H. (1973). The process of causal attribution." *American Psychologist, 40*(2).

Knopka, Gisella. (1971). Cultural differences in social work philosophy. *International Social Work,* January.

Lewis, M. (1980). Surprise and sense-making: What newcomers experience in entering unfamiliar organizational settings. *Administrative Science Quarterly, 25*(2), June.

Mannheim, Karl. (1936). *Ideology and utopia.* London: Routledge & Kegan Paul.

Martin, Joanne, Feldman, Marthe, Hatch, Mary Jo, & Sitkin, Sim B. (1983). The uniqueness paradox in organizational stories. *Administrative Science Quarterly,* September.

Mead, George Herbert. (1938). *The philosophy of the act.* Chicago: University of Chicago Press, 1938.

Merton, Robert. (1957). *Social theory and social structure.* New York: Free Press.

Olsen, Marvin E. (1978). *The process of social organization.* New York: Holt, Rinehart & Winston.

Pernell, Ruby B. (1970). Social work values on the new frontiers. In Katherine A. Kendall (Ed.), *Social work values in an age of discontent.* New York: Council on Social Work Education.

Smirchick, Linda. (1983). Concepts of culture in organizational analysis. *Administrative Science Quarterly,* September.

Specht, Harry. (1972). The deprofessionalization of social work. *Social Work,* February.

Van Wagner, Karen, & Swanson, Cheryl. (1977). From Machiavelli to Ms.: Differences in male-female power styles. *Public Administration Review,* February.

Wallach, Ellen J. (1983). Individuals and organizations: The cultural match. *Training and Development,* February.

Chapter 6

MAKING ETHICAL DECISIONS
Balancing Personal, Agency, Societal, and Client Values

WHO MAKES THE DECISION FOR THE CLIENT?

Betsy was nervous. She was scheduled to have her conference with Yolanda at 3:00. "Well, I think I've got all the details right," she thought to herself after reviewing her logs, "but I know I'm recommending something that Mr. Fenton might not agree with. Still, it's the only thing that makes sense. I hope Yolanda will agree with me." Looking over the notes she had prepared for her weekly supervisory session, Betsy was satisfied that the pertinent information was all there.

On entering Yolanda's office, she was really struck by the contrast between its neat and ordered look and the image, still vivid in her mind, of Mr. Fenton's dank, dark, and filthy apartment. Betsy got right to the point.

"Yolanda, I've tried everything," she blurted out. "I just don't see any way out. I have to refer Mr. Fenton to Protective Services. There's just no way he can stay in that apartment by himself. He needs to be taken care of. One of Harvey's group homes would be ideal for him. When you walk into the apartment, you're just overwhelmed with the stench of urine and feces. I don't think the window has been opened in years. There are old newspapers piled up, rotting food on the kitchen table and counters, dried catfood all over the floor. Oh, you know, you've read the logs." Yolanda listened attentively.

"He's 86 years old and I don't think he's been out of the apartment for the last two years. I'm not even sure he could handle the stairs. The place is a rat trap. The only time he gets food is when Mr. Galimbarry or Mrs. Striplin down the hall shop for him. And they're in their 80s, too, so sometimes they can't be very helpful. He could go two or three days without seeing anyone, and without any food. A human being shouldn't live like that. And not *this* human being. I mean, he was *some*body, once. I mean, he fought in the Spanish Civil War! And then in World War II.

"And he got a Master's Degree on the G.I. Bill and then taught high school until the mid-50s. And then they broke him. It was the McCarthy era. He was forced out of his teaching position because of the principles he believed in, and he wouldn't name names. I mean, he wouldn't rat on his friends. Since then, he sort of has given up. For a while, his brother was supporting him. But now his brother's dead, and there are no other living relatives. He gets some veteran's benefits and some Social Security, but it's barely enough to cover the rent. And last year, if Social Services hadn't intervened, he wouldn't have even had heat in his apartment.

"And I've tried everything. I don't think he minds my coming to visit him. I almost get the feeling that he enjoys it. So I'm convinced that he could be helped to relate to people in the real world again if somebody would show an interest in him. But he's been a recluse for so long. Just because he's old . . . I mean, old people shouldn't be left to die that way."

"I can see this is really eating at you," Yolanda interjected. "But before we look at your specific recommendations, Betsy, I want to explore two comments you made: 'He was somebody once,' and 'He shouldn't be left to die that way.' What did you mean exactly?"

"Well, look," Betsy replied. "He was an activist. He believed in something, and he was willing to risk his life for it. And he served his country well. He's an educated man. And then the system jumped on him. We, I mean society, owes him something. We owe things to all of our older people. And I think his situation is appalling. How much longer can he live without the right kind of medical care, without somebody to relate to, without proper nutrition?"

"Well, you've made some provocative statements, Betsy. And I see that you feel strongly about them. And I can understand why. But I wonder why you say that 'he was somebody, once.' Isn't he somebody now? He may be the same person, or he may be somebody different. Perhaps he's made a choice, not one that you're comfortable with, but one that he has made progressively, bit by bit, over the years. I'm not sure that he's being left to die. Perhaps he's made a choice about the way in which he wants to live. Let's take a look at the options that you've provided him. I looked at your records carefully. Apparently you've discussed VA health benefits with him, Medicare, the use of food stamps, Supplementary Social Insurance benefits, and a number of other options including moving to a nursing home. He seems to have rejected all of these. Did he understand what his options were?"

"Well, I think so. He didn't want to hear about VA health benefits. He's really down on the VA, I think because of the way he was treated after the McCarthy bit. And as far as Medicare, I just don't think he wants to see any doctors. And he's got a bladder problem. I know most older people do. But his could be serious. And food stamps, he won't even hear about. And I think that, as far as SSI goes, he just doesn't want any further trouble with the government. He'll accept Social Security checks and some Army disability because he figures he put money into the system and he served his time, and he should get that back, but he's a proud man. He just won't go on what he considers to be welfare. But to tell you the truth, he never really came out and said these things, It's just what I infer from the way he's responded to me. You know, when I first started visiting him, he wouldn't even talk. But he's sort of gotten used to me coming around. I think he even likes me. Sometimes I feel that he thinks he's doing me a favor by letting me visit him. And I think he can be rehabilitated."

"Betsy, are you really trying to rehabilitate this man?"

"Well, yes, I guess so."

"That's interesting," Yolanda continued. "You may actually have something else in mind. *Rehabilitation* implies helping someone change so as to assist the person to regain a prior level of functioning, or perhaps even achieve a higher level one. It presumes a maladaptive style of functioning. And its focus is to enable people, through some form of treatment, to achieve a higher level of social competence. But that seems to be quite different from the more radical solution you're recommending. Protective Services would require a court order to change his living conditions. And it would imply taking some freedom away from him. Let's look at a different term.

"*Habilitation*, in contrast to *re*habilitation, makes no assumption regarding the relationships among any past difficulties a person might have had and the current difficulties. It's an effort to make changes in the environment that would make it possible for somebody to function at a higher level, without requiring that he or she change him- or herself. I think maybe that's what you are striving for. Let's look at the ways in which Mr. Fenton could be habilitated in his current circumstances."

Betsy and Yolanda explored a number of options, including home visiting, making arrangements with a nearby church-sponsored meals on wheels, a home handy-person service operated by the county Area Agency on Aging, and periodic visits through the county Visiting Nurse Association. "But I just don't think that's enough," Betsy blurted out.

"Maybe not. But let me tell you an experience I had, some years back. I'd been working with a retired social worker in a nursing home. She'd been placed there by the hospital, after breaking her hip, because there no one who could provide her with care in her own home. I didn't like the nursing home. And I thought the service was demeaning. I also saw this woman as a person with a great deal of dignity, somebody who deserved something better than the treatment she was receiving. I arranged for some physical therapy, and then helped some old friends of her's find and fix up an apartment. She left the nursing home for the apartment. I felt that I had achieved something. My client died three months later. The move had just been too much for her."

Betsy thought for a moment. "At least she made the choice. And she could die in her own home."

"That's right," said Yolanda. "But aren't you telling me that Mr. Fenton has also made a choice?"

"But he's so helpless. I don't think he can really make a choice. Don't social workers sometimes have to act in the best interest of the client? To be honest with you, I'm not even so sure he's understood all of the options that I've presented him."

* * * * *

If you haven't faced a similar situation in your own practice, you may know others who have. Betsy's problem is not atypical. Social workers face agonizing quandaries in their practice every day. Betsy was struggling to make the right decision, but as Yolanda pointed out, the decision might not be entirely hers. Decisions like the one Betsy was struggling with are more than technical. That is, you can't just put the facts into a computer and hope it generates the right answers. What is "right" is often a matter of values.

First there are our own personal values. Then there are the client's values. Third, there are the agency's values, those of our employers or funders. These are generally expressed in policies and procedures. Both personal and organizational values operate within the context of larger societal values. There are also values held by specific professional and occupational groups and by the larger society. For example, Betsy tried to induce her client to make use of social entitlements (SSI, medicare, food stamps), which are an expression of society's commitment (albeit somewhat ambivalent) to serve those in need. Her client rejected some, apparently because of his feelings, about the society, about dependency, and about himself. The values of clients, workers, agencies, and the key publics with which they interact, and of the larger society, are not always congruent.

VALUES AND PROFESSIONAL ETHICS

Even one's own personal values may be in conflict with each other. The same is true of professional values. For example, the Council on Social Work Education in its 1982 *Curriculum Policies Statement* lists two core social work values that may conflict with each other when applied to Mr. Fenton's case. The first is a regard for human dignity, for the worth of the individual. The second is a respect for the rights of the individual to choose, to participate in or to take responsibility for the helping process. The right to choose presumes a certain amount of freedom, the freedom to select from among a number of different options. It presumes the absence of coercion.

It also presumes that the individual will be aware of all available options, will have received accurate information about the consequences of each option, and has a capacity to use that information as the basis on which he or she will make a realistic choice. But what if the individual does not have the capacity, or if the information is incomplete or inaccurate, or if the consequences of one or another action cannot be fully predicted (as was the case with Yolanda's client)? Does social work's regard for the individual then suggest that the worker, based on his or her best professional judgment, should make the decision, or that the decision should be referred elsewhere (to the court, as in a Protective Services case)?

At issue are both values and technical considerations. John Dewey once referred to *values* as criteria for selecting an appropriate course of action. Scientific knowledge and practice knowledge drawn from work-related experience also serve as guides to action. They provide the technical know-how that together with values are referred to as *practice wisdom.* Values may be challenged by knowledge, just as knowledge may sometimes be overridden by values, what we consider to be "right" or "good." This is because values often represent preferences strongly felt; that is, considered to be justified on the basis of some imperative.

But what imperative? *Teleologists* might argue that what counts are the results. Taken to the extreme, this would lead to an argument that the ends justify the means. Removing Mr. Fenton from his apartment, even if he does not agree to it, Betsy seemed to be implying, is the appropriate course of action because it will lead to a more healthful and humane environment, one in which he'll be treated with the dignity that he deserves. Is there a contradiction here? *Utilitarians* might argue that the decision should be based not only on what we know about Mr. Fenton, but on what we perceive to be the greatest good for the greatest number.

Here, we would have to take into consideration how we think society should respond to other people in Mr. Fenton's position, and to the extent to which society as a whole would benefit by routinization of one choice over another. *Relativists* might look at the costs and benefits of each of the possible solutions or sets of solutions. Assuming that there might be costs and benefits to each possible course of action, the appropriate choice would be that which reflects the greatest good (benefit) over evil (cost). In contemporary terms, we might express this as a Benefits:Costs ratio. But how do we assign weights to costs and benefits? Who benefits and who pays? The financial costs of providing various services to Mr. Fenton can be calculated for each of the organizations and programs involved (e.g., group home, SSI, the courts, the Visiting Nurses Association). Are there other costs for *not* providing services? To whom? Are there dangers to others in the building if Mr. Fenton is left in his current situation? Are there dangers to Mr. Fenton? Are these dangers acceptable costs, if we opt to maximize (the value of his) freedom of choice?

It may be correct that values guide us, but unfortunately, they are generally expressed at so abstract a level that they are not always clear guides. In practice, what do "freedom of choice" or "in the client's best interest" mean? Here professional *ethics* may be of some, if limited, help. Ethics are efforts to translate our perceptions of *good* and *desirable* (values) into *right* and *correct*. For example, the value "freedom of choice" can be expressed in the following ethical guidelines taken from the NASW *Code of Ethics*: "The social worker should appraise clients of their risks, rights, opportunities, and obligations associated with social service to them." And the client's rights should be protected by the social worker's efforts to "foster maximum self-determination."

The *Code of Ethics* was adopted in 1979 by the National Association of Social Workers' Delegate Assembly and was reapproved by the 1984 NASW Delegate Assembly. It reflects a democratic ethos, secular in nature, humanistic in orientation. You may be familiar with other, religiously based codes. How do they differ in source authority? You'll find the complete NASW *Code of Ethics* in Appendix A. We will have occasion to refer to it as we examine a number of other ethical dilemmas. An abbreviated overview appears in Figure 6.1. Look it over.

As we noted in the previous chapter, virtually all professions have codes of ethics; codes that may be periodically reviewed, modified, or reaffirmed. The arguments in favor of establishing codes are that they protect clients and, by regulating practitioner behavior, they also protect the general public. They do so by providing clients and the public with ways of assessing a professional's integrity, and so protect against practitioner charlatanism. In a way, they protect the profession, too, by establishing a baseline, a normative model against which professional behavior can be assessed by colleagues. They provide members of the profession with guidelines when they face ethical dilemmas. But even the best of ethical codes can only provide guide*lines*. They do not provide comprehensive guides to action in all circumstances. Choices still have to be made. You will discover, as we examine a number of other vignettes throughout this chapter, that these choices are often personal ones, your own interpretations of appropriate ethical behaviors.

Codes of ethics thus shape behavior, but in so doing also limit behavior. For these same reasons, there are those who argue against developing and using codes. There are leaders in every profession who feel that any code of ethics is likely to be somewhat coercive; that

(Passed by the 1979 Delegate Assembly. Implementation set for July 1, 1980.)

SUMMARY OF MAJOR PRINCIPLES

I. THE SOCIAL WORKER'S CONDUCT AND COMPORTMENT AS A SOCIAL WORKER

A. *Propriety.* The social worker should maintain high standards of personal conduct in the capacity or identity as social worker.

B. *Competence and Professional Development.* The social worker should strive to become and remain proficient in professional practice and the performance of professional functions.

C. *Service.* The social workers should regard as primary the service obligation of the social work profession.

D. *Integrity.* The social worker should act in accordance with the highest standards of professional integrity.

E. *Scholarship and Research.* The social worker engaged in study and research should be guided by the conventions of scholarly inquiry.

II. THE SOCIAL WORKER'S ETHICAL RESPONSIBILITY TO CLIENTS

F. *Primacy of Clients' Interests.* The social worker's primary responsibility is to clients.

G. *Rights and Prerogatives of Clients.* The social worker should make every effort to foster maximum self-determination on the part of clients.

H. *Confidentiality and Privacy.* The social worker should respect the privacy of clients and hold in confidence all information obtained in the course of professional service.

I. *Fees.* When setting fees, the social worker should ensure that they are fair, reasonable, considerate, and commensurate with the service performed and with due regard for the clients' ability pay.

III. THE SOCIAL WORKER'S ETHICAL RESPONSIBILITY TO COLLEAGUES

J. *Respect, Fairness, and Courtesy.* The social worker should treat colleagues with respect, courtesy, fairness, and good faith.

K. *Dealing with Colleagues' Clients.* The social worker has the responsibility to relate to the clients of colleagues with full professional consideration.

IV. THE SOCIAL WORKER'S ETHICAL RESPONSIBILITY TO EMPLOYERS AND EMPLOYING ORGANIZATIONS

L. *Commitments to Employing Organizations.* The social worker should adhere to commitments made to the employing organizations.

Figure 6.1 The NASW Code of Ethics.

V. THE SOCIAL WORKER'S ETHICAL RESPONSIBILITY TO THE SOCIAL WORK PROFESSION

M. *Maintaining the Integrity of the Profession.* The social worker should uphold and advance the values, ethics, knowledge, and mission of the profession.

N. *Community Service.* The social worker should assist the profession in making social services available to the general public.

O. *Development of Knowledge.* The social worker should take responsibility for identifying, developing, and fully utilizing knowledge for professional practice.

VI. THE SOCIAL WORKER'S ETHICAL RESPONSIBILITY TO SOCIETY

P. *Promoting the General Welfare.* The social worker should promote the general welfare of society.

Figure 6.1 Continued

it may stifle creativity or lead to ideological conformity and ultimately to conservatism in professional behavior and practice. Some professionals argue that because each case is unique, it must be judged independently. Precedents, based on previous practice (much as legal decisions are based on precedent), may be more appropriate than any guidelines adopted by a professional association. The professional association, they also argue, will always select a code that protects it against accusations of nonobjective actions more than it will protect the client.

Some social workers, while not disputing the utility of ethics codes, point out that effective practice is based less on a code that can become rigid and obsolete, than on competence and skill, technique if you will, that is continually developed, improved, and expanded. The client's best interest, along with that of society and the profession, is in the growth and development of competency, a competency that is empirically (scientifically validated) based.

While some of us may be in favor of a single code of ethics (even if we feel that any particular code might bear improvement), others are not. But whatever side of the argument we may be on, there is little question that there are ethical choices that are required when competing values or loyalties lead to quandaries similar to that Betsy faced. The costs and benefits of any course of action may be different for clients, co-workers, the agency and its various constituencies, or for the community at large. Choices often have to be made between values and even between beneficiaries.

Exercise 6.1
Identifying Ethical Guidelines

1. Look over the abbreviated overview of the NASW *Code*. Check those items that you think might provide ethical guidance for Betsy. Then turn to Appendix A and examine the more specific ethical guidelines provided for each section. Which of these complement each other? Which seem to be contradictory?

2. How would you choose among them: on the basis of the particular situation as described by Betsy (an ethical imperative); on the basis of a more universal or utilitarian notion of what is good; on the basis of anticipated outcomes or results; on the basis of some good/evil or cost:benefit (more good than evil) ratio? Jot down your thoughts in the space below.

DIVIDED LOYALTIES

Yolanda had been facing an ethical dilemma of her own. For some time, she had resisted joining the National Association of Black Social Workers (NABSW). Although she was aware that her Blackness shaped her personal identity, she didn't want it to shape her professional identity or her professional practice. Even here she was somewhat ambivalent, and that ambivalence made her subject to pressure. And the pressure was on, from other members of the BIB Club.

The pressure had been precipitated by action taken at a recent NASW delegate assembly meeting. At issue was interracial adoptions. NASW had taken the position that the best interest of the child (for whom adoption was deemed the most appropriate course of action), was best served by finding the family with the greatest capacity to help the child mature into his or her fullest developmental potential—whatever the ethnicity, race, or religion of either the birth or adoptive parents. Many Black social workers saw this as an expression of, or a possible basis for, racist policies and practices.

At best, it was seen as leading to a diminution of Black identity and a challenge to Black culture. At worst, it was a step toward cultural genocide. In its *Code of Ethics*, the National Association of Black Social Workers took the position that Black social workers must make commitments to the Black community's self-determination and apply their helping skills for the benefit of Black people. Professional activities must be guided by a Black consciousness and a determination to protect the security of the Black community. The *Code* is reproduced in Appendix B.

Carlotta Johnson, one of Yolanda's closest friends, and a colleague at the agency, put it to her as follows:

"Here are two key statements from the *Code*, Yolanda, tell me you can't accept them and make them your own." She pointed to the statements in the NABSW *Code* she had brought with her. "'I regard as my primary obligation the welfare of the Black individual, Black family, and Black community, and will engage in action for improving their social conditions.' 'I adopt a concept of a Black extended family and embrace all Black people as my brothers and sisters, making no distinction between their destiny and my own.'"

"Look, Carlotta," Yolanda responded. "The first statement makes me want to cry out 'yes.' But as a social worker I have to have equal commitment to any human being who's hurting. Look here at the *Code*, she pointed. "I've got no problem with the pledge that reads one up from the bottom: 'I stand ready to supplement my paid professional advocacy with voluntary service in the Black public interest.' But when it comes to the last statement, I've got a problem. It says that 'I will consciously use my skills, my whole being, as an instrument for social change, and with particular attention directed to the establishment of Black social institutions.' Well, I want to say 'yes,' again. But when I became a social worker, I took on a more universalistic position. And when I took a job in this agency, I made a commitment to serve all of our clients, without prejudice or priority based on race, gender, or anything else. It's not that I haven't thought of leaving the Center. Sure I have. And you know I have, and I might still leave for work in a Black agency. But right now I'm here. And this agency subscribes to NASW's position. And that has to be mine."

Sam faced a similar problem of dual (or was it multiple?) loyality. It was clear to him that there was no way in which he could win on the paraprofessional issue. "Let it lie, for a while, old buddy," Harvey had advised. But Sam wasn't about to let it lie. His conviction about the importance of involving new Americans in the "production and delivery" of services, he felt certain, represented not only their best interests, but the highest standards of professional practice. If new Americans could not become agency employees, he reasoned, perhaps they should be employed by and within their own community.

He raised the possibility with federal officials who visited the community to conduct their semiannual site visit on the New Americans Project. "You know," Sam broached the issue tentatively, "we've been successful in fostering a number of self-help groups, both in the Arab and Southeast Asian communities. I've been thinking. With more training and technical assistance from the agency, they might be encouraged to hire their own employees. I know that's a little bit strange to suggest employees for self-help groups. But what I have in mind is an arrangement where groups, once they are ready, might apply for grants. They could then hire their own people to do much of the work that professional staff from the agency are now doing. It shouldn't be difficult for us to train local people to do referral and even case management. The Center could continue to provide consultation, training and technical assistance."

"Interesting idea," one of the visitors had responded. "But if you're thinking about additional grant moneys, forget it. The Gramm-

Exercise 6.2
Selecting Between or Integrating Codes

1. Turn to Appendix B. Study the National Association of Black Social Workers' *Code of Ethics*. Do you agree with Yolanda that subscribing to both the NABSW and NASW codes creates a conflict that can only be resolved if the Black social worker works in an agency that provides services aimed primarily at the Black community? If so, flesh out Yolanda's arguments. If not, find the appropriate sections in the NASW Code that would support a social worker's total subscription to the NABSW Code.

2. Now, take the NASW position on interracial adoptions, and find the arguments in its favor in the NASW *Code of Ethics*. Can you find the arguments in favor of placing Black children only in Black families in the same *Code*? Do the same principles apply to Hispanic children, Native American children, Jewish children, children born to parents of other ethnic, religious, or racial minorities? Are there implications in your answers for cross-national adoptions (e.g., South Vietnamese or Brazilian children brought to the United States to be adopted)?

Rudman Bill and the mood on Capitol Hill right now means we're going to having less money to spend rather than more." "That's just the point," Sam responded. "I think we can make do with less and achieve more if we redirect our service activities." "Well," the federal official responded, "you write it up. You've still got two years on your grant. If you want to change the way in which the funds are allocated internally, and you've got a good rationale for it, I think I can get approval . . . so long as you don't go over your budget."

"I have to be honest with you," Sam replied. "I don't think the idea will fly around here without some prior encouragement from the funders. Let me share something with you in confidence." Sam reviewed the "paraprofessional incident" in his subsequent discussions with agency colleagues. "I think I understand," the site visitor nodded. "If I took some of the ideas we discussed today, and wrote them up in a letter suggesting to you that the Center experiment with the reallocation of part of the grant funds, your position would be strengthened. Well, we can do that. I'll even send you a report on a similar project we are funding to encourage and support self-help activities in Florida." "That would be very helpful," Sam replied. "It might require a reduction in agency staff," the federal official warned. "Well, your letter will help," Sam said. "We would have to cut back when the grant is over anyway."

THE SOCIAL WORKER'S CONDUCT AND COMPORTMENT

Potential conflicts between a social worker's commitments to the employing agency, the client population, funders, or other publics and the larger community or society are difficult enough. Equally difficult, although perhaps more subtle, are ethical issues that arise out of behaviors that some will consider private and personal, whereas others may define them as professional. In the next few pages, I'll present you with a number of real life situations. For some readers, the ethical issue will be clear and the appropriate action or decision will be unquestioned. But a discussion of these vignettes with others may suggest that there is no universal concensus on any one point of view.

* * * * *

Exercise 6.3
Commitments to One's Employer

Are there some ethical issues involved here? Look at Section IV in the NASW *Code of Ethics*. How do Sam's actions square with items L-1 and L-4? Are there potential conflicts between adherence to these positions and adherence to the ethical principles listed under II-F or V-M-2? Are there other ethical practice issues involved?

An article on the front page of the local press shocked members of the staff. Gertrude Dorsey, a social worker in the School Services Division, had just testified in court, as a witness in a divorce case, that she lived in a lesbian relationship with a woman who was suing her husband for divorce and for custody of their two daughters. As the court testimony revealed, Gertrude had two years earlier been the girls' therapist. The sisters had been referred to the agency because, as one of their teachers had discovered, they had been molested sexually by their father. Shortly thereafter, the girls' father had moved out of the home, to take a job in a different city. Their mother was brought into the treatment process, and over a course of months the mother and the therapist were drawn together. A strong bond of friendship emerged as client and therapist came to empathize with each other.

When Gertrude became aware of her sexual attraction to the client, she arranged for a different colleague to treat the mother while she continued working with the girls. Six months after treatment ended, Gertrude had moved into the girls' home. "While I'm no longer the family's therapist, for obvious reasons," she told the court, "I'm still a qualified social worker. And I can attest to this woman's competence as a parent. For her to lose custody to a father who has consistently molested the children would not be in their best interests."

On the morning the story broke in the press, Maria Ortez, Gertrude's supervisor, was in Bill Clapman's office. "Bill," she started, "it's about this Gertrude Dorsey thing. You must have seen it. Everybody's talking about it. I've always tried to separate my professional assessment of Gertrude's work from my feelings about her life-style . . . as long as she kept them separate. But now this . . ." she pointed to the newspaper article.

"Well, has she kept her professional and personal relationships separate?" asked Bill. "How could she?" Maria responded. "They are *living* together. I've never been so mortified in my life. I feel I'm responsible." At that moment, the phone rang. It was a member of the Center's board. "Have you seen the morning papers?" "You can't imagine how many times I've been asked that question today," Bill chuckled. "It's not a laughing matter, Bill," the board member reported angrily. "The agency's reputation is on the line, and so is your's as the director, and mine as a board member. You've got to fire that woman."

* * * * *

What are Bill's responsibilities in this matter? What are Gertrude's? What are Maria's? Are there causes here for disciplinary action on the agency's part, on NASW's? What would you need to know in order to arrive at a decision?

* * * * *

Mike Milbocker, the student assigned to Sam's department, had also been working in the School Services division on one of his practicum assignments. He served as a liaison between the Center and one of the grade schools that was heavily populated by children from Southeast Asian families. Early in the semester he had been mildly disturbed by the presence of a copy of *Playboy* magazine on Tim Mahler's desk. Mahler had explained the magazine's presence by pointing to an article on sex education in American public schools. But Mike suspected, especially considering all of Tim's off-color jokes, that this might not have been the principal reason Tim had purchased the magazine. Besides, he noted, it's got an address label on it. "That's no newsstand copy."

Working late one evening in Tim's office, Mike happened across a manila folder in the file box that included records on the school to which Mike was assigned. He was shocked to find that it also contained nude photos of children involved in simulated or real sexual activities with adults. Mike broke out into a cold sweat.

* * * * *

What should he do: confront Tim; share the "evidence" with Sam, his supervisor; keep things quiet, on the assumption that this was Tim's private business and there was no evidence of it interfering with his professional work at the agency? "If I rat on him," Mike thought, "Will I be exposing myself for having been snooping around? Was I really snooping? Could it jeopardize my position here as a student? Even if Sam protected me, how would other workers at the agency respond to me? And what about Tim? He seems like a pretty good worker, in spite all of this. Will I be putting his job into jeopardy?" If you were in Mike's position, what would you do?

* * * * *

Millicent Kapinski had been politically active since her return from South America. She spoke openly about her activities with colleagues at the Center. An active member of NOW (the National Organization of Women), she had campaigned for passage of the ERA (Equal Rights Amendment). And throughout his administration, she spoke of her dismay at President Reagan's politics, and her perceptions of his misguided effort to take apart the welfare state systematically. For Millicent there was no distinction between her political activism and her professional life. She saw them as consistent and integrated. It was clear that her political points of view were supported by NASW policies. There was no conflict.

But she was shocked to find that Cyndi Groten, the student whom she supervised, had recently become an active member of Lyndon Larouch's political organization. "This is bizarre," thought Millicent. "How can a social worker be affiliated with an organization that is so patently racist and anti-Semitic?" She determined to bring the issue up at her next supervisory conference with Cyndi.

"Look, Millicent," Cyndi defended herself. "You're politically active, and you've no problem with sharing your points of view around here. I know what people say about Larouch, that he's a crackpot. And some of the people around him may be. But Larouch is not. He speaks his mind about the things that he believes in. I'm no racist, and you know that. But there are issues on Larouch's platform that I think are right on target. Take this AIDS thing. Should kids with AIDS really be in the public schools? Should people with AIDS be allowed to immigrate to the United States and contaminate the rest of us? Should AIDS carriers be permitted to interact freely with the rest of the population? This is a public health thing. I couldn't agree with Larouch more. People with a serious and deadly communicable disease should be isolated from the rest of society. Why should parents of healthy kids have to take their children out of school and create alternative schools?"

* * * * *

Is this an issue of the greatest good for the greatest number? Is this a matter of balancing good over evil? Does NASW's *Code of Ethics* have anything to say regarding Cyndi or Millicent's political activism? Does it have anything to say about Cyndi's membership, on her private time, in a political organization with positions and platforms that may be abhorrent to the majority of the professional association's membership? Is Cyndi's freedom of expression in danger of being muted?

And what about Millicent's reaction? Should she undertake to "reeducate" Cyndi? Or are these issues not properly a part of the supervisory relationship? Should Millicent discuss Cyndi's political point of view with the faculty liaison from the School of Social Work, Cyndi's advisor?

* * * * *

A MATTER OF MONEY, AN ISSUE OF INTEGRITY

Carl Farrell is known as a straight arrow. No one would ever question his integrity. But there are some times when Carl questions whether he may be taking his integrity too far. A week or two earlier, Bill had asked Carl to scout around for a new printer. The firm that had done most of the agency's brochures and annual reports had just "busted" its union by hiring nonunion workers following a prolonged strike. And it was the agency's policy to put out bids only to union shops.

It happened that one of the members of the jazz combo with which Carl played on Thursday nights was himself a printer. When Carl explained to him, during one of the evening's breaks, what the Center was looking for, and asked if the printer knew of shops Carl might check out, his fellow musician replied: "Sure, why not us? We're a union shop."

"No reason. We'd love to get your bid. But we'll need at least two others to keep it fair." "Well, all right," the musician responded, "but you can't expect me to recommend others and possibly cut myself out of the competition." During the rest of the evening, there was a strain in their relationship, which was felt by other musicians in each of the three additional set they performed. Carl was surprised, therefore, when his musician associate called him on Saturday morning and invited Carl and his wife over for drinks that evening. Carl declined politely.

* * * * *

Would you have handled the situation in the same way as Carl? Why or why not? Are there appropriate guidelines you might be able

Exercise 6.4
Private and Professional Behaviors

NASW's *Code of Ethics* states that the social worker should treat colleagues with respect, courtesy, fairness, and good faith (III-J). It also requires that social workers should conduct themselves with propriety and integrity (I-A and I-D). And it also requires that social workers maintain the integrity of the profession, upholding and advancing its values, ethics, knowledge, and mission (V-M). Look over the three preceding vignettes focusing on Gertrude Dorsey, Tim Mahler, and Cyndi Groten, and think about your answers to each of the answers posed. Are there some general guidelines you might develop for yourself, so that you would know how to respond to each of these three situations? Or are the situations sufficiently different to require independent judgments in each case? Jot them down in the space below.

to turn to in the NASW *Code of Ethics* on which to base your decision?

* * * * *

"It's the damndest thing," Harvey told his wife. "You know that Alma Tetriakoff at the state agency I've told you about several times? A tough cookie. We had just finished negotiating a contract and gone out for a cup of coffee. As I reached for the check she nearly tore my hand off."

"You chauvinist bastard," Marsha responded, with a wink. "I would have done the same thing." "No, that's not it. I would have picked up a check if there was a male there, too. Alma let me have it because of the NASA, Pentagon, and New York City parking bureau kickback scandals. It's not exactly the same thing, is it? We're talking about a 50-cent cup of coffee, not a $50,000 payoff."

* * * * *

Is it or is it not the same thing?

* * * * *

Harvey, ever mindful of maintaining good relationships with "colleagues" in funding agencies kept them in mind when he ran across something that might be of interest to them. For example, knowing that Alma was a "nut on reprints," he always sent her copies of journal articles that he thought might interest her. He saw it as a professional courtesy. And unlike the coffee incident, Alma accepted it as such. Are there different principles at work here?

* * * * *

Mike, Betsy, Cyndi, and Mary Jo had just had an experience at school that gave each of them pause. During a class break, Sun Lee Nishikata had gone to the student lounge to purchase an apple from the refrigerated vending machine. She not only got her apple, but the machine kicked back her money and about four dollars in loose change. When she brought it to the instructor, asking what to do, he suggested she take it to the office downstairs where "complaints" were lodged when the vending machines did not work. Other students, overhearing the conversation, took off like lightning for the student lounge. They discovered that the machine not only kicked back quarters, nickels, and dimes, but that the door didn't lock. Within five minutes, it had been denuded, students bringing in two or three yogurts, apples, and pears, and other dessert items to class.

The instructor saw this as a good opportunity to explore the ethical issues involved. Some students clearly felt ashamed of their actions. "But what do we do now? If we put it back, someone else will take it, and in any case, it will probably spoil, because even the refrigeration isn't working."

"I don't think you should put it back," responded another. "That machine has been robbing us blind for years."

"I was amazed at how the conversation went," Mary Jo later reported to Harvey. "Professor Rafferty raised all kinds of issues, like taking paperclips or typing paper home from the office. One student told how she was so angry at her agency because of the way they treated staff and underpaid them, that she brought home everything she could, including staplers and paper cutters. And she apparently felt no guilt about it at all. Then Professor Rafferty asked the class if there was any difference between this behavior on the part of workers, or the student behavior of only a few minutes ago, and that which is associated with 'welfare cheating.' One of the students argued that one should, and she had, encouraged welfare clients to misrepresent their situation on their application forms, because she felt that the system was so punitive and so exploitive, that this was the only honest chance they would get."

* * * *

Should social workers and social work students impose a higher level of ethical expectations on themselves than on others? There probably is no doubt in most of the participants' minds that the incident with the vending machine was theft of something theft-like, even if it wasn't planned theft. Yet few students responded the way Sun Lee had. Sun Lee had come to the School of Social Work from Singapore to earn her Master's Degree. Might there be something in her background that generated a response that differed from others in the class? Does the incident say something about American society in general? About industrial society? What are the ethical implications of encouraging a worker's clients to misrepresent their situations? Is this a form of cheating as serious as taking staplers home? More serious, less?

* * * * *

Millicent was interviewing candidates for a new opening in the Community Education Department, an opening for a consultant on drug education. One of the applicants had exceptionally impressive credentials. In the course of the interview, she asked him to talk about some of his experiences as a private consultant. Here is the way he described his work:

"I've developed a style that may be a bit controversial, but it works. Here's what I would do when invited by a school board or a high school principal to help develop a drug education program. And let me say, in advance, that I always spell out my methods with whomever is employing me, so that they know what they are going to get and how they are going to get it.

"Once we settled on a fee, I'd go to the school in question and find the students and teachers who are most likely to take responsibility for developing an educational program, or who could block its implementation if they were not involved. I'd organize a committee. And since they were all expected to put in extra time, I offered to share my fee with them. My rationale was that since their involvement was essential, and since I was getting paid for my work, they should get paid for theirs. And I explained that I had clearance from the administration to do just that. I also offered to bring in a colleague of mine, an expert on drug education, who would put together a packet of articles and reports on drug education programs that had worked elsewhere. We would all read them, I would explain. And I would provide a checklist of things to look for. Each member would then identify those important principles on which we could design an educational program for this school and write a list of suggestions for action.

"Well, I must tell you that my assistant and I selected those items pretty carefully, based on what, in my nosing around the school, I thought might work. And frankly, any dunderhead who read those articles and followed the instructions on my checklist was likely to come up with some pretty similar kinds of solutions and suggestions. I then would take all of their written suggestions, and weave them into a comprehensive, integrated report. I'd then pass the report by everybody on the committee, asking them for their comments and suggestions. If there was general consensus, I would report that in a unified report to the administration. If some people had alternative ideas, and we couldn't arrive at consensus, I would include their alternative suggestions as well.

"Well, it almost always worked. People felt really involved. The splitting of the fee made them feel as if they were being treated as professional equals (whether they were teachers, students, or administrators). And the final recommendation almost always came with the approval and backing of the people whose support would really count if we were to install the new drug education program."

* * * * *

Millicent decided not to hire him, by the way, with some misgivings. Would you have decided the same way? On what basis do you think Millicent made her decision?

WHO'S THE CLIENT ANYWAY?

Kathy Springett approached one of the agency's social workers at Galloway Junior High. "I've got a friend, I can't tell you her name," she confided. "But she's pregnant, and she's even younger than me. And she can't tell her parents. She wants to have the baby, and then give it away. She knows she can't take care of it. I don't know what to do. If you tell her I told you, she'll kill me. So, how can I help her? What should I tell her?"

* * * * *

If you were the social worker, how would you respond? Suppose Kathy continues to refuse to tell you who her friend is. Is it your responsibility to find out? Who is your client, or who should be your client: Kathy, her friend, her friend's parents?

* * * * *

Mrs. Richards, a former client, called for an appointment. She missed it. This was not unusual. An examination of her earlier

Exercise 6.5
Integrity and Dollars

Once again, look over the NASW *Code of Ethics*. See if you can identify a set of principles that might serve as guidelines for each of the immediately preceding incidents (Carl and his fellow musicians, Harvey and the cup of coffee, the students and the vending machine, Millicent and the drug education applicant). Take them directly from the *Code*. Should these be modified or added to? How?

records showed that she frequently made appointments and then ignored or forgot them. But apparently pressures were piling up. She arrived at the agency, without a new appointment, three weeks later. Melvina Rhodes, an experienced social worker, was on rotation at the time, able to accept walk-ins. But when Mrs. Richards found she couldn't see her "regular worker," she became indignant, and was about to leave.

"The social worker you saw when you were last here in June is on vacation this month. But as long as you've made the trip," the worker told Mrs. Richards, "why not have a cup of coffee?" She did, sat down, and then she blurted out the story. Under the state's *workfare* guidelines, she had been "pressured" into accepting a job. Well, she liked the job all right, but there "was nobody to take care of the little ones." So she had left them in the care, early in the mornings, of her teenage daughter. "They be mostly in school and kin fend for themselves, later on," she explained. But now the eldest daughter, who had been a good student, was "doin' bad at school." The worker asked if she could make a home visit. Mrs. Richards agreed.

She found the home in a terrible state of disarray. In talking with the teenage daughter, the social worker discovered that Mrs. Richards not only left the children all alone when at work during the day (something she had frequently done even when she was on welfare), but was often out in the evenings as well. The teenage daughter was thus left with the responsibility of feeding her younger siblings, putting them to sleep, and taking care of them at night when they were ill. Sometimes her mother didn't come home at all until the next day. She was "out with one of her men," the girl explained. It was a wonder the teen went to school at all, the worker noted.

When the social worker raised the issue of the older teenager's burdens, and the apparent neglect of the younger children, Mrs. Richards became indignant. "I come in 'cause I needed help. Don't be takin' no side with that tramp. Don't come 'round here no more."

On the return to the Center, the worker raised the issue of continued service with her supervisor, Yolanda Stephenson. "I know Mrs. Richards will be back again when the pressures get too heavy for her. She won't accept much help from us, but she'll come here because she'll need someone to listen to her. But in the meantime, what do I do about her daughter and the younger children? The kids are neglected, but somehow except for the oldest girl, they seem to be OK physically and all go to school. I don't think this is a Protective

Services case. There's just not enough neglect for that. Welfare is no longer in the picture. What should I do?"

* * * * *

What should the worker do? Who is the worker's client? What is role of the former worker, the one with whom Mrs. Richards had originally made the appointment? Who is the client here, and who is the worker?

* * * * *

Sonya Gelman and her brother Richard Novetsky made an appointment to talk to one of the senior citizens workers at the agency. They had been referred by their attorney, who told them that their problem was not, at this point, a legal matter. It was a "family matter," and, he suggested, they might "benefit from some counseling." The problem was this.

Their father, Isador Novetsky, now 82 years old, had been living alone for the last 12 years, since his wife Lotte had passed away. Two years ago, he had become bedridden and the family, at their expense, had employed a practical nurse to care for him. Within six months, Mr. Novetsky had become almost totally dependent on the nurse, an attractive, fortyish woman, who was Jewish like Mr. Novetsky and had recently immigrated from Russia, from where he himself emigrated 68 years earlier. It became increasingly clear, Mrs. Gelman and the younger Mr. Novetsky explained, that they were no longer welcome. The nurse seemed overprotective, telling the children that their presence often upset their father.

The elder Mr. Novetsky seemed less and less interested in his children's visits. If they raised questions about his care, the food he was eating, or made anything that smacked of being a derogatory statement aimed at the nurse, he'd become nervous, even abusive, ordering them out of the house. Once he shouted after them: "Don't come around no more. You're only after my money." "What kind of money is he talking about? He doesn't have any," Sonya Gelman asked her brother. "Maybe he's lost touch with reality," he suggested. That's when the children decided to consult with an attorney.

The attorney advised them that they could declare him incompetent, but that a court hearing would be necessary. It might make sense to talk first to a social worker, and then if the social worker felt this was appropriate, a home visit might be necessary to get a sense of Mr. Novetsky's competence. The social worker, the attorney explained, might help the family think through a strategy other than the declaration of incompetency. Should the worker find that their father had indeed reached a point of senility and was no longer able to make proper judgments himself, then legal action might be warranted. On his children's request, the All-Families Service Center worker did, in fact, visit Mr. Novetsky.

She found the nurse suspicious. But Mr. Novetsky, although feeble, seemed fully lucid. "Look," he told her, "I know why my children sent you. They are money-grubbing and always have been. For 14 years, since Lotte died, they hardly ever came around. And they rarely invited me over, even to see my grandchildren. The grandchildren never come to visit. Then when I got sick, they saw their chance. They thought they'd put me in a nursing home. But I refused. So they got me a nurse.

"And did she turn out to be a honey! She takes better care of me than my wife did. She loves me. And I love her. Don't worry," he said with a twinkle. "It's not like when I was younger. I'm too old for that."

Before leaving, Mr. Novetsky invited the worker to "come back and visit anytime. You're a nice lady."

On returning to the Center, and writing up her site visit notes, the social worker expressed perplexity. Mr. Novetsky seemed perfectly lucid and aware of his situation. On the other hand, the children also seemed perfectly sincere in their concerns. Obviously, there was something in the family history that needed ferreting out. When the younger Mr. Novetsky and his sister Mrs. Gelman returned for a follow-up meeting, the worker raised a number of questions. "We're not here to wash our family laundry in public," the daughter told her. "This is not what we came for." Her brother agreed. "Maybe we've come to the wrong place."

* * * * *

What should be the worker's next step? Has she been "fired" by her original clients, the elder Mr. Novetsky's son and daughter? Is the senior Mr. Novetsky's invitation to come and visit again an opening to redefine him as a client? Are there guidelines in the NASW *Code of Ethics* that would suggest the next steps?

* * * * *

ETHICAL ISSUES

These are only a few of the ethical dilemmas you are likely to face in your practice. In the second edition of what has become a "standard" in many schools of social work, Loewenberg and Dolgoff identify 13 issues that require ethical decisions in social work practice. Let me review them with you. You may want to go to the original source for a more detailed discussion.

The issues are (1) professional knowledge versus client rights, (2) conflicting obligations and expectations, (3) informed consent, (4) ambiguity and uncertainty, (5) truth-telling, (6) privacy and confidentiality, (7) distributing limited resources, (8) priority of client's interests, (9) suspension of judgment; (10) limited nature of professional relationships, (11) choice of intervention modality, (12) relations with professional colleagues, and (13) adherence to regulations and policies. I'll take them one at a time.

(1) Social work, perhaps more than most professions, operates on the assumption that all persons have the right to make their own decisions, in particular, in relationship to the kind of treatment or other form of intervention in which they will be involved or that may affect them. Self-determination and participation are, in fact, themselves intervention modalities at the individual, organizational, and community levels. They are justified, not only on moral and ethical grounds, but also on the basis of their contribution to achievement of other desired outcomes. Thus, self-determination and involvement are defined as both ends (values) and means.

But social workers also possess other, more esoteric, to a certain extent empirically or scientifically based, knowledge. The actions a social worker will take on the basis of his or her knowledge might be in the best interest of the client, even when the client might choose another course of action. This may require ignoring, minimizing, or limiting the client's input. In the vignettes described earlier, were there instances in which the social worker might appropriately have utilized practice knowledge and skill without reference to the client's preferences?

(2) Professional social workers, like others, often have to balance conflicting obligations and expectations. Mrs. Gelman and her brother, the younger Mr. Novetsky, had expectations of the worker when they came to the agency on their attorney's advice. But the worker's expectations may have been somewhat different. Did she fully inform them of what she would do when she visited their elderly

father? And what about the senior Mr. Novetsky's expectations? Who was, is, or should be the client in this case? Does the worker have the right/obligation to redefine the client he or she will work with?

When Sam, not so subtly, let it be known to a site visitor that he was in favor or some changes in the New Americans Project, was he fulfilling the Center's expectations of him as an employee? Was he resolving a set of conflicting obligations in favor of his perception of what might be best for a client population? Are there ethical guidelines that can be universally applied to either one of these cases? Or are they so situationally specific that "situational ethics" must be depended on? Your decision might depend on to whom you consider the social worker accountable. These might include the person or persons who initiated a request for help; those who entered into formal, contractual, and goal-focused relationships with the social worker; and other beneficiaries, those who, in addition to the client, might benefit from intervention. But what of the employer and those other constituents of the agency, such as funders and collaborating agencies?

Some social workers resolve potential conflicts by defining their primary obligations to those with whom they have contracted to provide a service. And if contradictions exist, the first obligation is to the first contractor. Would this mean one's obligation is to the employer who makes its possible to contract with funders and clients?

(3) A related issue is that of getting consent—approval for taking action—but consent must be informed, and that means that the client or others must know what is likely to happen, how it is going to happen, and what the possible consequences might be. In the case of the client, he or she must voluntarily enter into the helping relationship. It's not enough for the client to enter the relationship of his or her own volition. The client must also be competent to make a decision. How competent was the 13-year-old who approached the worker at Galloway Junior High to decide whether or not the worker should intervene with her pregnant girlfriend? Without her friend's consent, should the worker have initiated an intervention process with the pregnant girl, with her parents, with school authorities? Who might be the client or clients have been? Who might be the targets of intervention? Does one need informed consent from those who are targeted for change?

(4) There is a certain amount of ambiguity and uncertainty in this case. But that's not unusual for social workers. At times, the ambi-

guity can be resolved by getting all the facts, or at least the facts that are relevant to the situation. But Loewenberg and Dolgoff also list other sources of uncertainty: (a) uncertainty about values and goals, (b) uncertainty about practice or the scientific knowledge base upon which decisions can be made, and (c) uncertainty about the consequences of intervention. Social workers may be beset by problems of ambiguity and uncertainty to a larger extent than practitioners of many other professions. First, the situations in which they intervene are often vague. Second, the knowledge base in which social workers draw is broad and general, rather than narrow and specific, and it is constantly subject to modification.

(5) On the surface of it, telling the truth, not deceiving clients, employers, and others, would seem to be a clear ethical imperative. Telling the truth is so basic and ethical an obligation that the NASW *Code of Ethics* does not even mention it. But here, too, there are ambiguities. Sam let it be known to the site visitor from a federal agency that he was interested in changing the nature of an agency program and its funding base. But he didn't tell others at the agency. Social workers do, on occasion, obscure facts, even if they do not misrepresent them. Sometimes, they do so in light of what they perceive to be a stronger imperative (in Sam's case, providing more appropriate services to the clients to whom he is personally and professionally obligated). But in some cases, holding back the truth may be important in order to decrease client uncertainty and anxiety, to protect the client from damaging truth, to simplify the options, when the worker judges the client not capable of dealing with the broad ranges of potential choices, or even to put a client at ease. How often have you said to a client, "You're looking good today," or "I'm glad to see you," or "I've been looking forward to this session," without really meaning it? Is it possible to mean it (professionally) and not mean it (personally) at the same time?

There apparently are good, or appropriate, reasons not to tell (all) the truth. But deceiving others for one's personal gain, or for papering over mistakes, or for increasing power over a client or some other group—these would be considered bad reasons for obscuring, withholding, or even telling a "white lie."

(6) The right to privacy is an essential value in our society. It forms the basis for the statement in the NASW *Code* that "a social worker should respect the privacy of clients and hold in confidence all information obtained in the course of professional service." And yet, as we

have seen in earlier chapters, social workers are likely to break this rule when sharing information about clients with each other. This breaking of the rules becomes permissible so long as it is not to the detriment of the client and it serves to engender a sense of comradery and trust among colleagues. But is it really ethical?

There may also be some compelling reasons that social workers will break a confidence. These include (a) advance knowledge that the law may be broken, (b) that the client may harm him- or herself and others in the immediate environment, or (c) when the worker makes an informed judgment that sharing information with relevant others is in the client's best interest. Look over the vignettes in this chapter. In which would the breaking of confidence have been justified? In which was the worker tempted to break a confidence with insufficient justification? Does the good over bad, right over wrong, benefit over cost ratio help to make an appropriate decision?

The answers may vary with whom one shares a confidence or how much is shared. The answers may differ when confidential information is shared with other social work colleagues (whom one trusts to keep the confidence), in contrast with colleagues from other fields (for example, a medical social worker giving confidential information about a child to a teacher whom she fears may share it with other teachers). Some information may have to be shared with the police or the courts, other information may have to be withheld. Some information, that which appears on computerized administrative records, may find itself inappropriately in the hands of other agencies as a result of a case management process, referrals, and the like. If confidences are broken, social workers are liable to litigation.

One way in which they protect themselves is by informing clients fully about the limits of confidentiality and receiving their "informed" consent to those limits. But would clients share all the information that they must, in order to receive proper guidance and assistance, if they knew that others might have access to the information? The signing of a consent form by a client may be an indication of trust, more than of an understanding of the consequences of that signature.

(7) An agency's resources are always limited; so are an individual social worker's. Often, decisions must be made about how those resources will be distributed, which client or clients will receive intensive services and which will not receive any service. Resources may include funds, services, or the worker's time. When Yolanda complained to Sam that Vietnamese immigrants were receiving

"$1000 each" while Black Americans were still suffering the consequences of slavery, she was talking about equity. And when Sam determined that money should go directly to new Americans, as employees of their own indigenous organizations, rather than to salaries for staff at the agency, he was making another decision. But who determines equity in our society? Who decides that one family deserves, requires, more service from an agency than another?

Equity considerations often form the basis of agency decisions about the length of service, the intensity of care, and even the selection of populations to be served. Vocational rehabilitation agencies have often been accused of "creaming" because they sometimes invest more time and energy in serving clients who can be easily rehabilitated, ignoring those they consider almost untreatable because of severe disabilities. "The choice," a director of a state rehab agency once told me, "is between rehabilitating and finding jobs for 150 persons in a locale, or for 30. We go for the greatest good to the greatest number. If we didn't, our success rate would be so low that we wouldn't even get funding from the state legislature for the 30." Yet some of those clients selected, he admitted, might make it on their own without agency help. A pragmatic decision? An ethical one?

(8) One ethical imperative that few would challenge is the primacy of client's interests over worker or agency interests. Yet here, too, we find substantial difficulties in application. If Harvey goes after a grant for a new program of services for the elderly (for whom funds are relatively available), he may have to give up on efforts to fund group homes for other less popular—but perhaps even more needy—populations. Is Harvey's decision based on a desire to be successful, or to expand services (to whomever) rather than fighting a losing battle? How does one weigh motivations when they may be mixed?

(9) Social workers are often expected to suspend judgment, that is, to hold judgments in abeyance until all the facts are in (at least those on which a rational decision can be made). But we, all of us, have our biases. Being nonjudgmental may mean that we attempt, in as disciplined a manner as possible, to withholding making a judgment about the character of a person or a situation, but not necessarily about the consequences of behaviors or actions for these same persons, their associates, or communities.

Loewenberg and Dolgoff point out that the withholding of judgment may be harmful to a client. They give the example of a client who might feel guilty about a certain behavior. If the worker addresses only the problem of guilt, the client may conclude that the worker considers the behavior acceptable. Perhaps, they point out, a more realistic way of dealing with the obligation to withhold judgment is to expect that social workers will never let their value judgments become the sole criteria for making a professional decision.

(10) Professional relationships are limited relationships. When they get mixed up with personal relationships, they can lead to difficulties. "Straight Arrow" Carl was well aware of this, and he refused to advocate solely for a friend's printing business. But what of the social worker who had a sexual relationship with one of her *former* clients? Does maintaining a professional relationship, a "correct" relationship, limit *any* kind of social interaction with clients or former clients? I know a community center director who refuses, as a matter of principle, invitations to dinner with members of her agency's board of directors. She views them, not only as members and volunteers, but also as part of her larger client population. Has she taken an ethical position too far, beyond the limitations that were intended?

(11) Are there "best ways" to help people? The choice of intervention methods always has ethical implications. There are, for example, ethical implications in using behavioral modification in contrast with ego psychological theories as the basis for interventions. Some social workers choose the intervention modality with which they are most familiar, most comfortable, or in which they feel most competent. "These are the competencies and the skills I possess," they are likely to conclude, and then ask, "what can I do with them?" Taken to an extreme, this may lead to Abraham Kaplan's "law of the instrument," mentioned in an earlier chapter. You'll recall his suggestion that if you give a small boy a hammer, he'll find that everything in sight needs pounding. Some agencies are the same way.

They will accept clients only with problems that are defined in ways in which they feel competent to cope, and they'll define their interventions in terms of the competence or skill of their employees, not necessarily or exclusively in relationship to the problems that clients present or perceive. This may be practical in a world in which specialization is the result of ever-increasing knowledge. But is it ethical? Would it be ethical to take action where one is not competent?

(12) Throughout this book, we have explored and we will continue to explore relationships between professional colleagues. If you'll turn to NASW's *Code of Ethics*, you'll find that Section III—

"A Social Worker's Ethical Responsibility To Colleagues"—includes almost as long a list as Section II, which focuses on ethical responsibilities to clients. Look over the first 11 items that explicate respect, fairness, and courtesy. I don't think you'll have difficulty with any of them. But the difficulties arise when these expectations contradict or conflict with responsibilities to one's employer, to one's clients, or even to the social work profession. And conflicts do arise.

Mike's concern about "ratting" on a professional worker whom he otherwise respects is perhaps an all-too-obvious example. Going public is not always the only way to proceed. Difficult as it may be to confront colleagues, some of their actions may require examination or censure. Social workers, perhaps like members of the general public, are too quick to accuse physicians of incompetence. The AMA, in a study published in the late 70s, concluded that a minimum of 5% of the medical practitioners in the United States were incompetent to practice medicine. Gloating, one of my colleagues at the university asked, "And if 5% are incompetent, can you imagine what percentage is only partially competent?" But how competent are social workers? We don't even have measures that are nearly as good as those that are used by the medical profession. And we rarely ask ourselves the question physicians have asked themselves. Why not?

(13) Most social workers are employed by social agencies or other bureaucratic organizations. Even those in private practice are subject to rules, regulations, and policies set by others (third party payers, state agencies that issue subcontracts, and so on). In all these relationships, commitments are made. One makes a commitment when one accepts a job, a commitment to adhere to an agency's rules or procedures. One makes a commitment when one signs a contract, to abide by the terms of that contract.

Unfortunately, these commitments are not always congruent with the objectives of the social work profession, and they sometimes place the social worker directly on the pointed horns of a dilemma: to follow directives by the employer (the one who pays), or to act in some other manner that the social worker considers to be more professionally or ethically correct. In practice, this is often defined as a matter of loyalty. And loyalties, as Yolanda recognized when she was invited to join the National Association of Black Social Workers, can be divided.

Sometimes, assuming advocacy responsibility for clients may conflict with one's sense of responsibility or duty owed to colleagues or employers. I used the term *going public* in reference to colleagues earlier. But there are times in which it may be necessary to "blow the whistle" on an agency, when its programs channel clients into services that are of no or limited benefit to them. Agencies sometimes do this to fufill quotas, to earn income through fees paid for services by clients or third party payers.

MAKING CHOICES

Perplexed? It's no wonder. The absence of clear guidelines that can be applied unequivocally to any situation cannot but be frustrating for any thinking social worker. But that frustration is the stuff of practice. And the resolution of ethical dilemmas, even when those resolutions are not perfect or even optimal, the struggle that goes into effort at resolution, that's what makes us true professionals. I don't mean to suggest that making ethical choices, without knowledge or skill, is all that anyone needs to be a real pro. But technique, by itself, is no substitute for making the right choices. And the term *right* always implies ethical choice.

I'm not certain that it will ever be possible to generate a set of principles that are more helpful than those implied in the discussion of the preceding 13 issues. Awareness of the issues and a process of conscious examination of their implications for practice is what contributes to ethical decisions. Like any professional, you'll have to accept responsibility for the choices you make and the actions you take. Yet, I think that you might find the following suggestions helpful in at least some of the choices with which you'll be faced. If you'll remember, in Chapter 1 we discussed a number of *need* theories.

Maslow postulated that all persons have a hierarchy of needs that can be described as ranging from the physiological through safety and security, to belonging and affection, on to esteem, and finally to the need for self-actualization. Alderfer regrouped these into *existence*, *relationships*, and *growth* needs. Using either Alderfer's or Maslow's formulation, can you develop a set of ethical guidelines for yourself or for your agency?

Let's take Alderfer's formulation. What this suggests is that when the client's existence is threatened, then the appropriate action is to preserve that existence, and this requirement takes precedent over concerns with relationships or with growth. If the worker makes a judgment that pregnancy, carried to term by a 12-year-old whose parents are not involved, endangers both the child and the unborn infant, then questions of relationship to another client or even the relationship of the 12-year-old to her parents take second place in order of priorities.

The first concern, then, has to be with the satisfying of the fulfillment of hunger, thirst, and other bodily needs, with protection from emotional and physical harm, with the provision of shelter, warmth, health, and mental health services. Only when these are assured, or not threatened by other interventions, should the worker focus on concerns for belonging, affection, acceptance, friendship, cooperative working relationships, respect, recognition, and esteem. The focus on growth, self-actualization, on a sense of achievement—these are the proper concerns of professional intervention once existence and relationship needs have been met. I don't mean to suggest that all three (or five in Maslow's formulation) cannot be worked on simultaneously. But I do think the "hierarchy of human needs" formulation can suggest priorities when choices have to be made.

"Needs-oriented" ethical choices can also be focused on families, groups, or communities. Thus, for community workers, or for organizational developers, the first concern is with the client system's survival needs. Helping an organization or community establish more effective intersystem exchanges or to grow into a mature and supportive entity would make sense only once survival is assured. But, here, we face some difficulty. Do we want to assure survival of a system that is not in the best interest of its human members or constituents? Of course not! Remember—not all individuals, groups, or organizations are our *clients*. Some are *targets* of change.

REVIEW AND TENTATIVE CONCLUSIONS

Social workers and social agencies are confronted with choices at every stage of interventions with clients. These choices may generate agonizing quandaries.

(1) At stake are a number of values that, in and of themselves, may be inconsistent and contradictory. These include the personal values of the social worker (and his or her colleagues), the client's or client system's values, those of the agency (as reflected in policies and procedures), those of other constituents and suppliers (e.g., funders and collaborating agencies), and of the society in which they are embedded.

Exercise 6.6
Choices by Order of Needs

1. Try using one of the need theories in reexamining the case illustrations presented throughout this chapter, or others of your own choosing, on cases that you've had more direct experiences with. Was the focus of intervention on the client's

   __ existence (survival needs)
   __ relationships (belonging, exchange, esteem, recognition)
   __ growth (individual or systemic development and achievement)

2. Give an example of how, in using this formulation, it may become necessary to redefine all or part of a client-system into a target-system. Why is this so? What were the ethical issues involved? Use NASW or NABSW *Code of Ethics* to justify your analysis.

(2) Values serve as general guides. They suggest preferences. We value what we consider to be more good than bad. This sometimes leads to a teleological conclusion that ends justify the means. It may presume a utilitarian conviction that choices should lead to the greatest good for the greatest number. Ethics are guidelines to behavior that are somewhat more specific than values. They may draw on a religious or secular/humanistic source of authority.

(3) Professional associations generate codes of ethics that provide guidelines by which professionals and their practices can be evaluated, and that may serve to give direction to the making of ethical choices when ethical dilemmas are faced. Such codes protect the worker, the client, the profession, and the public. They can never fully resolve contradictions, but they can be used to examine and weigh alternative choices. The NASW and NABSW *Codes* are presented.

(4) Thirteen sets of ethical issues were discussed: (1) decisions made on the basis of professional knowledge versus clients' choices, (2) conflicting obligations and expectations, (3) informed consent, (4) ambiguity and uncertainty, (5) truth-telling, (6) privacy and confidentiality, (7) distributing limited resources, (8) priority of client's interests, (9) suspension of judgment, (10) limited nature of professional relationships, (11) choice of intervention modality, (12) relations with professional colleagues, and (13) adherence to regulations and policies.

(5) One way of resolving some of the contradictions and prioritizing among ethical guidelines is to use a "hierarchy of human needs"

formulation. Choices about interventions, clients, or obligations would give priority first to questions of existence, then to questions of relationship, and finally to those of growth.

YOUR ADDITIONS

(6)

(7)

(8)

(9)

(10)

REFERENCES

Abrahamson, Marcia. (1981). Ethical dilemmas for social workers in discharge planning. *Social Work and Health, 6*(4).

Bergin, Alan E. (1980). Psychotherapy of religious values. *Journal of Consulting and Clinical Psychology, 48*(2).

Bermant, Gordon, Kelman, Herbert C., & Warwick, Donald P. (Eds.). (1978). *The ethics of social intervention.* New York: John Wiley.

Bok, Sissela. (1982). *Secrets: On the ethics of concealment and revelation.* New York: Pantheon.

Cohen, Robert. (1980). Ethics: Responsibility to more than the profession's clients. *NASW News, 25*(6).

Constable, Robert T. (1983). Values, Religion and social work practice. *Social Thought, 9*(1).

Council on Social Work Education. (1982). *Curriculum policy statement*. New York: Author.

Dillick, Sidney. (Ed.). (1984). *Value foundations of social work: Ethical basis for a human service profession*. Detroit, MI: Wayne State University Press.

Fishkin, James S. (1982). *The limits of obligation*. New Haven, CT: Yale University Press.

Frankena, William K. (1980). *Thinking about morality*. Ann Arbor: University of Michigan Press.

Goldberg, Matilda E., & Warburton, William E. (1979). *Ends and means in social work: The development and outcome of a case review system for social workers*. London: George Allen & Unwin.

Kanfer, Frank. (1979). Personal control, social control and altruism. *American Psychologist, 34*(4).

Keith-Lucas, Alan. (1977). Ethics in social work. In *Encyclopedia of social work* (17th ed.). Washington, DC: NASW.

Kranzberg, Melvin. (Ed.). (1982). *Ethics in an age of pervasive technology*. Boulder, CO: Westview Press.

Levy, Charles. (1976). *Social work ethics*. New York: Human Sciences Press.

Levy, Charles. (1982). *Guide to ethical decisions and actions for social service administrators*. New York: Haworth.

Lewis, Harold. (1982). *The intellectual basis of social work practice: Tools for thought in a healthy profession*. New York: Haworth.

Lewis, Harold. (1984). Ethical assessment. *Social Casework, 65*(4).

Loewenberg, Frank M. (1978). Professional values and professional ethics in social work education. In Betty Baer & Ron Federico (Eds.), *Educating the baccalaureate social worker*. Cambridge, MA: Ballinger.

Loewenberg, Frank M., & Dolgoff, Ralph. (1985). *Ethical decisions for social work practice* (2nd ed.). Itasca, IL: Peacock.

Maroney, Robert M. (1976). *Family and the state: Considerations for social policy*. London: Longman.

Maslow, Abraham. (1962). *The farther reaches of human nature*. New York: Penguin.

McCann, Charles W., & Cutler, Jane P. (1979). Ethics and the alleged unethical. *Social Work, 24*(1).

Miller, Henry. (1968). Value dilemmas in social casework. *Social Casework, 13*(1).

National Institute of Mental Health. (1981). *Ethical issues in the mental health policy administration*. Washington, DC: U.S. Department of Health and Human Services.

Pahel, Kenneth, & Schiller, Martin. (Eds.). (1970). *Readings in contemporary ethical theory*. Englewood Cliffs, NJ: Prentice-Hall.

Perlman, Helen Harris. (1976). Believing and doing: Values in social work education. *Social Casework, 57*(6).

Pumphrey, Muriel. (1959). *The teaching of values and ethics in social work education*. New York: Council on Social Work Education.

Reamer, Frederick G. (1982). *Ethical dilemmas in social service*. New York: Columbia University Press.

Reamer, Frederick. (1983). Ethical dilemmas in social work practice. *Social Work, 28*(1).
Ross, Judith W. (1982). Ethical conflicts in medical social work: Pediatric cancer case as a prototype. Health in Social Work, 7(2).
Shild, Sylvia, & Beck-Black, Rita. (1984). *Social work and genetic counseling: A guide to practice*. New York: Howarth.
Siporin, Max. (1982). Moral philosophy in social work today. *Social Service Review, 56*(6).
Timms, Noah. (1983). *Social work values: An inquiry*. London: Routledge & Kegan Paul.
Wells, Carolyn Cressy, with Masch, Kathleen. (1986). *Social work ethics day to day: Guidelines for professional practice*. New York: Longman.
Wilson, Suanna J. (1978). *Confidentiality in social work*. New York: Free Press.
Yelaja, Shankar. (1982). *Ethical issues in social work*. Springfield, IL: Charles C. Thomas.

Chapter 7

GETTING THE JOB DONE
Tasks, Responsibilities, and the Job Description

Carl Farrell was more than a little apprehensive when Bill Clapman, the Center's director, asked him to drop by for a chat. Things had not been going well for Carl. When he'd first come to the agency ten years earlier to take over the accounting department, Carl had been in his mid-30s, at the peak of his professional competence. Within a few years he'd helped the agency restructure its rather chaotic fiscal practices. Those had been exhilarating years.

In those days the agency was still in its growth phase, and Carl knew that the procedures he'd developed had given management greater control over its programs. Control was one of those things that Carl liked. There was something about taking a jumble of figures, even a mess of figures, and organizing them, that gave him a deep sense of satisfaction. It also felt good to get positive feedback from others at the agency. The others weren't like Carl; they were people-oriented. "I'm a numbers man," he often thought to himself, "but I really appreciate the kinds of things they (the social work staff) do." Nevertheless, over the years things had gone progressively sour for Carl. "Maybe it's the work, maybe it's me," he thought. Work had become routine. There wasn't much challenge to it. And Carl was feeling increasingly isolated. He'd never really shared much or had much in common with the other staff members. "Well, I'm an accountant and they're social workers," he reasoned. But there was something more to it than that.

"Midlife crisis," he'd reasoned. He had felt it coming on for some time. Perhaps that's why he'd gone back to playing the bass a couple of nights a week at Renfrew's. Jazz was Carl's one real outlet. It provided him the structure through which he could be really free, at least for the few hours each night that he played. "Improvisation without commitment," that's how he saw it, an opportunity to let loose. And an opportunity to really relate to other people. "It's like a sexual thing," he confided to his wife. "When we're playing off each other, it's really an act of love. We're saying things that we could never say in words. But then when I leave it, when the gig is over, I really can leave it behind. It's no commitment. I can pack up my fiddle and never look back. It's a real love affair while you're playing, but with no commitments. No strings. When the set's over, it's over."

But work wasn't like that at all. It was more like writing a score that sort of played itself. And there was no intensity in the relationships with the other players. That's the way Carl had wanted it, or so he thought. But it wasn't satisfying. He knew something was missing in his work, and he was certain that Bill saw it too. That's why he wasn't looking forward to what he thought might be coming as he walked into Bill's office.

FROM MANAGING FINANCIAL ASSETS TO MANAGING PEOPLE AS ASSETS

"Carl," Bill began, "over the years, you've helped us all learn to manage our assets more effectively. Now I've got another challenge for you. Tell me what you think." Bill then went through a litany of issues he felt needed to be addressed. "I realized something was wrong," he explained, "when the staff reacted the way it did to Sam's proposal. There's no reason we should not explore alternative staff arrangements for the New Americans Project. Clearly, we've got all kinds of staffing arrangements operating already. Maybe too many. Maybe not enough. Maybe some of our people are trying to defend their own turf or their own ways of operating, I don't know. What I do know is that we've got to get a handle on what's going on. We can be more efficient, and we've got to be more accountable. I think what we need is a job analysis.

"Here, look at this stuff," he continued, handing Carl a number of notebooks. "Take a look here, at this 'task bank' developed by a guy by the name of Sydney Fine at the Upjohn Institute. Mary Jo, one of our students, brought this in. It's a system for identifying every task that's performed in an agency like ours and then rewriting the tasks to the specifications of the job. You then reorder the tasks, as I understand it, and reassign them in some more functional way. I don't understand it all, but I think you should take a look at it. Then I'd like you to pull together a little task force—some key staff people who can help you put together a task bank for our agency. What I'm looking for is some way of rationalizing, of making more systematic the way we assign tasks to different people and to different departments. It's not so different from managing financial assets; it's managing people assets."

Carl was slow to respond at first. "I'm not sure I know enough about what people are doing around here." "That's the point," Bill responded. "I'm not sure any of us really does. But I have a feeling that if we could specify the tasks that have to be performed, we might be a little less defensive about who should perform them." Carl thought about it a bit longer. "I like the idea," he began slowly. "It's a challenge. I'm really not sure I'm the right person for it, but I need a challenge right now. Let's talk about who should be involved. I think Yolanda, Sam for sure, Millicent and Harvey—he's always full of ideas." "And Ali," Bill suggested. "She seems to be trusted by everyone, and it would give her a little more stature around here. Besides, she knows what the clerical staff do. And why not add Mary Jo? It would be a good assignment for her. We should involve our students more."

"I'll give it a try," agreed Carl. "But before I do, I'll want to talk to each of these people to make sure that they really want to participate. I'm not too good at this interpersonal stuff, and I need to feel secure, to be sure, I guess, that they'll want to work with me." "Good," Bill responded. "I'll call them and tell them I asked you to chair a task group to do some exploring into ways in which we might make better use of our staff. I'll explain that I think you're the right person, because you've got a good systematic mind and because you've no stake in any particular department's operations. That should give you the legitimacy you need. Come back and tell me how you decide to proceed after you've had a chance to talk to them all." "Well," thought Carl as he returned to his office, "if I'm going to help write this score, the first thing I better find out is just what the score is." He gave his boss a few days to contact the others and then called Mary Jo.

TASK ANALYSIS: FINDING OUT WHO'S DOING WHAT

Mary Jo explained what she knew about task analysis to Carl. "I think it's real exciting. I worked on a similar process in a job I had before returning to school. I learned more about it in a class on personnel practices, and it gave me a chance to rethink the work I had done at the agency where I worked before. We organized a small team and interviewed everybody at the agency. We used a standard form and got everybody to spell out, as precisely as they could, the tasks that they performed. We tried to group these tasks into 'people' tasks, 'materials' tasks, and 'ideas' tasks. What I mean is that some tasks were almost exclusively related to working with people, like interviewing, counseling, and advising. Other tasks were related to materials, such as filing and typing. Still other tasks were related primarily to ideas—for example, diagnosing, assessing, and evaluating.

"What I mean by *task* is the smallest unit of work that can be described. And to describe a task, you have to build it around an action verb, like some of those that I mentioned: 'counsels,' 'files,' 'records,' 'refers' and 'distributes.' But you need more than just an action verb. You also need a sentence that you build around it.

"A sentence includes the following components: (1) who, (2) performs what action, (3) to whom or to what, (4) using what tools or methods, (5) to what end or for what purpose and (6) using what directions or under whose instructions. For example, you could say, 'The adoption worker writes letters to adoptive parents confirming agency decisions to place a child in their home and informing them of the necessary procedures in order to provide them with the information needed to begin the adoption process, under the direction of the adoption supervisor.'

"Whenever I forget the order in which a sentence should be written, I just think of an example I learned. It works like this: '(1) The butler (2) laces (3) Mrs. Scarlett's tea (4) with arsenic (5) in order to do her in (6) at the behest of the upstairs maid.'

"One of the nice things about getting everybody to identify the tasks they perform is that you quickly learn that what they are actually doing may be different from what it says in their job descriptions. Not only that, but some people may be performing tasks that they really hate, or that they're not very good at. By finding that out, you can help people share tasks, or shift responsibilities for tasks from one person to the other. That way, people who are better at certain things or who like to do them might take on more responsibility for certain tasks than for others. It's also possible to specify the level at which the tasks should be performed. For example, you could develop criteria for determining whether the letters that the adoption worker writes are clear, warm and empathic in style and contain all the pertinent information. That way you can train people to perform tasks more effectively, correct them if they're making mistakes and use those criteria in supervision.

"But it's not so easy to do, sometimes. Some people are pretty defensive about the tasks they perform and are not so willing to give them up or to let anybody else know what they are doing. I mean, it's like if anybody else knew exactly what they were doing, they would have some of their strength or their power stripped away. And if somebody else decides to reassign tasks from one person to another, there might be some resistance on the part of the people who were getting new assignments and those who were having old and cherished assignments taken away. Know what I mean?"

Carl looked over the forms and procedural manuals that Mary Jo shared with him. He was comfortable with the technical aspects of task analysis. It fit his sense that everything should be kept neat and accountable. "That's what accountants like, after all," he smiled to himself. But he was troubled with what he perceived to be some political aspects of this whole process that could mean potential conflict among staff members. Putting things neatly down on paper, fitting them in appropriate boxes, and showing the relationships between them—these were things Carl felt both at ease with and competent in doing. Dealing with interpersonal relationships, especially if conflict were involved—that's not something he felt comfortable with.

"The best way to handle things is to be straightforward," he thought. "I'll just approach each of the members of the task force, tell them what I've learned from Mary Jo and discuss the charge I got from Bill Clapman. And then I'll ask them what they think."

* * * * *

Millicent's reaction: "Interesting idea. Intriguing. You know, I think I can use this approach in our department's work in training agency volunteers. People come in with all kinds of skills and all kinds of backgrounds. And we've had no way of assessing what they can do and what they can't do. If we could clarify the tasks that we expect them to perform, we could train them for those tasks more adequately, maybe even help them develop their own standards for effective performance. If people know what's expected of them, and where they are in terms of being able to meet those expectations or what they are, they're more likely to be motivated to improve.

"As to using it with the agency's professional staff, I'm not sure. I think about my own work. It's not something I can easily define. No, that's not altogether correct. I suppose I could lay out all the major tasks that I perform. But, you know, my work isn't routine. I'm often involved with the public, particularly when I'm doing community education or family life education. And often I find myself responding to other people's expectations or their definitions of the problems that they're presenting. What I mean is that other people are likely to shape my work as much as I do myself.

"It's not that I'm not responsible for my work but that my responsibility is to be responsive to others. No, as I think about it, there really are too many external demands and expectations for me to be able to spell out all the tasks that I perform. And I suspect the same would be true with many of the other professional staff members at the agency. Certainly I'm willing to sit down with the rest of the task force to discuss these issues. But I'm not sure it would work, or how. What I am concerned about is any potential limitation on our autonomy and flexibility."

* * * * *

Yolanda responds: "Carl, you've got to be kidding! I can't imagine what Bill has in mind. Sure, it might work for our secretaries, although the routines around here are so clear that I'm not sure that it's worth the effort. But for the caseworkers and other clinicians? No way.

"There's something that happens in the relationship between client and worker that you just can't define in neat little boxes. Oh, maybe they can teach clinical practice at the university, but when students get here it's a different world. It's not so much the tasks that we perform, the things that we do, as the way we do them. I guess it's the difference between task and 'technique.' And I don't mean by that anything mechanical. I mean something artistic. What good would it do you to describe the kinds of tasks that Picasso performs? Or what

Coleman Hawkins does? Would it yield better understanding? Could you supervise or train people to become a Picasso or a Hawkins?

"You know, clinical practice can be pretty intense. And sometimes there's no way of predicting at the beginning of a session exactly what kinds of things a therapist will do. The more disturbed the client or the more difficult his or her circumstances, and the more emotion involved, the more creative we have to be. We (therapists) are likely to have to draw on a wide variety of skills.

"I mean, we listen, we attend, we mediate, we diffuse, we probe, we redirect, we calm and we energize. Those are all action verbs, like you've been describing for task analysis. But I'm not sure we could ever get a complete inventory. Even if we did, I'm not sure we could properly use them either for allocating responsibilities, for training or for supervising. What really happens in a treatment session, the real stuff of practice, just can't be described with these verbs alone. There's something very personal, almost a magic dynamic that makes true therapeutic communication work. You just can't put that down in a simple sentence."

* * * * *

Sam responds: "I like it. I really do. This is maybe just the thing that we need to clarify the distinctions between the work of professional staff, volunteers, clericals and paraprofessionals. It's not that we don't know who is who, but we may not know what is what. A lot of us perform similar tasks. Some may even be identical. But the expectations we have of ourselves, in different professional roles, may be quite different. The performance standards we impose on some staff may be at a higher or lower level than we would impose on other staff.

"When I think of my job description, what it really does is it spells out what my official role is at the agency. And it's the same for other staff members. But sometimes we have different expectations of each other in our role performance. This would help clarify what the appropriate expectations might be. And I can see where it could even lead to some negotiations within a department or across departments for the allocation of specific tasks or responsibilities. Maybe even some reshuffling that would lead to greater efficiency and effectiveness. But most important, it would spell out the differences in roles or the jobs that we expect different levels of staff to perform. Yeah, I really do like it.

"You know, as I think about it, while it may not always be so important for clinicians to clarify their own tasks, it is important for them to spell out those tasks for other people with whom we interact. You know, clients don't come here directly. They go through an intake and an assessment process first. Sometimes they are referred by other agencies. After we see them, we may send them to rehabilitation, to the child guidance clinic, to a housing worker, and to a variety of other people who perform a lot of other kinds of tasks. In effect, while we provide them with intensive treatment within our own program, we are really part of a processing chain. That is, the client gets processed at a number of different stations, either here, within the agency, or outside. And sometimes the tasks that are performed by different workers are contradictory to the tasks that are performed by other workers, or else they are duplicative. Sometimes, of course, and if we're lucky, they complement each other.

"But we have no way of really knowing that. Recently, we've begun to do more in the area of case management. And the case managers are the people who could really benefit by some clarity about the tasks that are performed for the client at different stations. Yes, I do think that we could benefit in some ways from doing a more clear analysis of the tasks that we perform in making sure that they are in fact performed by the right people."

* * * * *

Harvey responds: "Hmm. Got to think that one over. Interesting idea. One of the dangers I see is that in clarifying all of the tasks that need to be performed at the agency, or even in my own department, well, it might lead to some rigidity. We might even find ourselves trying to train staff to fit the tasks instead of trying to fit the tasks to the staff. You know, there's always a tendency in every organization, even as loose an agency as this one, to try to make people fit.

"What we really ought to be aiming for is making the workplace fit the person. Look, if we try to do task analysis here and allocate tasks to each of the staff members in my department, we'd have a heck of a time. I mean, we don't have a formal organization structure here. We're really informal. If you try to design an organization chart for this department, it would look more like a bowl of spaghetti than a neat hierarchy of positions and responsibilities. If anything, we're constantly sharing tasks, reassigning them, picking up each person's load when there's a heavy burden on that person and expanding, redefining, and creating new tasks to perform. That's what makes us as dynamic as we are, and that's why we've grown so rapidly.

"Still, as I think about it, when new people come into the department, it can be awfully confusing. And sometimes we'll leave important things undone because we haven't paid enough attention to tasks that might seem less important at the moment, or that may be less popular. I'll think on it some more. Got some material for me before we get together as a task force?"

* * * * *

Ali responds: "I've got to tell you, Carl, when I first heard I was being appointed to this task force, I just didn't know how I could be helpful. I'm only the receptionist around here. But now that you've explained it to me, I do have some ideas. First of all, I have a good feel for what the other support staff at the agency are facing, the kinds of problems that they have to attend to every day. When we went through a cutback last year and consolidated the clerical staff into an agencywide pool, there was a lot of bitching. It made work so impersonal. And then there was the problem of everybody doing similar things. Some of the secretaries not only felt lost because they weren't close to their old bosses anymore, but because they were being required to do all kinds of things that they either didn't like to do or didn't know how to do well. This (task analysis) could have helped them.

"But there's something else that bothers me, too. It's not just what people do but how they relate to each other. I guess I have the reputation around here of getting along well with everyone. But some people don't get along well at all. You know, people have different styles, and there's some real resentment about two of the girls—I won't mention their names—in the pool who, I guess you would say, are lesbians. Now, don't get me wrong, and maybe I shouldn't even be saying this. I don't mean that people shouldn't have the right to be what they are. But it makes people uncomfortable. For me, this place is like a family, and I guess family members ought to take care of each other. Is this something we should be discussing in a task force, too?"

* * * * *

At first, Carl wasn't sure what to make of the apparent differences in the way in which his colleagues had reacted to the challenge before them. Systematic as he was, he had taken notes following each of the meetings. He now went over them. Four sets of issues seemed to have been presented by one or more people. One had to do with the *nature of professional practice* and the apparent difficulty that some staff members had in clarifying the tasks that were to be performed by professional staff. This seemed to be especially problematic for those who thought of practice as relatively indeterminant, involving "people changing versus people processing."

A second issue had to do with the *roles that people perform* in the agency. And there seemed to be a difference in people's minds between routine versus nonroutine tasks assigned to those roles. There were also concerns about the nature of the relationships between incumbents and different roles. Third, the nature of *people's interpersonal relationships* seemed to be an issue, particularly when people behaved in ways that violated either agency norms or the values held by some members of the staff. Finally, there seemed to be an issue that had to do with what Carl defined as *"creativity and autonomy."*

"Funny," Carl thought, "I'm beginning to think like a social worker. Maybe it's a good thing I'm an accountant and not so personally involved in these issues. Maybe I can help us arrive at some clarity." He decided to put these issues on the agenda for the first meeting of the task force.

PEOPLE CHANGING VERSUS PEOPLE PROCESSING

The core tasks—that is, those that are most central to the missions of a human service organization—are generally those that entail staff-client relationships. They help to define what the organization is in business for. From the staff's perspective, these relationships are aimed either at categorizing the client and his or her needs or at changing the client in some way. The more critical the need, or the more significant the change sought, the more important the nature of the relationship and often the more significant the demands made on the client. From the client's point of view, his or her relationship to the staff member is aimed at securing some sought-after benefit: a change in status or position, greater access to needed resources or perhaps more control over his or her circumstances.

There may even be a perceived intrinsic value built into the relationship itself, one that increases the client's sense of belonging, self-esteem, or pleasure in the social interaction with a staff member. If, however, the client perceives the nature of the relationship to be less than beneficial, even punitive, he or she may attempt to manipulate that relationship by controlling the degree of information provided, refusing to cooperate and circumventing the agency's rules or perhaps even opting out of the relationship altogether. After all, clients are people, each with their own sense of self and identity, only part of which is connected in some way to the agency. When clients are not forced to accept agency services, as might be the case when participating under a court order or seeking service out of desperation, they can resist the agency's efforts to categorize them or to change them.

Thus the agency is always limited in its ability to coerce or demand compliance. From your own experience, you know that a university may set up rules and procedures for satisfactory completion of academic requirements, but short of refusing to award a degree, it can do little to force students to comply. A physician can recommend surgery, but short of using emergency procedures cannot force the patient to accept the recommendation. In general, the more important the agency's services are to the client, and the less likely the client is to find a substitute elsewhere, the more likely the client will comply. On the other hand, the greater the need for the client's willing compliance, the more likely the agency will be to accommodate the client's perception of appropriate demands and services.

These limitations on an agency's authority require that it establish procedures to minimize conflict in staff-client relationships, and that it increase staff control over those relationships. Sometimes this is done by appealing to common values ("We both want Susan to do better in school," or "We all agree that better relationships in the family are of central importance"), by pointing out the benefits of compliance ("If you register, we can assure you that the checks will keep coming on a monthly basis") or by threatening dire consequences for noncompliance ("If you don't register early, you may miss the opportunity to send your child to camp," or "If you miss three sessions, the rules require that I report this to the probation department"). Staff can also control the relationships through the establishment and maintenance of a set of procedures that keep the client at a certain distance, and with limited access to information ("Sorry, that's privileged information," or "It takes several sessions before you get the hang of it," or "If the time is convenient for you, we'll meet here every Tuesday at 10:15").

These client control tasks, central as they are to most agency practice, are difficult for members of helping professions to face squarely. They prefer to redefine them as "helping" rather than controlling. But when performing a task analysis, it soon becomes clear that many of the activities performed are directly related to controlling client behavior. And this may be one of the reasons that some members of the helping professions find it difficult to engage in the process. There may be some aspects of task analysis that are simply too threatening to their perceptions of themselves, and to the ideological frameworks that infuse and provide direction to their practice. This may be less so in people-processing than in people-changing situations.

People-processing activities tend to be composed of what James D. Thompson calls "long-linked technologies." The *assembly line* method might be a more familiar description. People processing includes several steps: reception, recording, labeling, routing, treating, and referral or discharge. Think about your own experience at the university. *Reception* would include all those activities that were involved in your recruitment (sending out brochures and application forms, other promotional activities including individual meetings or interviews, and so on). *Recording* would include collecting all the relevant materials on you as an applicant (including the material from your application forms, references, high school or undergraduate records, and so on).

Labeling would include the process of categorizing applicants on the basis of strengths and weaknesses, interests, and aptitudes. *Routing* would then include sending the student applicant to the appropriate department. *Treatment* would include all of the educational programs and processes. *Referral,* or *discharge,* would include graduation, referral to higher educational opportunities, job referral or job routing, and the like. Clients and other human service organizations go through the same kind of process. Sometimes the process is handled by a number of different organizations, each responsible for one or two of these stages.

There is the danger that, in part of this process at least, the client may feel as if he or she has been turned into nothing but a piece of paper. Becoming a student or a client, in fact, requires becoming an artifact of the service organization. Regardless of its rhetoric or ideology, the organization is virtually never interested in the whole person. It is interested in those characteristics of the person that make it possible to serve the person or refer him or her elsewhere (that is, to change the person or to process the person in some way). In other words, the agency is interested first in transforming the person into a client and then helping the client deal with specific parts of the self.

Because people-processing tasks tend to deal only with certain aspects of the person or certain stages of the service process, they tend to be somewhat easier to describe in task terms. That may be why Sam felt it would be more appropriate to use task analysis to get a better handle on what different staff members did as a client was processed through the agency, so as to assure that each of the tasks was done appropriately and that staff members at different stations (on the assembly line) would know what had been done before and would be prepared to do the appropriate thing at their point of intervention. This may also be why Yolanda was not sure that task analysis was an appropriate approach to use in examining the treatment or clinical program. And it may account for Millicent's skepticism.

Clinical programs focus directly at changing or improving the client. Such improvement may include becoming better educated, cured of a disease or rehabilitated. One might distinguish such people-changing activities into categories like socialization, education or rehabilitation (that is, changing people because of some physical or moral defect). These changes often require an intensive involvement of a staff person, or an intensive relationship between the staff member and the client. It also requires that the client participate actively in the process of change.

The client has to want to be educated, to want to change, to want to overcome a drug habit and to work actively toward self-improvement. Social workers, educators, and other human service helpers use a wide variety of methods to induce the client to want these changes and to provide clients with the skills to achieve such changes. But these methods are sometimes hard to categorize. "It's not so much what we do as what happens in the relationship," Yolanda explained at one of the early task force meetings. There is a certain mystique in this process. And that mystique resists definition, although it certainly can be defined. But it requires a careful delineation of the tasks

Exercise 7.1

Client Processing and Client Changing

1. On a separate sheet of paper, in two or three paragraphs, describe a client-processing procedure at an agency with which you are familiar. Describe all the tasks that are performed in processing the client from reception through referral or discharge. Underline the action verbs.

2. Now describe a more intensive client-changing activity (teaching, family treatment or rehabilitation). Again, underline all the action verbs.

3. Which was more difficult to do? Why? If you had to interview staff members at your agency involved in either one or more of the steps in people processing, or in an intensive treatment or people-changing approach, who do you think would have a more difficult time in describing the tasks that they perform? Why?

performed and an understanding of how those tasks relate to each other.

I am a professor at a school of social work. If somebody were to examine all the tasks that I perform, they might wish to group them under teaching, research and knowledge development, knowledge dissemination (including writing books like this one), and service (both to the community and to the institution by which I am employed). Taking one of those functions, teaching, we might further identify a wide variety of tasks that include lecturing, counseling, preparing course outlines, selecting library materials, grading and so on.

Because faculty members are notorious in their demands for academic freedom (what we earlier referred to as professional autonomy), they resist having their activities categorized into discrete tasks. Doing so would make it possible for others to evaluate the effectiveness of their lecturing, selection of books, grading and so on. In fact, categorizing tasks might make it possible to develop performance criteria by which faculty would evaluate themselves or be evaluated by others (including students). This would also lead to identifying weaknesses in a faculty member's performance and to developing training programs aimed at overcoming such weaknesses or improving competence. Would this be a violation of academic freedom? I think not. But I think it would be so perceived by many faculty people. Hence the resistance to task specification and the development of clear performance criteria.

Many professionals are similarly resistant, reluctant to have the very heart of what they do examined and compared to the work of others. It may be less threatening (and also less productive) to maintain a shroud of mystery. That shroud, by protecting the professional's work from scrutiny, increases the profession's authority over others.

Moreover, some professionals argue that a task analysis would provide only a limited view of their professional behavior. Because students, campers, and other clients are themselves individuals with unique characteristics, needs, and behavioral patterns, the helping professional must respond to those characteristics. Thus, in every helping situation (like those alluded to by Millicent), the professional can be expected to behave somewhat differently. This is more true in intensive relationships characterized by people-changing activities than in people-processing activities (in which only part of the client is subject to review or classification).

TASKS AND RESPONSIBILITIES

The description of tasks, and their allocation to staff members performing different roles, can lead to the writing of more comprehensive and accurate job descriptions. No job description, however, is ever fully comprehensive or accurate. Organizations could not operate effectively if people did only what was contained within their job descriptions, nor could staff members operate effectively if they tried to do everything contained in their job descriptions. Yolanda was quite correct in suggesting that innovation and experimentation would suffer if, as Harvey suggests, someone tried to unscramble his "bowl of spaghetti-like" organization chart.

Under normal circumstances, Harvey's staff might not be expected to do any counseling of individual residents in group homes. Their primary functions are to establish group homes, locate them in the community, and make sure that they meet all the licensing standards. But in a crisis or emergency situation, staff may very well be called on to do crisis counseling and sometimes to locate people in group homes. In other cases they may refer a home resident to the appropriate professional service in the community. These nonroutine tasks are common to other fields of practice as well.

Within a particular agency or department, internal allocations of responsibilities may result in specially tailored task assignments that do not appear on the official job description.

Despite her initial resistance, as the work of the task force continued, Yolanda began to see the possibilities of using task analysis to build on strengths of some of her staff, while overcoming the weaknesses of others. Before exploring the utility of task analysis with her staff, Yolanda tried to analyze her own job. Although all members of the clinical staff each have the same basic job description, she realized, it was necessary for each to do the same things. Some staff were already doing more family and group counseling than others because of their interest or competence in these methods. To get a feel for the procedures Yolanda used, and how they might work for you and your agency, you might want to complete the following exercises.

DOING TASK ANALYSIS

Doing your own task analysis[1] generally begins with an examination of your job description. A job description is a general statement of what a person does on the job. It is not a description of what he or she knows or at what level of skill a person should be performing. A functionally written job description should include all of the major tasks that are performed on the job. Unfortunately, most job descriptions are not written in this way, so that they may not serve their functions—as guides to

the tasks that are to be performed. The excerpt from a sample job description that follows is a bit sketchy, but it will give you some idea of what goes into one.

Sample Job Description Excerpt

The worker greets clients, obtains necessary case information from clients and from other relevant sources, and assesses this information. He or she records this information on prescribed agency forms and sends it to the appropriate department, according to agency rule. The worker also informs clients of their rights and refers them to the appropriate department in the organization or to an external source of service.

Exercise 7.2

Examining the Sample Job Description

Before you begin working on your own job description, examine the sample we have provided you. Then proceed as follows:

(1) Underline all of the action verbs in blue pen or pencil (for example, "greets," "refers").
(2) In black ink, underline to whom or to what the action is referring (for example, "clients," after the word "greets").
(3) Finally, with any color, circle those words that describe tools the worker might be using.

You may have noticed that "to whom" or "to what" the action refers is not always clear. Nor is it always clear what tools or methods are being used. Both are astute observations, and we will address them shortly. But before we do, you should complete **Exercise 7.3**.

Action verbs serve as a basis for writing task statements. For each action verb in the job description, it should be possible to generate a task statement.

On the form in Figure 7.1, one action verb has been taken from the job description excerpt to show you how to write a task statement. (You will need more than a single copy of the task statement form. Feel free to photocopy or otherwise duplicate the form for **Exercise 7.4**. For practice purposes, it might be good to start with five or six copies of the form.)

Let us begin with the example of the task we identified as "obtaining case information." This is a task requiring work with people. Some tasks require working with "materials" almost exclusively (for example, filing, typing, addressing). Other tasks involve working with "ideas" (for example, designing a computer program, generating research hypotheses, preparing proposals). While there is certainly some work with ideas and with materials involved in "obtaining case information," the task is basically one in which interaction between people takes place.

We'll postulate that the task is performed in a family service agency. What basic expectations might we have of all persons performing this task? They might include fulfillment of certain entry-

Exercise 7.3

Writing Your Own Sample Job Description

On a separate sheet of paper, write up your own description. If one already exists at the agency, use that. Otherwise write one up in your own words. Try to keep it to a single page. Do not forget to include action verbs. If you are finding it hard to work on your own job description, pick a colleague's job with which you are familiar. When you are finished, go back over your statement and underline all of the action verbs. Did you leave any out? If so, add sentences with action verbs that you think should have been included. Underline them.

level requirements—completion of a BA degree in social work or psychology or their equivalent, empathy and understanding, entry-level interviewing skills, and so on.

Most tasks can be done poorly or well, effectively or ineffectively. Once performance measures have been identified, it is possible to set performance standards, that is, to rate them along some agreed-upon scale. By *performance standards* we mean the level at which we expect the work to be done. This generally requires describing how we think the workers should perform the task. For example, if a worker's task is described as follows:

> receives, routes, transfers incoming telephone calls to the office requested by the caller, eliciting information as necessary to ascertain proper routing, using agency directories as required, in order to enable the caller to complete his call,

the performance standards might include the following:

- is tactful and pleasant with callers
- routes calls correctly and promptly
- operates equipment properly
- does not leave caller hanging or disconnect caller prior to indicating to caller that call cannot be completed at this point because of difficulties in routing the call.

Title of Task: Obtaining Case Information	*Task Cluster: XXX*
Who	The child welfare worker
performs what action	obtains case information
to whom or to what	from clients
using what tools or methods	interviews by telephone, in the office or in home visit
to what end or for what purpose	to determine nature of service needed
using what directions or under whose supervision?	according to procedures found in the agency's manual and under guidance of the child welfare supervisor or the supervisor's designate.

Figure 7.1 Sample task statement.

Each of these might be ranked on a five-point scale, from acceptable to highly acceptable work, as follows:

5	4	3	2	1
high	better than average	acceptable	barely acceptable	unacceptable

It is also possible to set some numerical measures for evaluating performance, such as

- Over a two-week period, fewer than five complaints of incorrect routings will be made.
- Over a 30-day period, no more than eight complaints will be made that the worker was tactless or unpleasant with the caller.

There are many ways tasks can be clustered. One is to group them according to whether they reflect work with people, ideas, or materials. These are rather broad categories, however. You may prefer to group the tasks you perform under functional categories. For example a manager might group the tasks she performs under (1)

Exercise 7.4

Writing a Task Statement

Title of Task ________________ *Task Cluster* ________________

Who	1
performs what action	2
to whom or to what	3
using what tools or methods	4
to what end or for what purpose	5
using what direction or under whose supervision?	6

People	Concepts	Materials

Entry-level requirements	Performance criteria

Rating:

Importance	Hi 5 4 3 2 1 Lo	Difficulty	Hi 5 4 3 2 1 Lo
Frequency	Hi 5 4 3 2 1 Lo	________	Hi 5 4 3 2 1 Lo

orientation and training, (2) supervision of worker assignments, (3) work-flow planning, (4) data collection and reporting, and (5) performance evaluation. Any one of these clusters could include more discrete tasks. For example, orientation and training might include

- *assessing* worker performance
- *establishing* training objectives based on assessment of worker performance
- *organizing* orientation and training workshops
- *arranging* for experts to provide needed training

You have probably noticed that I did not write out each statement completely. This is not necessary when doing a preliminary clustering of tasks. We know, after all, *whom* we are discussing. Chances are that the answer to "under what direction or under whose supervision" will remain the same for each cluster. This may not be the case when you begin the task analysis process with other staff members in your organization. Notice also that any of the tasks listed above could be broken down into smaller units of work. For example, action verbs associated with "arranging for experts . . ." might include "calling," "interviewing," "orienting," "scheduling," and so on. And some of these might be further broken down into smaller tasks. When do you break a task statement into smaller units of work? There is no simple answer. My own rule of thumb is to connect the decision to the *frequency* with which a task or task cluster is performed. For example, in defining the job of a person whose full-time responsibility is training and orientation, I would err on the side of comprehensiveness. For a worker whose involvement in these activities is minimal, I would err on the side of "skimpiness." A supervisor who may only occasionally be responsible for training could always look at the job description or task clusters assigned to a trainer if she or he wanted more details on what is to be done, how, and at what level of proficiency. Information gathered on the task summary workshop may be rewritten in the form of a job description.

You are probably surprised at what your job really looks like. But what do you do next?

First, you can share the experience you have just had with others at the agency. Feel free to duplicate the entire activity for use as a training or assessment tool in your own agency. If you are going to use task analysis, you might want to explain to others that it is an assessment approach based on the following:

(1) use of a *standard (controlled) language* that introduces precision, clarity, and understanding to job descriptions;
(2) disaggregation of *jobs* into the series of *tasks* of which they are composed (tasks are the fundamental units of works);
(3) a *filing system* that makes it possible to inventory tasks and their definitions and combine them to describe existing or possible future job titles; and
(4) identification of tasks and description in a *task definition* format.

The task definition is composed of the following components:

(1) use of a prescribed method for formulation of *task statements*;
(2) division of all work activity into three *functional areas* (people, data, things) that encompass what workers do in the entire world of work;

Exercise 7.5

Task Clustering

Identify the major categories under which the tasks you perform tend to cluster. You can do this in one of two ways:

(1) Write down all the shorthand task statements you can in the following space for *Notes*, and then look for some order or logic by which these might be clustered; or
(2) if you are pretty certain of the categories, put them down in the *Notes* section and add some notes about the tasks that might fall under each.

Complete the exercises on the *Task Summary Worksheet*. You will need between five and seven copies; feel free to photocopy the sample for your own purposes. To complete it, use the following procedures:

(1) Take one of the categories of work that you have just identified and write it in the upper left-hand corner of the task summary worksheet. Now, write all of the task statements that fall under that category of tasks. If there are more tasks than fit, use an additional sheet.
(2) Do the same for the other categories that you used for grouping your tasks.
(3) Rate each of these tasks for importance. Use a scale of five to one, with five signifying very important, and, one, not at all important.

Notes

Task Summary Worksheet

Category: ____________________

(Cluster Description) ____________________

Task	Importance	Frequency	Difficulty
1			
2			
3			
4			
5			
6			
7			
8			
9			
10			

(3) ranking of the work functions on standard *worker function scales* for each of the three areas, to clarify requisite functional level of performance; and
(4) derivation of precise *performance standards*, *training needs*, and *worker qualifications* for each task from the task statement and worker function scales.

This approach can be used for supervision, the evaluation of worker performance, training and recruitment, and organizational analysis. As a supervisory tool, it provides the supervisee and supervisor with an opportunity to (a) clarify each worker's job, and (b) arrive at some agreement about the level of performance expected.

Supervisors have found that good job descriptions, especially those derived from task analysis, may be utilized to improve a work unit's function by increasing the clarity and precision of job descriptions. Misunderstandings are prevented when points of potential disagreement over job definitions and responsibilities are explicated. Task analysis also provides a basis for mutual bargaining and negotiations between staff and line personnel.

As an evaluative tool, task analysis provides the supervisor with standards for assessing what the worker does in relationship to what he or she should be doing, and a guide against which the worker can compare his or hew own accomplishments in relation to an agreed-upon norm.

As a training or recruitment device, task analysis establishes clear statements about the tasks that workers are to perform, a means of assessing where current staff and potential recruits are in relationship to those norms, and a way of spelling out in detail the requirements of the job.

Learning objectives for staff development or in-service training can be formulated in accordance with the task statements and the standards associated with each. These standards include expected levels of performance as well as required levels of skill or competence prior to entry into a particular job.

As a tool for organizational analysis and redesign, task analysis provides information necessary for job restructuring so as to make the most efficient use of available human resources, and access to information on the part of all members of the agency staff for use in problem solving.

DRAWING ON EXISTING TASK BANKS

Yolanda had gone through a set of similar exercises before testing out the approach with her staff. "If we are to go this way," she reasoned, "we had better test out the procedures and find out how people will react." But instead of starting from scratch, she decided, "I think it might be easier if we drew on an existing 'task bank,' a listing of all the tasks that might conceivably be performed by social workers in a particular area of practice." She looked first into some of the materials that Mary Jo had prepared for the task force. These seemed a bit general. She then found a new book, recently published by Sage. In it, the authors, Pecora and Austin, had developed a new task bank of over 100 discrete activities. "Very useful," she thought, "but a bit overwhelming. What I need is a smaller, more focused collection of tasks, tasks that better reflect what a specific cadre of workers do." She found just what she was looking for in the same Pecora and Austin book—a list of 28 tasks performed by child protective service workers.

The list, drawn from earlier works by Selinske, is found in Figure 7.2. Although none of her own staff was him- or herself involved in protective services work, examining a focused listing for people doing other social work jobs, she thought, would help members of her staff to examine the utility of task analysis. Moreover, the fact that it described someone else's practice might be less threatening than a list of clinical tasks. "There won't be any reason to say, 'Hey, that's not what I do.' Later on, we can focus on what we do do."

Along with the Selinske list, I have included a more comprehensive job description, also borrowed from Pecora and Austin. Look it over. Are the job descriptions in your agency as well written? What would it take to describe your job as thoroughly and accurately? For the agency to develop comparable job descriptions for all current positions?

REVIEW AND TENTATIVE CONCLUSIONS

Getting the job done and getting along may conflict with each other. The conflict need not be debilitating, however, especially if roles and the tasks assigned to those roles are clearly understood, and as long as consensus exists among the key parties on how a role should be performed.

I. Screening Reports of Suspected Child Abuse and Neglect

A. Receiving referrals of cases of suspected child abuse and neglect.

Task 1 Elicits information from the reporter regarding the facts relevant to the situation which led the party to report suspected child abuse or neglect in order to assist in determining the validity of the referral.

Task 2 Obtains information for individuals making self-referrals regarding the facts relevant to their referral in order to assist in determining the validity of the referral.

Task 3 Solicits information about the reporter's relationship to the child and his/her motives for making the report in order to assist in determining the validity of the referral.

Task 4 Asks questions about the identification and location of the subjects of the referral in order to gain enough information to contact them for further investigation.

Task 5 Listens carefully to the reporter's statements in order to record the information provided as accurately as possible.

Task 6 Asks for and obtains the name and telephone number of the reporter in order to be able to clarify information at a later time.

Task 7 Identifies him/herself in order that the individual making the referral can recontact him/her if necessary at a later time.

Task 8 Supplies information to reporters regarding the agency's legal mandates, policy and procedures, the investigation process, and legal anonymity for reporters in order to keep them informed.

Task 9 Elicits comments from the reporter regarding his/her fears and concerns about making the report in order to facilitate completion of the referral.

Task 10 Conveys a nonthreatening and supportive tone and recognizes and addresses the reporter's hesitancy in order to make him/her more relaxed and comfortable about the referral.

Task 11 Offers reassurance and support to the reporter, encouraging and reinforcing the individual's decision to report in order to facilitate completion of the referral and to encourage future referrals.

Task 12 Solicits information from the reporting service agency about the facility's action to date regarding the referral and its intent for continued involvement in order to gather complete information and to assess the present status of the situation.

Task 13 Suggests that reporting service agencies inform and openly discuss their referrals with the family in order to facilitate open communication and continued rapport between service agencies and their clients.

Task 14 Suggests that relatives, who are making referrals, inform and openly discuss the referral and their concern for the child's safety in order to preserve their existing relationship.

Figure 7.2 Tasks from a comprehensive child protective service task bank.

Task 15 Explains to individuals making inappropriate referrals the reasons why their referrals are so considered in order to discourage inappropriate referrals in the future.

Task 16 Refers individuals making reports to appropriate agencies when the matter is inappropriate for protective service intervention in order to facilitate their receipt of needed or desired service.

Task 17 Closes the discussion with persons making referrals by thanking them for their concern and acknowledging the merit of their actions in order to reinforce their decisions to report and to demonstrate the agency's appreciation.

B. Determining the urgency and appropriateness of referrals.

Task 18 Determines whether the information in the report constitutes a CPS referral in order to screen out inappropriate referrals.

Task 19 Evaluates the validity/appropriateness of the referral in order to determine whether to initiate a CPS investigation.

Task 20 Evaluates the reported circumstances, according to the agency's guidelines for emergency response, in order to determine whether the agency should initiate an immediate response.

Task 21 Considers and assesses the intent/motivation of the reporter in order to gather more complete information about the potential validity of the report.

Task 22 Checks to see if there is a history of unsubstantiated reports from the reporter in order to supplement information gathered from the reporter.

Task 23 Consults with supervisory staff in determining the urgency and/or appropriateness of referrals in order to facilitate sound decision making regarding the agency's response to referrals.

C. Recording referral information.

Task 24 Summarizes, records and labels the factual responses and statements made by the reporter in order to document the referral.

Task 25 Summarizes, labels and records impressions about the suspected child abuse and neglect in order that the record will reflect the referral and accurately distinguish between facts and impressions.

Task 26 Labels and records his/her own impressions of the report in order to supplement the referral information received from the reporter and to facilitate determining the validity of the report.

Task 27 Completes all necessary forms and paper work within the designated time frame in order that the referral is properly entered into the agency's recording system.

Task 28 Maintains a system for filing written records in order that information can be retrieved.

SOURCE: Selinske (1981) as reported in Pecora and Austin (1987).

Figure 7.2 Continued

DEFINITION OF POSITION:

Under the agency's policies and professional requirements this outpatient therapist position provides direct management of assigned clients, is responsible for the facilitating team work for Adult Outpatient Services, engages in consulting and informational activities for the community and other professional disciplines, participates in program evaluation procedures and professional record keeping, makes referrals to other local and state facilities, coordinates mental health services with other community and state resources, engages in supervision of graduate student interns and works under the direct supervision of the Coordinator of Adult Outpatient Services.

MAJOR RESPONSIBILITIES AND RELATED TASKS:

I. *Direct Clinical Services* (40%)

1. Establishes initial data of a potential client's presenting problems, mental status, treatment history, medical problems, and assesses client diagnostically according to best professional standards and agency policy in order to determine treatment modalities, assignment priorities, and/or provide information and make appropriate referrals to other treatment resources in the community (brief screenings).
2. Implements crisis or pre-crisis intervention procedures with potentially suicidal, homocidal, or gravely disabled clients in order to prevent destabilization, enhance adaptive functioning, and move clients toward an appropriate treatment program.
3. Gathers treatment related information with respect to client's presenting problems, mental status, relevant psychiatric, medical, developmental history, in order to make decisions regarding diagnosis, treatment objectives, and ongoing treatment plans (intake).
4. Evaluates and assesses clients based on state and DSM III categorizations, in order to provide professional treatment planning, consultation, or referral assistance.
5. Shares information on Mental Health Center's philosophy, procedures, policies, and treatment modalities in order to help prospective clients, interested citizens, or ongoing clients make treatment decisions, set appropriate goals, or better understand the functions of the mental health center.
6. Interviews collateral contracts, previous and current treatment professionals, and significant others in order to further establish a data base for assessment, treatment, planning, or treatment involvement.
7. Develops therapeutic relationships with ongoing clients (involving hope, trust, empathy, compassion, congruence, team work, etc.) in order to provide an environment whereby clients can make appropriate changes.
8. Constructs a conceptual scheme of the development of client's presenting problems, maintenance of presenting problems, and consequences of presenting problems in order to strategize for possible therapeutic interventions.
9. Clarifies priority problems, goals for change, and session limits according to agency policy in order to assist clients in developing appropriate expectations for treatment in relationship to the agency.

Figure 7.3 Position description for a Mental Health Specialist II, adult outpatient services.

10. Utilizes broad based insight and cognitive behavioral treatment approaches and interventions in order to change targeted behaviors and stabilize adaptive behaviors with individuals, couples, and families.

11. Manages the termination process and discharge planning in order to enhance client's ability to retain treatment changes, utilize community social supports, treatment professionals, and/or continue work on therapeutic change.

II. *Client Information System* (30%)

1. Establishes appropriate professional files (including initial brief screening assessments, intake evaluations, progress records, treatment objectives and plans, previous treatment records, client's consents for current treatment, confidentiality, and release of previous records, exchange of information with other agencies and health care providers) in order to demonstrate psychotherapeutic work to agency and State of Washington.

2. Provides necessary client information to other agencies or health care providers (psychiatrist, mental health professionals, mental health agencies, schools, courts, hospitals, etc.) in order to coordinate services to identified clients.

3. Gathers information as available from all potential clients information resources in order to maintain a current and comprehensive fund of client information for treatment purposes.

III. *Administrative Activities* (20%)

1. Participates in required staff meetings and inservice meetings in order to keep abreast of agency policy and administrative procedures, meet requirements for continuing education, upgrade professional knowledge, improve adult outpatient team work and service coordination, engage in mutual consultation, and share professional support.

2. Utilizes weekly direct services supervision under the direction of the coordinator of adult outpatient services in order to facilitate professional accountability in the agency.

3. Supervises graduate student interns on a weekly basis according to best professional judgment and agency policy in order to facilitate student development of professional expertise in client relations, therapeutic interventions, professional interfacing with other treatment providers and services, constructive participation in agency functions, and client information management.

4. Evaluates/coordinates student work with the university in order to maintain and improve the ongoing student internship program.

5. Monitors psychotherapy literature in order to be abreast of helpful information for delivery of mental health services.

IV. *Enhance Adult Outpatient Team Functioning* (10%)

1. Provides information to prospective clients or interested citizens in order to promote the program of the agency, increase community interest in mental health, refer clients to other appropriate community resources, provide treatment linkages, assess mental health concerns, desires, and facilitate development of appropriate health care planning or connections with appropriate treatment resources.

Figure 7.3 Continued *(continued)*

2. Monitors the adult outpatient waiting list for the satellite office in order to provide for an orderly and fair client intake process in conjunction with the other satellite office.
3. Engages in appropriate team work functions (such as mutual support, clarification of office responsibilities and procedures, mutual assistance) according to best professional judgment and agency policy in order to provide a professional working environment and effective service delivery.
4. Develops cooperative relationships with families, physicians, public officials, and all interested agencies or individuals in order to interpret the Mental Health Center services and provide for the development of mental health services in the community.

V. *All Other Responsibilities as directed by Supervisor or Executive Director*

KNOWLEDGE AND SKILLS

Activities are governed by a professional code of ethics and rules of confidentiality; thorough knowledge of the techniques and principles of psychological, behavioral and social disorders; skill in dealing with the public in advocating for mentally and emotionally disturbed, developmentally disabled and drug dependent persons; ability to develop cooperative relationships with families, physicians, agency personnel and executives and public officials; ability to interpret mental health services; ability to prepare precise, complete records and maintain updated client records; ability to participate in social and community planning and to carry out recommendations and directions.

TRAINING AND EXPERIENCE

Must have at least a masters degree in a mental health related discipline from an accredited college or university and at least two years appropriate experience in the direct treatment of mentally ill clients under the supervision of a mental health professional. The appropriate mental health experience could be acquired in any of a variety of settings, e.g., alcohol, drug, mental retardation, physical rehabilitation, etc. As such, these requirements meet the state definition of mental health professional, and this staff person can provide clinical supervision to other staff.

SOURCE: Pecora and Austin (1987).

Figure 7.3 Continued

(1) People, like other resources, are important assets to any agency. Like other assets, they can be managed. But unlike other assets, they also manage themselves and their relationships, and to a certain extent are managed by those relationships.

(2) Task analysis is one approach to defining who does what to whom or to what, with what tools (how), for what purpose, and under whose directions or what specifications. Tasks are the smallest unit of work one can define. Once tasks are described, it becomes possible to specify both qualifications of their performance and criteria for evaluating that performance.

(3) Some human service tasks may be more difficult to define than others. These tend to be associated with intensive client-staff interactions, such as tasks associated with people changing (education and treatment). Others, those related to people processing, can be defined more concretely, much as one might define assembly line tasks.

(4) The tasks described tend to be related to specific roles performed by agency staff. But the ways such roles are performed are subject to the interpretation of the role performer and the significant others in his or her role set.

(5) Task analysis can be used for defining worker responsibilities, specifying performance requirements, orientation and training, and for job design. Whatever its use or uses, the effort requires acceptance and legitimation by staff at all levels in the organization and a sense of trust: trust that the effort is in the best interest of both the staff and the agency.

Once again, it's your turn to add conclusions from this chapter.

(6)

(7)

(8)

(9)

(10)

NOTE

1. The activities and exercises that follow in Chapter 7 are taken from Lauffer (1982).

REFERENCES

Austin, Michael J. (1981). *Supervisory management for the human services* (esp. Chapter 4, Appendix A). Englewood Cliffs, NJ: Prentice-Hall.

Debloois, Michael, & Melton, Raymond C. (1974). *Functional task analysis: The training module*. Tallahassee: Florida Department of Education.

Epstein, Irwin. (1970). Professional role orientation and conflict strategies. *Social Work, 15*, October.

Fine, Sydney, & Wiley, Wretha W. (1971). *An introduction to functional job analysis*. Kalamazoo, MI: W. E. Upjohn Institute for Employment Research.

Gouldner, Alvin. (1959). Organizational analysis. In Alvin Gouldner & Robert K. Merton et al. (Eds.), *Society today*. New York: Basic Books.

Hasenfeld, Yeheskel. (1972). People processing organizations: An exchange approach. *American Sociological Review, 37*, June.

Hasenfeld, Yeheskel, & English, Richard A. (1974). *Human service organizations*. Ann Arbor: University of Michigan Press.

Haynes, Michael G. (1978). Developing an appraisal program. *Personnel Journal, 57*(1).

Lauffer, Armand. (1982). *Assessment tools for practitioners, managers and trainers* (esp. Chapter 3). Newbury Park, CA: Sage.

Lewis, M. (1980). Surprise and sense-making: what newcomers experience in entering unfamiliar organizational settings. *Administrative Science Quarterly*, June.

McCormick, E. J. (1981). *Job analysis: Methods and application*. New York: AMACOM.

Morrisey, G. L. (1983). *Peforming appraisals in the public sector: Key to effective supervision*. Reading, MA: Addison-Wesley.

Patten, Thomas H., Jr. (1977). Job evaluation and job enlargement: A collision course? *Human Resource Management*, Winter.

Pecora, Peter J. (Ed.). (1978). *Human services management project task bank*. Milwaukee: University of Wisconsin School of Social Welfare.

Pecora, Peter J., & Austin, Michael J. (1987). *Managing human services personnel*. Newbury Park, CA: Sage.

Ritzer, George, & Trice, Harrison M. (1969). *An occupation in conflict: A study of the personnel manager*. Ithaca, NY: Cornell University Press.

Selinske, J. (1981). *A guide to improved service delivery: Analysis of the tasks, knowledge and skill requisites and performance criteria of the child protective functions*. Washington, DC: American Public Welfare Association.

Thompson, James D. (1967). *Organizations in action*. New York: McGraw-Hill.

Thompson, James D., Carlson, R. O., & Avery, R. W. (1956). Occupations, personnel and careers. *Educational Administration Quarterly*, Winter.

Vinter, Robert D. (1963). Analysis of treatment organizations. *Social Work, 8*, July.

Chapter 8

DESIGNING JOBS AND RESTRUCTURING WORK

Job Restructuring, Recruitment, and Placement

Bill Clapman was nobody's fool. He rarely took major steps without carefully thinking through the rationale for, and possible consequences of, the actions to be taken. And asking Carl Farrell to undertake chairing a task force on task analysis was part of a larger formulation of problems and prospects. That the final outlines of the process were only shadowy shapes on the horizon of Bill's mind didn't trouble him. It was giving shape to ambiguity, Bill had always thought, that energized the creative impulse.

Bill Clapman's confidence in both the agency and the staff was borne out by the events set in motion by the task analysis process.

JOB REDESIGN AND RESTRUCTURING

Although Yolanda was initially resistant to task analysis (she had worried that it could not possibly reflect the richness and diversity of the tasks performed in her unit), it didn't take long for its values to become evident. First, the process articulated nicely with the task-centered approach used by the clinicians in the unit she supervised. One could use it to help clients think through "who is responsible for what, where, and how." Even before completing the process of analyzing their own tasks, a number of caseworkers were already applying what they had learned of task analysis to their practice with clients. That generated confidence, which, in turn, lead some workers to examine the possibilities of restructuring their jobs.

One of the first innovations they attempted was *task sharing*, that is, the reallocation of tasks among staff members so as to articulate better with their personal interest and with individual strengths. This made it possible for some workers to avoid performing undesired tasks, while permitting others to increase the variety of tasks performed. For example, Marge Davidson took on several staff members' responsibilities for working with the schools even as those other workers continued serving families whose kids were having school-related difficulties. Task analysis also permitted staff to consider establishing a job sharing process in which two more persons divide a single job. For Steve Sanchez, this was a godsend.

He had wanted to return to school, but the demands of a full-time job (and the unavailability of well-paying part-time alternatives) had made this impossible. Now, with Yolanda's help, he was able to divide his job into two parts, sharing it half and half with Kitty McPherson. Kitty worked mornings, so she could spend time with her children in the afternoons. Steve went to school in the mornings, and began work at the agency at 2:00 every afternoon. When school work was light, Steve sometimes "banked" time by putting extra hours in, then took a "withdrawal" during exam week.

Other changes in work schedules were instituted. Three staff members opted for a four-day work week (9½ hours per day) while two others extended their schedules to include Saturdays and two evenings, while reducing the number of morning hours they had to work on Mondays through Fridays. In each case, they worked the same number of core hours each week. "I'm not sure Bill had flex-time in mind, when he started us on the task analysis process," Yolanda had remarked to one of her staff members, "but it has certainly lead to some interesting discretionary time arrangements without any additional hardships in terms of coordination or getting the job done." Had she asked Bill, she would have found that this was precisely the kind of openness he had hoped to promote.

* * * * *

REDEFINING JOBS AND REDESIGNING PRACTICE

Taking the cue from the changes being instituted in the clinical services department, Sam undertook an even more innovative and comprehensive approach to job restructuring in the New Americans Project. Earlier in the year, he had been intrigued by a conference paper presented by the staff of Homebuilders, a small agency in Seattle, Washington, that worked with families in crisis. Instead of carrying a caseload of 20 to 24, typical of most traditional agencies, Homebuilders staff members see no more than two families at any given time. But they work with those families intensely, and for no more than a month, on call 24 hours a day.

The Homebuilders staffer might spend an entire day with family members, perhaps even the better part of a week, helping them learn how to shop and prepare meals more effectively, arranging for home repairs (even getting in there and cleaning up the kitchen or painting the front door), and helping members of the family learn how to communicate with each other. Learning how to listen and to accept each other might be new to families with histories of violence and neglect. Homebuilders staff acted as role models, teachers, and coaches.

The problems faced by New Americans were not necessarily the same as those of Homebuilders clients. But, it seemed to Sam, the principles upon which services, aimed at New Americans in crisis, might be based should be no different. Intensive counseling, available on a 24-hour basis, he reasoned, made more sense than the typical service pattern that included counseling sessions once a week, sometimes complemented by referrals and the often time-consuming process of case management.

Sam was certain that his staff would respond enthusiastically when he suggested that they study the Homebuilders approach with the view in mind of adapting it to the New Americans Project. He wasn't mistaken. A complete restructuring of the project, however, was neither possible nor desirable. Some families would continue to need ongoing services. Those staff members that worked with community groups, building on the natural self-help process in the immigrant communities, and who served as linkage agents between those groups and public and private service sectors, would have to continue performing their much-needed tasks.

But about a third of the staff, he calculated, could be reassigned (and retrained) to work along the lines of the Homebuilders model. Initially, they might copy the model as it was developed in Washington: no more than two families in any worker's caseload at any given time (averaging about 23 cases a year, pretty much the monthly average for workers in the more traditional track). They would provide intensive treatment, available for a time-limited period (no more than four weeks), with the worker involving him- or herself in every aspect of the family's internal life and its external relationships—wherever problems might manifest themselves and wherever intensive learning might enable the family to cope more effectively on its own. Eventually, Sam knew, the New Americans Project would be able to develop its own variations of the model based on its own experience and the needs of immigrant populations. Sam's staff agreed to experiment with the Homebuilders model.

As experience with the approach unfolded, enthusiasm continued to grow. What staff members particularly liked about the new work style was that it gave them the feeling of being responsive when clients needed their help the most. And they could see a process through from beginning to end. It wasn't like the more traditional counseling approach in which a worker might help the client with one or two aspects of a larger problem, not see other family members, and perhaps have to depend on the services of another agency without ever being sure that these services were properly provided, if at all. The Homebuilder approach lead to almost instantaneous feedback. You could see the impact of your efforts almost as they were expended. You knew when things were going right. And you knew when things weren't going well.

Perhaps the biggest motivator for those staff members involved in the Homebuilders "experiment," as staff of the New Americans project were now calling it, was the sense that they were themselves responsible for the outcomes of their own work with families in crisis. "When you can't slough it off on somebody else, you're responsible. And when you know you're responsible, you have to live up to that responsibility. I feel myself more alive now, even though I'm working harder than I ever have before in my professional life. It's not only that my job has been enlarged, its that my life has been enriched," reported one of the social workers in an evaluation session, about four months into the experiment. By that time, most of the other staff members wanted in, at least for a limited period. Others didn't want to give up all the other things they were doing, while some could not devote the kind of intensive time required because of other family and personal obligations. Yet everyone wanted some time on the experiment.

A few months into the experiment, Sam looked over the range of tasks his staff performed. They tended to cluster into three kinds of jobs: community and neighborhood development; standard casework and case management; and intensive crisis-oriented homebuilding, the "experiment." Although some staffers preferred one of these jobs over the other two, others were anxious for at least limited experiences in all three. After several months of trial and error, they finally hit on a job rotation scheme that seemed to have more advantages than disadvantages.

Every staff member would be assigned to one of the three basic jobs. At the end of six months, he or she could ask for reassignment of that job, or assignment to one of the other two. As a rule, no one could stay in a single job for longer than four terms (two years). Thus, somebody in the homebuilding project might work intensively with two families at a time for, say, 18 months, and then shift either over to community work or to caseworker/case management and then back to the experiment. Another staff member might rotate every six months between the three kinds of jobs. Still a third might remain in the more traditional casework/case management job, shifting into homebuilding for the six-month period, and then back again to her "base" period.

RECRUITING NEW STAFF

The response to the task analysis process in Harvey's department had been different than in Yolanda's or Sam's. There already was a considerable amount of flexibility in the way in which tasks were assigned, and a good deal of job sharing and job rotation. There was hardly any question about the need for job enlargement or job enrichment. At various times, the community placement staff were involved in complex tasks such as consulting with or setting up new group homes, preparing communities for group home placement, and direct work with clients of both an advocacy or *ombudsman* nature. And at any given time during the year, staff members might be involved in speech making and public relations activities, legislative lobbying, or the preparation of proposals for contract or grant funding. If you liked variety, could deal with ambiguity, and could stand the pace, you liked working with Harvey Marcus.

For Harvey, the biggest challenge wasn't in motivating staff, it was in their proper selection. Shortly after the agency had begun the task analysis process, Harvey's department had been awarded a major contract from the state department of public welfare. It called for

The following terms are used in the literature and in personnel work to define some of the work restructuring arrangements described in this chapter.

Discretionary time systems (sometimes referred to as *alternative work schedules*): arrangements whereby staff members, generally in consultation with their supervisors, arrange for variable work schedules on the ad hoc, perhaps changing every week or more, scheduled basis (e.g., putting in evenings instead of mornings). Technical terms sometimes associated with DTS and AWS include:

Band Width—the total number of hours in the interval between the earliest possible starting time and the latest finishing time of the job (e.g., the eight-hour day).

Core Hours—total number of hours the employee must be at work daily or weekly.

Length of Work Week—number of days the worker must be on the job.

Variable Daily Schedule—schedule may vary from day to day or week to week without prior approval from the supervisor.

Banking—carrying forward a surplus or a deficit of hours worked from week to week, with a balance generally required at the end of the month.

Compressed Work Week—generally 38 to 40 hours of work performed in less than five days, or *extended work week*, the same number of hours extended to six or seven days.

Flex time—workers choose when to start or stop work on any given day, so long as the total required hours—generally eight—are performed.

Other terms that deal with the job redesign process include the following:

Job Enlargement—adding variety or widening the range of tasks workers perform. Sometimes referred to as *horizontal job loading* or *horizontal job enlargement*, suggesting that simple tasks are added to a job that was initially simple in nature.

Job Enrichment—this is sometimes referred to as *vertical job enlargement* (adding more complex responsibilities, often implying self-management or the management of others). Typical tasks include those associated with coordination, planning, coaching or teaching, representing, and so on.

Job Sharing—arrangements whereby two or more workers divide up the tasks in a single job, and each perform that job on the basis of an agreed-upon portion of the job with appropriate portions of the salary and other benefits, for example, a 40-hour job may be split into two half-time jobs.

Job Rotation—arrangements whereby an entire job or major complex of tasks within it are rotated between workers on either a fixed schedule or on an ad hoc basis, generally but not always with an understanding that the worker will return to his or her base job.

Task Sharing—the reallocation of tasks within a unit of several staff members to articulate with the personal interests, individual capacities, or inherent characteristics of the tasks—some being undesired and boring, others being especially demanding.

Figure 8.1 The job restructuring and redesign terms defined.

establishing six experimental small group homes for the elderly. This would be the first time that the All-Families Service Center would be expected actually to manage a set of group homes (in contrast with helping set them up, consulting with them, and evaluating their management). The award required hiring some 60 professional and semiprofessional workers within a two-month period, then assigning them to their jobs, and orienting them to a particular work style and philosophical approach. The agency had agreed to manage the group homes for three years as a demonstration project. Later, a decision would be made about whether the homes would become part of the Center's ongoing programs, or transferred to some other legal and organizational entity.

Harvey did not underestimate the magnitude of the task, or the impact of 60 new staff or relationship within his department. His experience as a young adult in Israel had taught him that you can't absorb three or four times your population without some major dislocations—regardless of how strong the initial population, its ideology, and its commitment. In the early years of Israel's statehood, the Jewish community had absorbed a population nearly three times its size in refugees from the DP camps from Europe and refugees from Arab lands. In his professional life, Harvey had witnessed a number of agencies attempting to expand rapidly without giving careful attention to the human resource issues involved. You couldn't just expect that new staff members would absorb and integrate the norms and styles of other workers, particularly if new staff members so far outnumbered those already on board.

What was required was a careful process of recruitment, orientation, and intensive initial supervision. Harvey's first concern was with the recruitment process itself. As he saw it, there were four steps involved: (1) defining the jobs to be performed, (2) determining the criteria for selection of people for those jobs, (3) establishing a recruitment strategy and putting it into effect, and (4) hiring and placing staff. Orientation, supervision, and training would follow.

Putting together the job descriptions wouldn't be an easy task, but given the recent experience with task analysis, it certainly was manageable. Mary Jo was nearing the end of her field placement at the agency and graduation from school. He knew that Bill was considering hiring her as an assistant to Carl Farrell to work on other personnel issues. His first step was to ask Bill if Mary Jo might be temporarily assigned to his department to work on job descriptions. Permission was granted. He also involved Billie Jean Elving. In the two years since Billie Jean had joined the staff, Harvey had been much impressed by her careful attention to details and her unflappable manner. "We don't need another empire builder," he mused, comparing Billie Jean's style to his own. "We need somebody who can *operate a program*, not an *operator*."

Mary Jo and Billie Jean took just under three weeks to put the new job descriptions together. They began by looking at what the project grant called for. They then interviewed supervisory personnel at the state level to get their perspectives on how the jobs should be structured. The state had detailed guidelines regarding the qualifications for personnel to be employed in group homes, along with a list of tasks that would have to be performed. There was some flexibility, however, about how those tasks could be grouped into specific job assignments.

They each visited several group home facilities in the state and in nearby states, homes that had reputations for progressive practice. They read dozens of articles on group homes and the evaluation reports of a nationally recognized project in California. Then they called the director of that project and several other well-known gerontologists and group home operators. Finally, Mary Jo and Billie Jean put their findings to paper, coming up with what they thought were, at least theoretically, pretty sound job descriptions that included not only the tasks to be performed, but also the qualifications and requirements for people who were to undertake those jobs.

In the meantime, Harvey had begun to assess the job market. In terms of *in*experienced but educationally qualified workers, it looked like it might be a buyer's market. The first homes were scheduled to begin in the summer, in time for the new crop of BSW (Bachelor of Social Work) and MSW (Master of Social Work) graduates. Finding *experienced* staff, especially supervisors and medical personnel, would be more difficult.

For some supervisory staff, the agency might have to look inward. In addition to Billie Jean, there were at least three other members of his staff who might be ready for positions as group home managers. He made a note to talk to Yolanda and Sam about the possibility of reassigning staff from their departments. There were some values associated with internal recruitment. It's an encouragement, he noted, for workers to be promoted from within and it serves as a morale booster for others. Internal recruitement helps maintain loyalty to the agency, and it requires less extensive orientation.

In addition to experience and training, Harvey was interested in a balanced staff, that is, a staff balanced in age, gender, and racial and ethnic identity. It wasn't a matter of affirmative action. The agency had a good record on that. But it was a matter of finding staff whose backgrounds were similar enough to those of the elderly residents of the group homes to assure sensitivity to cultural and other identity issues.

Before beginning their recruitment effort, Billie Jean and Mary Jo joined Harvey in his rec room one evening. "Assuming all other things being equal, that is, the people we interview have all the right paper qualifications—you know, in terms of experience, training, and background—what are some of the personal characteristics we're looking for?" After several hours of deliberation, they came up with the following list. They would be looking for new staff members who

(1) liked working closely with people, both clients and colleagues, and were tolerant of differences in style and personality;
(2) were interested in jobs in which there was a great deal of variety, in which they would be challenged to use different kinds of talents and skills, even those that might not appear in their job descriptions;
(3) liked to know how they were doing, were self-critical, and looked for clues in the job itself for signs of success of difficulty, and who were not reluctant to get criticism from co-workers and supervisors;
(4) could make decisions on their own, if they had to, and were not afraid of working autonomously when it was necessary; and
(5) were sensitive to the way in which their behavior affected the lives of others, and were concerned about being helpful to others.

"We haven't said anything about pay, benefits, and job security," commented Mary Jo. "I'm particularly sensitive to these issues, now that I'm about to finish school and enter the job market again myself." "There's not much we can promise about job security," responded Harvey. "Our contract with the state is good for three years. I don't imagine we'll be going out of business after that, but there's no way in which we can promise people long-term career opportunities—especially since most will be coming on with less than an MSW, and most of the other professional jobs in the agency require a Master's degree in social work, or a professional degree in some other field." "I don't think that'll be a major factor," responded Billie Jean.

"This agency has a superb reputation for its professionalism and commitment to professional training. We can offer training opportunities and we do encourage junior staff to continue their education, often at agency expense and at least with release time." "Well, that leaves the question of pay," Harvey concluded, "and I guess there's not much we can do there. The state sets the salary rates for these jobs, and they're not particularly good. But the agency benefit package is excellent. It should be a plus in our favor."

Billie Jean made an inventory of the factors she thought might be most attractive to potential recruits. In her characteristically systematic manner, she listed the issues she felt would lead to an increase in motivational potential, and to job satisfaction. As the basis for her list, she drew on research by Yale sociologist Richard Hackman, whose work she was familiar with.

What was left was the establishment of a recruitment, application, screening, interviewing, and decision-making procedure. The job openings were posted in the agency, advertised in the local press and in both the state and national newsletters of selected professional associations (the National Association of Social Workers, the National Association of Black Social Workers, the American Nursing Association, the Group Home Association), and brief announcements were mailed to schools of social work and other agencies in which recruits might be sought. The letter was followed up by phone calls by Harvey and Billy Jean to agency administrators to avoid any misinterpretation about "raiding" and to increase the likelihood of good referrals.

The agency's standard application form was modified somewhat. It continued to request desired biographic information, employment history, educational background, related life experiences, and references. But it also included two brief vignettes. Each presented a practice problem that workers were likely to encounter in a group home. Applicants were asked to analyze the factors that contributed to the problem, and then describe how they would deal with it within the position for which they were applying. Harvey wanted to know if they could think on-the-job and how they felt about certain practice issues.

Harvey delegated responsibility for screening and interviewing to Billy Jean. She convened a small group of five staff members, three from her department, one from Millicent's, and one from Yolanda's. They screened the applications as they came in, dividing them into

The Variable Billie Jean Selected	How She Scored Each (out of a Score of 10)	
1. Variety of skills to be used on the job, opportunity to use one's capacities and talents.	+8	*Multiple skills required for most jobs–interpersonal and managerial*
2. Multiple, interrelated-related tasks (task-identity) and responsibility for a unit of work from beginning to end.	+6	*Each of the staff members will be responsible for much of a client's care, from beginning to end*
3. Task significance–the importance to others of performing tasks well, making a difference on someone's life–co-workers or clients.	+9	*Very high–what these people will do may affect the life expectancy, not just life circumstances, of our clients*
4. Autonomy, workers can set some of their own owrk responsibilities, norms, and so on.	+6	*Staff will be expected to take independent initiative*
5. Feedback built into the job, staff can see how they are doing or get feedback from clients and supervisors.	+9	*High–you know when you're doing well and when you aren't when you aren't when you work ultimately with older adults in a residential setting*
6. Job security.	+5	*So-so; not sure the grant will be extended beyond the three-year award; agency might transfer responsibility to another organization*
7. Compensation: How good are the salaries and benefit package?	+4	*Not the best: State grant does not permit high salaries; only part of regular agency benefit package, which is pretty good, is available to these staff, pending decision about whether this would be an ongoing agency department or division*
8. Relationship with co-workers.	+9	*If we select them right, considering the kind of working relationships in the rest of this department, it should be pretty good*
9. Supervisory competence.	+9	*We do pretty well here; should not have any major problems; build a lot of responsibility into the work itself*
10. Possibility for growth and personal development.	+10	*Should be really high, like for all staff in this department*

Figure 8.2 Billy Jean's list.

three piles: *sure bets*, *no chances* (if applicants clearly did not have the right educational or experiential backgrounds, or responded incompetently to the test questions), and a "*let's reexamine*" pile. The "no chances" were sent a polite thank you letter. The "sure bets" were invited for interviews, and the "let's reexamines" were held pending a reference check.

BENEFITS AND WAGES

For Ali, the task analysis process had been unsettling. At first, she felt honored to be involved in the task force; it was a good feeling to be respected by professionals at the agency. And she learned a great deal about what social workers do. It gave her a new and added respect for the kind of work in which the clinicians and others were involved. But as the process continued, it became clear to Ali that she and others in the support staff were performing tasks that were defined as professional, but for which they were receiving clerical wages.

This might not have bothered her so much if AFSCME (the American Federation of State, County and Municipal Employees) hadn't begun some probes with the agency's clerical staff about unionization. Many of the other voluntary agencies in the community were already unionized. Initially, Ali didn't have an opinion on the issue, one way or another. Although her dad had always been a union man, and she appreciated the protections it had afforded her family, the Center was more like home to Ali than a job.

But as a number of the other clerical employees began raising issues about fairness, and as union organizers made her increasingly aware of the discrepancies in salaries and benefits between clerical and professional staff, Ali began raising some of these issues at meetings. And as she did so, she found herself becoming a representative of other support staff (unofficial, to be sure). She was relieved to find that this in no way adversely affected her relationships with members of the professional staff. Most were, in fact, sympathetic with some of the issues she raised.

Yet Ali was perplexed. No one in Yolanda's department seemed to have considered the clerical staff in the job restructuring process. Secretaries might also be interested in flextime. Mary Jo was, in fact, the only "professional" staff member who consulted her about the concerns that support staff might have in the new program Harvey

1. Decide whether to conduct a structured, semistructured, or unstructured interview. *Structured* interviews follow a set order of questions or issues. Often questions are forced-choice in style. Unstructured interviews are more spontaneous. They might begin with a list of issues to discuss, or they might be left out for the interviewee to initiate issues. A typical opening might be "What would you like to know about the job or the agency?" A semistructured interview is based on a set of issues or questions that the interviewer will probe (e.g., responses to the problem vignette on Harvey's application form, or the list of five personality characteristics developed by Harvey, Billie Jean, and Mary Jo).
2. Be prepared to answer questions about the job and the agency. Make it easier for the applicant by providing information in advance (perhaps in a packet sent in the mail, or with information made available in the lobby prior to the interview). Such information might include facts about the agency, the department, and the particular job; information about what is being sought in applicants; procedures that will be used both in the interview and in other parts of the hiring process. If the packet is sent out in the mail, it might include information on who the applicant will be talking to, what to bring along, how to get to the agency, and when the job will be available.
3. During the interview, help the applicant ask questions if he or she is ill at ease (in such situations it is easy for one's mind to go blank), and inform the applicant about what you're looking for, and what will happen after the interview (e.g., reference check, follow-up interviews with other staff, and so on).
4. Wherever possible, try to set up the interview as close as possible to the actual place of employment, the worksite itself.

Figure 8.3 Tips for conducting an interview.

was setting up. And Mary Jo was still a student. Nevertheless, Ali was intrigued by the list of five sets of personality characteristics to be used in interviewing new staff for Harvey's department. "You know, Mary Jo," she was surprised at her own boldness, "I think you're saying as much about the job as about the people you're looking for to fill jobs. You know, I'll bet there are a lot of secretaries who'd like more feedback, more control over their own work, more responsibility for seeing a job through from beginning to end, and more of an opportunity to be helpful to people."

THE JOB CHARACTERISTICS MODEL

Ali's, Harvey's, Yolanda's, and Sam's experiences may seem disparate and not connected. They are not disparate. They are all related to the way in which work is designed for individuals and groups in an

1. Get as much information about the agency as you can in advance of the interview. Find out who you'll be meeting with and what the focus of the interview will be. Will there be subsequent interviews, other people to talk to?
2. Sometimes it's possible to speak to other agency staff even before the formal job interview—people already on the job, friends or former acquaintances, friends of friends. The more you know in advance of the interview, the more impressive you can be with your knowledge and the clearer you can be about the kinds of questions to ask or issues to explore.
3. Be prepared to talk not only about what you've done and your educational background, but also about the specific skills you have or interest in developing or expanding those skills. For example, if you've prepared a *curriculum vita* (always a good idea), you might describe where you've worked but not much about what you've done. And even if the C.V. describes what you've done, it might not highlight specific competencies or experiences that might be of interest to the hiring agency. If you've done your research well, you'll know enough to tell the interviewer that you've had experience in such activities as translating a line-item budget into a functional budget, writing a project proposal, doing single-case studies, training volunteers, or researching innovative programs in other parts of the country.
4. Be clear about what you're looking for in terms of salary, benefits, and job tenure or security. Be knowledgeable about the range of benefits generally available in other agencies. If there's a variable benefit package in this agency, be ready to say something about what configuration you might be interested in. And be prepared to ask appropriate questions about legal issues.
5. Be prepared with a list of questions about the job itself, what you'll be expected to do, the kind of supervision or learning opportunities that will be available, your potential co-workers and the decision-making or management style employed.
6. And last but not least, be punctual, dress properly (neither overdressed or underdressed). If you're nervous at the early part of the interview, say something like "I always need a few minutes to warm up at the beginning of an interview. Perhaps you'll tell me a bit more about the agency and the job. Then I'll be ready to ask some more specific questions." First impressions are important. And nervousness and anxiety need not count against you.

Figure 8.4 Tips for job applicants.

organization. In order to get a better conceptual handle on the changes that were set in motion by the task analysis effort, it may be useful to look at some of the work done by Richard Hackman. Hackman has been interested in those aspects of work design, in effect the *characteristics* of the job, that affect work motivation and the critical, psychological states that lead to greater effectiveness and satisfaction with one's own growth and development on the job.

Exercise 8.1

The Job Interview

1. Think about the last job you applied for. What kinds of issues or questions was the agency interested in? List the five or six items that it seems to you were of greatest importance.

2. What else should the agency have been interested in? Did you present that information? Why or why not?

3. If you had conducted the interview (as the recruiter), how would you have restructured it? Why?

In Hackman's model, work is perceived as satisfying and motivating when it is experienced as (a) *important and worthwhile*, (b) *responsible*, and (c) *results-oriented*.

According to the model, every job has similar dimensions or characteristics. These include (a) skill variety, (b) task identity, (c) task sigificance, (d) autonomy, and (e) built-in job feedback. The first three dimensions are related to the experiencing of the job as meaningful—*important and worthwhile*. In which of your previous jobs were you required to perform a wide variety of activities involving a number of different skills and talents? To what extent did they tap into or test your intellect, your affect, and perhaps even your motor skills? This is what Hackman refers to as the *skill variety* dimension of a job.

Task identity refers to the degree to which a job requires that you complete a whole and identifiable piece of work, doing the job from beginning to end with a clearly definable outcome—like matching a potential adoptive child with a family, and seeing the process through until an adoption process is completed. There's a qualitative difference between that kind of job and one in which you might be responsible for only a piece of the overall action, as in a hospital when a patient goes to a variety of stations along the way from admissions, through multiple testing, leading to diagnosis, treatment (perhaps including surgery), to a process of aftercare and discharge. Only a few of the 30 or 40 actors involved, perhaps the admitting physician or surgeon, will feel a great deal of involvement in the overall process. Others, such as the admissions or billing clerk, or perhaps even the x-ray technician, will identify with only a minimal number of tasks. For them, "task identity" will be hardly "identifiable."

A related concept, *task significance*, refers to the degree to which a job has a substantial impact on the lives or on the work of others—colleagues in the organization, clients, workers in other agencies, or perhaps even the general public. When social workers understand that the results of what they do will significantly affect the well-being of other people, when they feel they have some responsibility for completing the whole job, and when they are challenged to use a wide variety of competencies and skills, they will tend to experience their work as *meaningful*. The work can be difficult, it may even be overwhelming, but it will be experienced as important, valuable, worthwhile.

People will feel a personal *responsibility* for the work they do when that work allows substantial discretion, when they make their own decisions and assume independence of action. You'll recognize this as a definition of *autonomy*. The more autonomy people have on the job, the more they're likely to view the outcome of their work as being based on their own efforts and initiative. And the more the effort and initiative is one's *own*, the more responsibility one feels for one's work.

Some jobs have, within them, a built-in *feedback* mechanism; that is, you know how well you've done or whether you've finished the job based on some aspect of the process itself. For example, workers who know they've helpled families get housing, or helped an unemployed worker get a job, or have found a foster placement for a child, know what the results of their work are. When work is experienced as meaningful, and when workers feel a sense of responsibility for the outcomes of their work, and when they, in fact, know the actual results of that work, they're likely to be much more highly motivated to invest in their jobs. Such investment reflects what Hackman calls a job's Motivation Potential Score (MPS). His formula for arriving at that score is as follows:

$$\text{MPS} = \frac{\left(\begin{matrix}\text{Skill}\\\text{Variety}\end{matrix} + \begin{matrix}\text{Task}\\\text{Identity}\end{matrix} + \begin{matrix}\text{Task}\\\text{Significance}\end{matrix}\right)}{3} \times \text{Autonomy} \times \begin{matrix}\text{Job}\\\text{Feedback}\end{matrix} = \underline{\qquad}$$

What can you do with the MPS score? Not much if you have only an MPS for your own job at a given point in time; a great deal if you have comparable data.

You might use the resulting score to compare how much a particular job motivates different workers at the agency, perhaps in different jobs or departments. You might also examine the extent to which different jobs motivate you differently. For example, if you use this formula as a way of evaluating jobs at the All-Families Center, you might discover that staff members in Harvey's department get a relatively high MPS, in particular, because they are called upon to use a variety of skills, have a great deal of autonomy, and feel that what they do has a significant impact on the lives of others.

In Yolanda's department, autonomy might be a bit lower, and job feedback (you can't always tell how well clients are doing) might not be as high as in other departments. But clinicians are likely to score high in skill variety, task identity, and task significance. One of the reasons that workers in Sam's department were so motivated to move into the homebuilders experiment is that it increased all five dimensions that contribute to a high MPS.

I suspect that, except for Ali in the receptionist's role, other support staff might score a good deal lower on skill variety, task identity, task significance, and autonomy, although there might be a good deal of feedback built into their jobs. And yet, a number of clerical staff may also be highly motivated, whereas some professional staff in Sam's, Yolanda's, and Harvey's department might not be. Does this prove the formula wrong? Not necessarily.

There are a number of moderators that increase the extent to which some employees take off on their jobs and others are turned off by the same jobs. Hackman identifies two moderators: (1) growth needs and (2) knowledge and skill. The first presumes that a number of people, you and I included, may have strong need for personal accomplishment, for developing ourselves beyond where we are now. Those with strong growth needs are likely to have high internal motivation when working on complex and challenging jobs.

People who have less powerful needs for growth and personal development may be less eager to explore the opportunities for accomplishment provided at work, or may find other sources of satisfaction for their growth needs (say, at the university, or in recreational activities). Some people are in high-MPS jobs, but they have neither the background, knowledge, or skill to perform well, and so they may experience a good deal of personal failure leading to unhappiness and frustration. But because their work is not done well, they may tend to withdraw from it. Some, in fact, "burn out," because neither their knowledge nor their skills are sufficient to overcome the enormous pressures inherent in the job that once motivated but now depresses.

How valid is the job characteristics model? It's hard to tell. There is considerable evidence that it is more on target than off-base. But no single model is going to explain all behavior, whether on the job or anywhere else. Hackman himself notes that evidence about the proposed moderators is both scattered and inconsistent. These certainly don't adequately account for the job stress or burnout factor. And we know that people experience their psychological states differently. For some, experiencing work as meaningful or responsible may be less important than for others. No one has really tested out the relationships between this model and some of the trait factor theories we explored earlier.

There's another problem, too. The model treats job characteristics as if they were independent, that is, not interdependent or dependent on each other. A more accurate algorithm would show the intersections of various job characteristics and experienced psychological states. You probably caught onto this as you were reading the preceding pages. For example, I suspect that an increase in task identity often leads to a greater sense of task significance. Research on the question is not yet conclusive.

Hackman feels that the concept of feedback in the model is flawed because workers, their supervisors, and outside observers often disagree about how much feedback a job actually does provide. Sometimes feedback from non-job sources, for example, from family members and co-workers, is most important in shaping a worker's perception about success or failure. There's another issue too. People tend to try to overcome cognitive dissonance. That is, they may perceive a job as unsatisfying and unmotivating, but it's hard to live with that perception and stay with it for long. You either have to give up on your aspirations or leave the job and look for another one. But sometimes there aren't too many options for finding a new job. So people scale down their expectations and become more "realistic" (some would say fatalistic).

These cautions notwithstanding, I think you may find the model quite useful in assessing your job, the jobs of others, and even jobs that you may be applying for in the future. It may lead you to some clues about ways in which a particular job or complex of jobs might be enlarged, enriched, or otherwise modified to increase motivational potential, satisfaction, and perhaps even effectiveness.

Do you see any relationships between Hackman's job characteristics model and the earlier work we examined on needs (Maslow's, Alderfer's, or McClelland's)? How does it articulate with Lawler and Porter's or Vroom's expectancy theories? Note that these all focus on the individual, whereas Hackman's approach pays primary attention to the job itself.

In the pages that follow, I've designed three sets of exercise and scoring instruments that are takeoffs of the more comprehensive "Job Diagnostic Survey'" developed by Hackman and Oldman. You might find it helpful in assessing your own perceptions of your current job or in assessing the characteristics of a position in which you may be interested.

Remember that the scores you arrive at will have little meaning, in and of themselves. They are useful only for comparative purposes. The following are some uses to which you might apply the exercises:

(1) to compare your assessment of the job over time, say at six-month or at one-year interval (what might this teach you about yourself or the job?);
(2) as a way of assessing new job possibilities, and comparing them with your current or previous jobs;
(3) as an assessment tool applied to specific groups at the agency (co-workers, supervisors, workers in a particular department or sub-group), perhaps as a way of helping staff and management to develop greater awareness of those aspects of the work situation that lead to higher motivation, or to head off problems as they begin to emerge (especially if the instruments are used at specific intervals); and
(4) as a baseline for job restructuring as well as for evaluating the impact of the changes made.

Before beginning the exercise, a few words about the scoring procedures. You'll note later that there are some instances in which you'll have to total the scores of two, three, or four items. If this is the case, your final score will be an average of these. There are some places in which you are instructed to "reverse the score." This is because some of the assessment items are written in the negative. To reverse the score, use the following formula: an item that you scored "1" would now receive a total of 7 points; 2 would equal 6; 3 would equal 5; and 4 would remain 4. Everything else should be self-explanatory.

Exercise 8.2

Job Characteristics and Their Motivational Potential

Describe your current job (or one you recently held) as *objectively* as possible. Questions about what you *like* or *dislike* about the job will come later.

Circle the number that most accurately describes the job.

1. To what extent does your job require you to work closely with other people (clients or colleagues in related jobs at the agency or other agencies)?

   1-----------2-----------3-----------4-----------5-----------6-----------7

Very little; not necessary for the job.	Moderately; job requires some work with others.	Very much; crucial and essential part of job.

2. How much autonomy is there in the job; to what extent are you permitted to decide how to go about doing your work?

   1-----------2-----------3-----------4-----------5-----------6-----------7

Very little.	Moderately.	A lot.

3. To what extent does your job involve doing a "whole" and identifiable piece of work? Does it have a beginning and end or is it only a small part of the overall work begun, finished by others?

   1-----------2-----------3-----------4-----------5-----------6-----------7

Only a tiny part of the whole piece of work.	Moderate-size chunk.	The whole job from start to finish.

4. How much variety is there in your job? Do you do many things, using different skills and talents at work?

   1-----------2-----------3-----------4-----------5-----------6-----------7

very little; work is routine; repetitive.	Moderate variety.	Lots of variety.

5. How significant or important is your job; are the results of your work likely to affect the lives or well-being of other people significantly?

   1-----------2-----------3-----------4-----------5-----------6-----------7

Not very significant.	Moderately significant.	Very significant.

6. To what extent do managers and co-workers let you know how well you are doing or the job?

   1-----------2-----------3-----------4-----------5-----------6-----------7

Hardly ever get feedback.	Yes and no; moderate.	Lots of ongoing feedback.

7. To what extent does the actual work itself provide clues to how well you are doing, apart from any feedback from co-workers or supervisors?

   1-----------2-----------3-----------4-----------5-----------6-----------7

Could work forever without knowing how I'm doing.	Get some feedback.	Job is set up to give almost constant feedback.

Scoring for Exercise 8.2

To score the extent to which the characteristics of your current (or a recent) job contribute to your motivation to exert effort on that job, review the numbers you circled for each question in **Exercise 8.2**. These are your "scores" for each of the five characteristics listed below.

Job Characteristics and Their Motivational Potential	Your Scores
1. Skill Variety—#4	________
2. Task Identity—#3	________
3. Task Significance—#1 and #5 (average the two)	________
4. Autonomy—#2	________
5. Feedback from the Job—#6 and #7 (average the two)	________

$$\text{Motivational Potential Score} = \left[\frac{\overset{(1)}{\text{Skill Variety}} + \overset{(2)}{\text{Task Identity}} + \overset{(3)}{\text{Task Signif.}}}{3}\right] \times \overset{(4)}{\text{Autonomy}} \times \overset{(5)}{\text{Feedback from Job}}$$

$$\left[\frac{(\quad) + (\quad) + (\quad)}{3}\right] \times (\quad) \times (\quad) = \underline{\qquad (\text{MPS})}$$

If changes were to be made to increase the job's motivational potential, where should those changes occur?

Exercise 8.3

How the Job Feels: Experienced Psychological States

Section 1.

Now indicate how you personally feel about the job. Using the scale that follows, indicate how much you agree with the statements below by writing in the appropriate number. In each statement, you will be referring to "on this job."

1	2	3	4	5	6	7
Disagree Strongly	Disagree	Disagree Slightly	Neutral	Agree Slightly	Agree	Agree Strongly

☐ 1. It's hard for me to care very much about whether the work gets done right.

☐ 2. My opinion of myself goes up when I do this job well.

☐ 3. Generally speaking, I am very satisfied with this job.

☐ 4. Most of the things I have to do on this job seem useless or trivial.

☐ 5. I usually know whether or not my work is satisfactory on this job.

☐ 6. I feel a great deal of personal satisfaction when I do this job well.

☐ 7. The work I do on this job is very meaningful to me.

☐ 8. I feel a very high degree of personal responsibility for the work I do.

☐ 9. I frequently think of quitting this job.

☐ 10. I feel bad when I find I have performed poorly on this job.

☐ 11. I often have trouble in figuring out whether I'm doing well or poorly.

☐ 12. I feel I should personally take credit or blame for the results of my work.

☐ 13. I am generally satisfied with the kind of work I do on this job.

☐ 14. My own feelings are not generally affected by how well I do, one way or the other.

☐ 15. Whether or not this job gets done right is clearly my responbility.

Section 2.

Using the same scale as for Section 1, please indicate how much you agree or disagree with the following statements about how *other people* in your agency or at work who hold similar jobs to yours feel about their work. If no one holds exactly the same job, think about persons whose jobs are very similar. If lots of people hold the same jobs, and their feelings are likely to diverge a lot, pick those whose feelings are most important to you.

☐ 1. Most people on this job feel great personal satisfaction when when they do it well.

☐ 2. Most of these people are very satisfied with their jobs.

☐ 3. Most of them feel that their work is useless or trivial.

☐ 4. Most feel a great personal responsibility for what they do on the job.

☐ 5. Most have a pretty good idea of how well they are performing.

☐ 6. Most find the work very meaningful.

☐ 8. People on this job often think of quitting.

☐ 9. Most feel bad when they find they have performed their work poorly.

☐ 10. Most have trouble figuring out whether they are doing a good or bad job.

Scoring for Exercise 8.3

To determine how you experience your job psychologically—how it "feels" to you—score the following statements as directed.

Categories and Items	Your Scores (averaged)
1. My Work Is Meaningful—Section 1, #4 (reverse scoring) and #7; Section 2, #3 (reverse scoring) and #6.	______
2. I Am Responsible for My Work—Section 1, #8 and #12 and #15; Section 2, #4.	______
3. I Know How I'm Doing—Section 1, #5 and #11 (reverse scoring); Section 2, #5 and #10 (reverse scoring).	______
4. I Feel Good About Myself When I Feel Good About the Job—Section 1, #2 and #6 and #10 and #14 (reverse scoring); Section 2, #1 and #9.	______
5. My General Satisfaction for the Job—Section 1, #3 and #9 (reverse scoring) and #13; Section 2, #2 and #8 (reverse scoring).	______

First, total the scores you gave yourself for every item in each of the categories below.

Note that some items require "reverse scoring." That is because the original item was written in the negative. Here is how you "reverse score": If your score was *7*, "reverse scoring" would be *1*, for *6* it becomes *2*, for *5* it becomes *3* and vice versa.

Finally divide your total score for each category by the number of items covered. Thus for category 1, below, you would divide your total score by 4. This figure goes on the line for averaged scores.

Exercise 8.4

What I Look for in a Job and How Much I Get

Section 1

This time, please indicate how satisfied you are with each aspect of the job listed below. (If you are using this form to assess a prospective job, substitute "desirability" for "satisfaction.")

1	2	3	4	5	6	7
Extremely Dissatisfied	Dissatisfied	Slightly Dissatisfied	Neutral	Slightly Satisfied	Satisfied	Extremely Satisfied

☐ 1. The amount of job security I have.

☐ 2. The amount and kinds of pay and fringe benefits my job provides.

☐ 3. The opportunities for personal growth and development on this job.

☐ 4. The people I work with on the job.

☐ 5. The degree of respect and fair treatment I receive from my supervisor.

☐ 6. The feeling of worthwhile accomplishment I get from my job.

☐ 7. The chance to get to know other people while on the job.

☐ 8. The amount of support and guidance I receive from my supervisor.

☐ 9. The degree to which I am fairly paid for what I contribute to this organization.

☐ 10. The amount of independent thought and action I can exercise in my job.

☐ 11. How secure things look for me in the future in this organization.

☐ 12. The chance to help other people while at work.

☐ 13. The amount of challenge on the job.

☐ 14. The overall quality of supervision I receive in my work.

Section 2

The characteristics listed below could be present in any job. To what extent would you personally like to see each present in your job? Use the scale below to indicate the degree you would like to see each present in the job. Note that the scale is numbered differently than those you used earlier.

4----------------------5----------------------6----------------------7

Would like this only moderately.	Would like this a lot.	Would like this *extremely* much.

☐ 1. High respect and fair treatment from my supervisor.
☐ 2. Stimulating and challenging work.
☐ 3. Changes to exercise independent thought and action in my job.
☐ 4. Great job security.
☐ 5. Very friendly co-workers.
☐ 6. Opportunities to learn new things from my work.
☐ 7. High salary and good fringe benefits.
☐ 8. Opportunities to be creative and imaginative in my work.
☐ 9. Quick promotions.
☐ 10. Opportunities for personal and professional development in my job.
☐ 11. A sense of worthwhile accomplishment in my work.

Scoring for Exercise 8.4

Average the scores for each item.

Categories and Items	Your Scores (averaged)
I Feel I can Grow in this Job—Section 1, #3 and #6 and #10 and #13	________
I Am Satisfied with My:	
(a) Job Security—Section 1, #1 and #11	________
(b) Compensation—Section 1, #2 and #9	________
(c) Co-workers—Section 1, #7 and #12	________
(d) Supervisor—Section 1, #5 and #8 and #14	________
Growth, Relationship, Security, and Pay Needs Compared	
(a) Growth Needs—Section 2, #2 and #3 and #8 and #10 and #11	________
(b) Relationship Needs—Section 2, #1 and #5	________
(c) Security/Pay Needs—Section 2, #4 and #7 and #9	________

REVIEW AND TENTATIVE CONCLUSIONS

Sometimes an agency's administrative "structure," embodied in its rules, regulations, and job descriptions, seems as rigid as its physical structure. But buildings can be redesigned and so can jobs—often to the advantages of the agency, its clients, its staff, and other concerned parties.

(1) Jobs, any jobs in an agency, can be redesigned or restructured to accommodate the achievement of the organization's missions, and the competence, interests, and skill of staff members. Redesign requires careful attention to the tasks assigned, the competencies associated with those tasks, and the criteria by which performance will be measured.

(2) Job *restructuring* generally refers to the design of alternative work schedules (ANS) using discretionary time systems (DTS). Terms associated with DTS and ANS include *length of work week, variable daily schedules, band width, core hours, flextime, compressed work week,* and *banking*. These terms were defined in Figure 8.1.

(3) Terms associated with job *redesign* include *job enlargement* (adding variety or widening the range of tasks), *job enrichment* (adding more complex responsibilities including self management), *job sharing*, *task sharing*, and *job rotation.*

(4) Recruiting staff to fill agency positions (persons new to the agency or others who may be recruited from different divisions or departments) requires careful matching of job and worker characteristics. Some of the variables to be attended to are the skills to be used on the job; the range of interrelated tasks and their significance; the extent to which workers are expected to operate independently; the kind of feedback available on the job and that which may be needed by workers; compensation and job security; the opportunity for building meaningful relationships with co-workers; the availabililty of competent supervision; and opportunities for personal, work-related, and professional growth.

(5) A job characteristics model that can be used to explain motivational potential was presented. The formula is found below.

$$\text{MPS} = \frac{\left(\begin{matrix}\text{Skill}\\\text{Variety}\end{matrix} + \begin{matrix}\text{Task}\\\text{Identity}\end{matrix} + \begin{matrix}\text{Task}\\\text{Significance}\end{matrix}\right)}{3} \times \text{Autonomy} \times \begin{matrix}\text{Job}\\\text{Feedback}\end{matrix} = \underline{\qquad}$$

YOUR ADDITIONS

(6)

(7)

(8)

(9)

(10)

REFERENCES

Austin, Michael J. (1981). *Supervisory management for the human services* (see esp. Chapters 4, 7, and 10). Englewood Cliffs, NJ: Prentice-Hall.

Beer, Michael, et al. (1984). *Managing human assets* (see esp. Chapters 4 and 5). New York: Free Press.

Cohen, A. R., & Gadon, Harold. (1978). *Alternative work schedules: Integrating individual and organizational needs*. Reading, MA: Addison-Wesley.

Fein, Mitchell. (1983). Job enrichment: A reevaluation. In J. Richard Hackman et al., *Perspectives on behavior in organizations*. New York: McGraw-Hill.

Ford, Robert N. (1969. *Motivation through the work itself*. New York: American Management Association.

Hackman, Richard J. (1983). Designing work for individuals and for groups. In J. Richard Hackman et al., *Perspectives on behavior in organizations*. New York: McGraw-Hill.

Hackman, J. Richard, & Oldham, G. R. (1980). *Work redesign*. Reading, MA: Addison-Wesley.

Harrison, Roger. (1973). Role in negotiation: A tough minded approach to team development." In Warren G. Bennis et al., *Interpersonal dynamics* (3rd ed.). Chicago: Dorsey.

Katzell, R. A., & Yankelovich, Daniel, et al. (1975). *Work productivity and job satisfaction*. New York: The Psychological Corporation.

Chapter 9

SUPERVISING AND BEING SUPERVISED
Authority and Authority Structures in an Agency

Millicent Kapinski took Thursday and Friday off—well, not really off. Following her meeting with Bill Clapman a few days earlier, she decided to do some reading and hard thinking before responding to his request.

Millicent had been bothered for quite some time about the rapidity with which changes were occurring at the agency ever since Bill had initiated the task analysis business. She liked a lot of the things she saw happening, but she felt that all this dynamism led to a certain weakening of the agency's central thrust. Originally, she hadn't been sure what exactly she meant by that. It was more of a gut feeling than anything else. But it had all become crystal clear in her second meeting with Bill.

"Millicent," he had begun, "I appreciate the work that you and Carl and the others did on the task analysis task force. But you must have known this would be only the beginning of a process. Frankly, things are moving along much as I had hoped."

"Bill, I'm confused," Millicent cut in. "I've been afraid we may be losing control over the change process." Bill leaned forward. "That's curious, Millicent, tell me what you mean." "Well, I've been talking to a number of the department heads and supervisors. Everybody seems to be going off in their own directions. And I suppose that's not so bad, it does loosen us up quite a bit. But some of the supervisors seem to be at a loss. The way we've reorganized jobs requires a lot more knowledge, and maybe some more skill, than a great many of the line workers possess. And supervisors seem to be in the middle of it all. The problem, it seems to me, is that staff may not be able to perform competently in all the new directions we seem to be moving in."

"So, the key issues are competence and performance?" probed Bill.

"Yes, that's it."

"As usual, you're right on target, Millicent," Bill leaned back on his chair.

"Oh oh," thought Millicent. "When Bill leans backward in a relaxed position, it means he's about to pounce."

"Look Millicent. I've already asked Carl to expand his job description from managing our fiscal accounts to managing the agency's personnel function. And as you know, we've hired Mary Jo to be his assistant. They will be working on issues that relate to the agency's hiring practices, and our wage and benefit packages. Both will have to be readjusted to deal with new job descriptions, and with the kinds of work that we'll be requiring of staff. And I've begun to work with the personnel committee of the board of directors on a new wage/benefits package. But to be able to do what the agency requires of staff, and to be sure that they'll continue to innovate, we've got to provide them more than financial benefits and job security. We have to provide them some educational support.

"While we all take pride in the level of education of the staff, I don't think we have thought systematically enough in the past about the educational functions of supervision, about job training and development, and all the kind of things that I know you know something about."

"Do I detect that you're about to ask me to design a training program for supervisors?" Millicent asked. "You know I'm a community educator, not a staff developer. That's not in *my* job description." Bill leaned back farther. "Not yet, perhaps." He then leaned forward. "Oh oh, that's it," thought Millicent. "He's pouncing."

"With all the changes taking place, all the new developments," he looked at Millicent squarely, "we're going to have to develop our own people. And that means investing in training, education, and all kinds of other support activities. We've got a competent staff. We're competent at what we're doing now. But we won't stay competent long, unless we continue developing. I want you to coordinate the development function." "But what about the supervisory staff?" asked Millicent.

"I said *coordinate*, not *do* everything. As far as I'm concerned, our middle management people are central to the success or failure of this agency and its programs. But you can't expect more of supervisors than they're capable of doing. You may have to do some training of trainers. You may also have to develop new kinds of training and continuing education opportunities that are outside of the supervisory process."

"You know, Bill, I've been an educator all my life. But this is the first time I've been challenged to be an educator in the organization in which I'm employed. When I was a school teacher, I was teaching kids. When I was a community developer, I was educating peasants in rural villages. In most of my years at this agency, I've been involved with family life education, focusing on clients and community people. I think I would like the new challenge. Do I get a new title?" she laughed.

"Well, you may at that, let's think about it together later. First, I'd like you to do some thinking about what needs doing. Check out the different supervisory styles around here. Find out how much of the supervision is focused on management issues, and how much on education leading to better performance. Do an inventory of the kinds of training activities the staff have taken advantage of in the last few years, those with and without agency support. And do some reading. Why don't you hit the library at the university? Talk to Margaret Antell on the faculty. I understand she's the *maven* on supervision at the School of Social Work."

Millicent did talk to professor Antell, who suggested a list of books and articles as a way of becoming familiar with social work's unique struggle over the meaning of supervision. "When you've had a chance to read and to think about the issues some more, let's talk again." For Millicent, nothing could have been more delicious. Here's what she did, and what she found out.

THE EVOLUTION OF SUPERVISORY STYLES IN SOCIAL WORK

Before going to the School of Social Work Library, Millicent reviewed some of her reading notes. Although not a social worker by training, she had become increasingly identified with the profession, as the outcome of her work at the Center. Two years earlier, she had begun reading the "classics," books written by the profession's founders in the 1920s, 1930s, and early 1940s. The recent rediscovery and republication of Bertha Reynolds's writings by NASW was in particular gratifying to her. She found in Reynolds a kindred spirit, someone committed to the oppressed, objective in her analyses, and yet passionate in her commitments. In "The Art of Supervision," an article published in *The Family* more than half a century ago, Reynolds had written about supervision as

> enlarging perspective, stimulating imagination, and cultivating sturdy independence of thought and sound personal relationship with human beings . . . supervision . . . becomes an art of teaching on the job, a relationship that gives new life, a force that builds for the future in the lives of a questioning and virile generation.

In her landmark work, *Learning and Teaching in the Practice of Social Work*, Reynolds specified the following as the essential aspects of social work supervision: (1) that it operate through a relationship between supervisor and supervisee in which workers are individualized as persons as they are helped to perform their particular jobs; (2) that the supervisor operate as a "specialized" worker rather than as a superior officer, whose qualifications are based on skill and experience rather than on the basis of hierarchical positions; (3) that the ultimate objective of the supervisory process is achievement of the agency's deepest purposes; (4) that supervision is essential to administration but not identical with it, in particular, because it has educative as well as administrative functions; and (5) the art of supervision is one of building creative human relationships.

Millicent smiled to herself as she reread these "principles." "How naive and how profound at the same time," she reflected.

Following Professor Antell's suggestion, Millicent went first to the *Social Work Encyclopedia* at the library. She looked up "supervision" in each of the last three editions, took notes on journal articles she wanted to pursue, and then she looked for other books in the card catalog Professor Antell had suggested. She found one by Austin, another by Middleman and Rhodes, one by Paul Abels, and a fourth by Gambrill and Stein. Under the general heading of "supervision," her eye lit on a book by Margaret Williamson, published in 1950. She'd remembered seeing it on Bill's shelf. "Oldies are sometimes

Exercise 9.1

The Supervisory Relationship

Why do you think Millicent reacted as she did?

1. Underline some of the words that you think are key to Reynolds's assessment, words such as *relationship*, *individualization*, *agency function*, and so on.

2. Do you agree with Millicent about the profundity of Bertha Reynolds's assessment? Why or why not?

3. Do you agree with Millicent about the naïveté of Reynolds's assessment? Why or why not?

When you've completed the chapter, come back and reexamine your own answers. How would you modify them? Use a blank sheet of paper if necessary.

goodies," she reasoned. "And I do want to get a historical perspective before trying to sort things out for the agency." And she got one.

THREE INTERRELATED FUNCTIONS

Clearly influenced by Reynolds, Williamson had written about three interrelated functions of supervision: administrative, educational, and what she called "secondary leadership." Williamson saw the three functions held together in one person, the supervisor, doing one job, with supervision and administration being indistinguishable from each other. Administrative tasks included recruiting and assignment of workers, their induction and orientation, assistance in organization of the job, interpretation of agency policies and explanations of administrative requirements, arrangements for protecting the health and physical safety of both workers and program participants, and administration of the personnel policies of the agency.

"Well, that might work in a small, traditional agency, or even one like ours whose departments have a lot of autonomy," Millicent thought, "but what of large multipurpose or multifunctional agencies, like public welfare offices with separate personnel departments and relatively tall hierarchies of positions? And what about the supervision of social workers who operate as independent clinicians, private practitioners, or consultants, social workers who might not even have an agency base?"

Williamson's treatment of the educational function of supervision focused on the development of capacities to learn and to do within the context of the job—that is, doing the job more effectively in pursuit of the agency's missions. Movement, Williamson pointed out, à la Reynolds, should progress from consciousness-of-self to a conscious *use*-of-self. Central for the worker's growth, it presumed a relationship with a supervisor that is supportive and directive. "Amazing," thought Millicent, "in addition to administration, the supervisor is expected to function as the master teacher and therapist all rolled into one. Interesting," she thought, "the supervisor is case working the supervisee."

The same might be said of the "secondary" leadership function, a term Williamson had borrowed from Walter Kindelsperger, an early group worker and social educator who saw the supervisor as the backup person, someone you could use as a sounding board, someone who helps the worker analyze and evaluate what's happening in his or her practice; a person who, not directly involved with clients, might be able to take a more objective and broad point of view.

Millicent immediately connected this function with an article she had read only a week earlier by Resnick and King, "Shadow Consultation," which had appeared in *Social Work*. Although they referred to it as new organizational change strategy, the indebtedness to Kindelsperger was undeniable. The social work *consultant* in the article (she substituted the word *supervisor*) observes a manager (in industry) in a typical day of work, and then provides feedback on the manager's effectiveness in relating to and directing his or her associates. The purpose of this intervention is to promote change in the manager's leadership behavior, helping the manager become more open to change.

Despite differences in emphasis, Millicent found Williamson's three functions continuously referred to in the subsequent social work literature on supervision. For example, in what has since come to be thought of as a modern classic, Alfred Kadushin's book, *Supervision in Social Work*, the author defines social work supervision as serving three major interrelated functions: (1) the administrative, (2) the educational, and (3) the supportive. Although the language is contemporary, and the treatment is much more exhaustive, Kadushin's orientation is much the same as Williamson's.

THE ADMINISTRATIVE FUNCTION

To begin with, he defines administrative tasks as including staff recruitment and selection, inducting and placing the worker, unit work planning, work assignment, work delegation, monitoring, reviewing and evaluating the work, coordinating work between supervisees, acting as a channel of communication within the administrative structure, plus administrative buffering (protecting the worker where appropriate), and community liaison. This administrative function, it appeared to Millicent, had received increasing attention over the years.

In Irving Miller's article on supervision that appeared in both the 1971 and 1977 editions of the *Encyclopedia of Social Work*, the emphasis is on administrative functions. And it parallels Kadushin's definition of the supervisor as primarily an "administrative officer." The administrative orientation was supported and elaborated by Michael Austin in a 1981 publication, *Supervisory Management for the Human Services*. Austin, whose work on task analysis influenced the Center's own efforts, places social work supervision, as he defines it, squarely within the management function. In his book, he deals with management by objectives, the deployment of staff, the monitoring of worker performance, the delegation of work, and the management of task groups.

THE EDUCATIVE FUNCTION

All of this made sense to Millicent. Yet despite these definitions of supervision, definitions that paralleled and reflected much of contemporary management literature, there was something about social work supervision that was different. Whatever else they might say, beginning with Reynolds, all of the authors seemed to her to place inordinate emphasis on the educational and supportive components of supervision. An earlier *Encyclopedia* article had, in fact, defined social work supervision as primarily educational in focus. And so did Paul Abels in a book written about 10 years earlier. Abels defines the essence of supervision as a

> process by which people assist each other in learning the norms, attitudes, and knowledge which they will need to perform their functions in the agency in an effective and satisfying manner . . . (Supervision) is a consciousness-raising process, in which the awareness of all the parties in the transaction is increased on behalf of effective practice.

What Abels calls a "synergistic" model employs systems concepts to define the supervisory process as one in which learning contributes to change, with the major agent of change being the supervisor, and the supervisee being treated as the client system. Abels also discusses the multiple responsibilities of different parties for sharing, often on an equal basis, in the developmental process.

"This is really the core of it," thought Millicent. "Social work has put the supervisor at the center of the developmental process, much as the worker is a key element in the development of the individual client, the group, or even the community. In a sense, the supervisor role models professional attitudes, values, insights, perspectives, and even the application of scientific knowledge and professional ethics to problem solving and decision making. But is it realistic?" she asked herself. "To a certain extent, yes," she decided. "But somehow, the model seems a bit anachronistic today, despite the fact that it seems to be so well ingrained in the profession's psyche."

When she thought about how Yolanda and other supervisors in the clinical services department performed supervisory tasks, she saw much evidence of the educative approach, modified and informed by the administrative. In fact, when the clinical supervisors at the agency had completed descriptions of the tasks they performed, over 30% seemed to be educational in orientation. They'd recorded only a slightly higher percentage of administrative tasks. But when workers in those units had recorded the kinds of tasks that they depended on their supervisors for, more than half the tasks were administrative in nature, and less than one out of seven were educational. Are workers telling us something different than supervisors? Were supervisors idealizing something that did not exist, she wondered?

Millicent found the answers in a study by Kadushin. In his research on supervisors and supervisees in a large public agency in the early 1970s, the Wisconsin educator found that more than one-quarter of the supervisors surveyed saw themselves as teachers, but barely 3% of the supervisees saw themselves as students. Moreover, supervisors reported a great deal of satisfaction from their teaching activities, whereas workers tended to report satisfaction with help they received in dealing with specific client or administrative problems. "It seems," Millicent reflected, "that supervisors and supervisees may be perceiving their relationships differently, or at least the supervisors want to teach more than supervisees want to be taught."

"I know what Yolanda does with her staff, but does Harvey emphasize education in the same way?" she asked herself. On reflection, she realized that Harvey's approach to supervision was quite different. He encouraged education and training, but primarily by getting staff to share information with each other, or by allowing them to take time off to educate themselves in areas that were important to their work. Harvey is not a case worker, she realized, and that may be the reason for the difference. He involves his staff in problem solving and decision making. Harvey, she reckoned, is more of an administrative-type supervisor, albeit with a participatory style.

But, while analysis of individual supervisory styles might yield some insights, Millicent reasoned, it wasn't going to get her very far. Better to take Kadushin's discussion of the educational function and think about who should be responsible for its conduct. Kadushin

Ten Highest Sources of Supervisor Satisfaction in Supervision	*Percentage of Supervisors Checking Item as a Strong Source of Satisfaction (N = 469)*
1. Helping the supervisee grow and develop in professional competence.	88
2. Ensuring more efficient and effective service to more clients through my supervisory activity.	75
3. Sharing my social work knowledge and skills with supervisees.	63
4. Greater opportunity and leverage to affect changes in agency policy and procedures.	45
5. Stimulation provided by curious, idealistic, and enthusiastic supervisees.	44
6. Helping the supervisee grow and develop as a person.	37
7. More diversified job.	31
8. Having others look to me for leadership, advice, direction.	24
9. Providing emotional support to supervisees when needed.	23
10. Increased salary that goes with job.	23

Ten Highest Sources of Supervisee Satisfaction in Supervision	*Percentage of Supervisors Checking Item as a Strong Source of Satisfaction (N = 348)*
1. Sharing responsibility with, and obtaining support from, somebody in administrative authority for difficult case decisions.	44
2. Help from my supervisor in dealing with problems in my work with clients.	40
3. Help from my supervisor in my development as a professional social worker.	34
4. Administrative access to agency resources I need to help my clients.	27
5. Stimulation in thinking about social work theory and practice.	27
6. Critical feedback I need in order to know how I am doing as a social worker.	24
7. The emotional support I need to do my job more effectively.	21
8. Some sense of agency appreciation of my work.	19
9. A sense of belonging in the agency.	12
10. Growing toward greater maturity as a person.	9

SOURCE: Abstracted from Kadushin (1985).

Figure 9.1 Partial results of Kadushin's study

distinguishes between educational supervision, staff development, and in-service training. *Staff development* refers to all of the activities that an agency might employ to enhance job-related knowledge, attitudes, and skill. In my own research I found that agencies tend to take either a "service" or a "change" orientation to staff development. The service orientation presumes that the individual worker has the right and responsibility to choose his or her own directions. This might include participation in the planning and development of courses and workshops at the agency, or in selection of courses and conferences to attend outside of the agency. It may include independent learning projects.

The training orientation, on the other hand, presumes that someone other than the trainee determines the goals and the means of instruction. For example, a supervisor or department head might determine that all staff must learn a new approach to family treatment, or must be taught to fill out a new set of forms properly. *In-service training* refers to the training conducted within the agency. Other training efforts might be conducted outside the agency, as when selected staff are sent to a workshop or course on budgeting or grantsmanship by agency management. Thus, training is oriented more toward agency needs, whereas service-oriented staff development is more oriented toward the worker's perceptions of his or her own work-related and professional needs.

Service-oriented educational supervision focuses on the needs of a particular worker (or those in a work unit) carrying a particular case load or encountering particular problems on the job. Change-oriented educational supervision had more in common with administrative supervision; the focus is on learning to do the job better. Both can be carried out on a one-on-one basis, in a group setting, and with considerable amounts of worker(s) input. Austin gives specific attention to four clusters of tasks performed in educational supervision: (1) assessing, (2) orienting, (3) updating, and (4) upgrading. To what extent should the supervisor be responsible for each? With whom should the responsibility be shared: the worker or other members of the supervisor's staff, other supervisors within the department, the department head?

Assessment, Millicent decided, is clearly a supervisory function. A supervisor does educational assessment when he or she is involved in performance appraisal. But assessment shouldn't be limited to the here and now, on the ways in which the worker is currently performing on the job. It also requires an anticipatory process, thinking through what kinds of challenges the worker is likely to be faced with on the next assignment, next week or next year. This means carefully thinking through the worker's career and occupational goals, so that educational assessment might lead to a process of personal and professional development. And it requires a normative orientation; one that might begin with defining performance standards (much as the staff had already done in the task analysis process)—standards against which current practice might be evaluated.

This may be too big a job to be left to the supervisor alone. It involves not only the worker being assessed, but also other members of the work group or work team who should not only be involved in setting the standards, but in sharing their assessments of each other and their capabilities to perform according to some agreed-upon norms. Moreover, those norms must also be shaped by the agency's standards, set by the board, or those set by an outside funder or contractor (like the state agency that had just awarded Harvey's department a huge grant). There might even be some useful "generic brand" assessment instruments that could be used by many agencies. Millicent found one in the appendix to the Austin book. She xeroxed it, and made a few modifications to take back to the agency. You'll find it referred to as *Counseling Behavior Check List* (Figure 9.2).

Orientation focuses on the who, what, how, and why of a particular job or of specific agency practices. The supervisor, according to Austin, has the responsibility for introducing the new worker to the agency, or for changes in the agency to people currently on staff. But here, too, the job is shared. In some agencies, formal orientation programs are conducted by a training division or department; the supervisor may orient workers to the particular department, its operations, its programs, and services. One of the problems with expecting the supervisor to do all of the orientation, or even take a major role in it, Millicent noted, is that it expects a great deal from one person. Are all supervisors equally knowledgeable about the community context within which the agency functions, the source of supply for the agency's resources, the range of its benefit programs, the norms that govern work in a particular department? In many settings, this would be an unrealistic expectation. But shifting full responsibility for orientation to a formal training department has

I. Personal Characteristics

A. Relationships with Others

____ Shows an exceptional ability to relate to others.
____ Demonstrates a high degree of relating to others.
____ Relates adequately with most people.
____ Has difficulty relating to some others.
____ Often relates in a manner which "turns off" other people.

B. Warmth and Caring

____ Displays these qualities appropriately.
____ Usually presents self as warm and caring.
____ Displays some concern and support, but with some observable limits.
____ Displays these qualities inappropriately, or in a highly limited manner.

C. Tolerance for Ambiguity and Stress

____ Recognizes a stressful situation; adjusts and tolerates accordingly.
____ Sometimes behaves inappropriately under stress.
____ Low tolerance for stress.
____ "Falls apart"' when under stress.

D. Flexibility Regarding Environment and Time Commitment

____ Able to function effectively regardless of environment and, if necessary, is willing to devote more time than expected to complete the task.
____ Able to function effectively regardless of environment but reluctant to be flexible in time commitment.
____ Needs a particular environment but flexible in time commitment.
____ Needs a particular environment to function in and is not willing to be flexible in time commitment.

E. Openness and Acceptance of Others' Values and Lifestyle

____ Genuine and demonstrated acceptance of values and lifestyles other than own.
____ Limited acceptance of values and lifestyles other than own.
____ Closed to values and lifestyles other than one's own.

F. Self-Awareness and Understanding

____ Has an awareness of own personal stages of growth and shows continuance of this growth awareness.
____ Generally seems aware of current growth process but appears not equipped theoretically for inward probing.
____ Sometimes appears unaware of feelings and motivation.
____ Appears to have minimal awareness of feelings; does not appear to have accepted own problems; responds in stereotyped manner.

G. Self-Esteem

____ Self-directed and confident; accepts responsibilities; maintains sense of identity; functions independently.
____ Good sense of identity and rootedness; needs only occasional reassurance.
____ In frequent need of reassurance; lacks a significant degree of self-confidence.
____ In constant need of reassurance; does not function well independently.

Figure 9.2 Counseling behaviors checklist.

H. Motivation Toward Continued Learning
- ____ Shows openness and enthusiasm for learning new ideas, methods, and approaches.
- ____ Can be encouraged to be open to some new ideas, methods, and approaches.
- ____ Is generally uninterested in exploring new methods, ideas, and approaches.
- ____ Closed to new knowledge and techniques.

I. Ability to Relate to the Population that the Agency Serves (if applicable): Ethnic, Sexual, Cultural, etc.
- ____ Shows considerable ability along with some language familiarity, where applicable.
- ____ Reflects an openness for cultural and lifestyle differences among client populations.
- ____ Generally lacks cultural awareness.
- ____ Resistant to people from different cultures and lifestyles.

II. Counseling Skills

A. Attending and Listening: Attention paid to the physical and psychological communication of the client, communicates attention to the client through verbal and physical action.
- ____ Displays attentive listening to both verbal and nonverbal messages of the client and self.
- ____ Usually shows attentive listening as described above.
- ____ Attentive listening is not commonly displayed.

B. Empathy: Responsive to client in a way that shows an understanding of what the client experiences emotionally and intellectually and what the client is communicating verbally and nonverbally.
- ____ Demonstrates understanding of client's thoughts and feelings enriched at a level deeper than client expressed verbally.
- ____ Reflects accurately client's expressed surface feelings but does not show understanding of client's deeper feelings.
- ____ Shows awareness of client's thoughts and feelings though responses are often mirror images and occasionally are "off base" from client's feelings.
- ____ Displays little interest andunderstanding of client's thoughts and feelings.

C. Process: The awareness of, and the ability to work with, the dynamics that underlie the content of the therapeutic relationship.
- ____ Frequently aware of underlying process and, when aware, able to use it in a manner that facilitates the therapeutic process.
- ____ Frequently aware of underlying process though has difficulty integrating it into the therapeutic session.
- ____ Seldom aware of underlying dynamics, slow to formulate understanding.

D. Communication of Respect: Belief in the worth of the individual (i.e., respects the right and responsibility to make own decisions and encourages the potential for change).
- ____ Displays respect for client in a manner that enhances the client's self-esteem.

Figure 9.2 Continued *(continued)*

____ Displays feelings of value for the client but occasionally allows limitations in feeling and communication.

____ Frequently allows own prejudices to interfere with acceptance of client, subtracting from client's feelings of self-worth and capabilities.

E. Limit Setting.

____ Sets and maintains clear consistent limits with the client appropriate to situation and dynamics.

____ Experiences occasional difficulty with limit setting, maintains them well once set.

____ Seldom sets realistic limits in the therapeutic relationship.

F. Clarity of Expression: Use of clear language, within the client's frame of reference, to express thought, feelings, experience.

____ Uses vocabulary appropriate to particular client.

____ Occasionally speaks in vocabulary and terminology which the client cannot relate to.

____ Frequently speaks at a different level than that of the client.

G. Timing: Use of intervention, techniques, clarifications, interpretations, and self-disclosure at a time when most beneficial to the client's growth.

____ Consistently displays an accurate sense of timing which enhances the therapeutic process.

____ Usually displays a good sense of timing, only occasionally interrupting and taking away the flow of therapeutic process.

____ Frequently interrupts and redirects the client preventing a smooth flowing process.

H. Confrontation: Constructive challenges of the client's discrepancies, distortions, and defensive behavior.

____ Frequently uses confrontation in a manner that enhances the client's self-awareness and moves toward therapeutic growth.

____ Occasionally confronts the client in a manner that enhances self-awareness, occasionally does so inappropriately.

____ Seldom able to act confrontively; inappropriately confrontive.

I. Self-Disclosure: Willingness to tell the client something personal about self which is pertinent to their therapeutic process and yet does not lay another burden on the client.

____ Possesses an ability to share self-disclosure when appropriate without changing the direction of the therapeutic session.

____ Shares self-disclosure when appropriate though occasionally this information appears vaguely judgmental.

____ Shares self in a way which takes up a significant part of the therapeutic session; displays judgmental, superior, directing quality.

J. Termination

____ Displays appropriate insight into and ability to handle skillfully the dynamics that are particular to ending a case.

Figure 9.2 Continued

—— Usually shows the skills that are necessary for adequately dealing with termination; occasionally unable to sense and deal with termination issues.

—— Displays inability to handle ending in an effective way.

K. Variety of Techniques:

—— Can accurately use a variety of counseling skills, as needed.

—— Is open to a variety of techniques but lacks expertise in more than one general area.

—— Seems inappropriately limited in use of techniques.

III. Case Management Skills

A. Diagnostic Evaluation

—— Is able to make knowledgeable, sound evaluations and communicate them to the client and to coworkers when necessary; evaluations are based on sound knowledge of clients' themes and dynamics.

—— Has adequate diagnostic knowledge and skills, occasional difficulty formulating and communicating.

—— Seems unsure of evaluations of clients, seldom formulates evaluations.

—— Avoids evaluating client's abilities to function.

B. Treatment Planning

—— Has ability to formulate, develop, and implement sound treatment plans which prove effective for client.

—— Develops sound, treatment plans but finds implementation difficult.

—— Develops treatment plans which are sometimes questionable.

—— Formulates treatment plans which prove ineffective for the client.

C. Agency Specific Skills: Ability to learn to use specific skills appropriate to the agency, if any (e.g., reading and understanding medical records/charts, preparing court reports, being an effective advocate in the community, communicating the relevance and needs for rules, use of milieu therapy).

—— Considerable ability to learn and use agency specific skills.

—— Some ability to learn and use agency specific skills.

—— Limited ability to learn and use agency specific skills.

D. Crisis Intervention Management

—— Consistently is able to act effectively and swiftly at point of crisis.

—— Action in crisis situation is usually effective and appropriate.

—— Becomes flustered in an emergency situation; does not act swiftly or effectively.

E. Identification of Crisis

—— Usually able to identify the dynamic situation "beneath" the crisis.

—— Aware that a crisis is occurring but has trouble identifying the underlying issues.

—— Cannot distinguish the crisis that is occurring.

F. Intake Interview Skills

—— Gets necessary information and makes appropriate communication and referrals.

Figure 9.2 Continued

(continued)

____ Gives basic information but lacks ability to provide a clear picture of the problem.
____ Performance on intakes is unsatisfactory.

G. Recognition of Consultation Needs
____ Is aware of present abilities and limitations in seeking consultation in regard to working with different clients.
____ Aware of limitations but uncomfortable in seeking consultation.
____ Is aware of personal limitations but has difficulty in utilizing consultation.
____ Unable to use consultation when in difficulty.

H. Ability to Write Case Summaries, Reports, Evaluations
____ Submits excellent reports which are current, orderly, and appropriate.
____ Gives reports adequate to agency's needs, limited as to richness and appropriateness.
____ Reports are disorganized and difficult to read.

I. Presenting Cases
____ Discusses feelings and events in some detail, showing relationship of the two.
____ Includes detail but lacks relevant discussion.
____ Speaks in generalities with small amount of supporting detail.
Speaks in generalities.

IV. Professionalism

A. Reliability
____ Communicates sense of enthusiasm and commitment (e.g., tries to be on the job on time, completes tasks).
____ Occasionally late for appointments, meetings. Usually makes sure that breaks and leaves do not inconvenience other staff members. Tasks most often completed on time.
____ Tends to be late; tasks sometimes not completed on time; takes unusual amount of time for breaks; leave privileges are used about the same as others but with little concern for effects.
____ Seldom on time; often tasks are not completed on time; takes longer or more frequent breaks than others; tends to take advantage of leave privileges.

B. Confidentiality
____ Always maintains client information in a confidential manner.
____ Reveals client information in inappropriate ways.

C. Judgment
____ Conveys exceptional professional judgment by conduct that is appropriate to the setting.
____ Conduct is usually appropriate to the setting.
____ Inappropriate conduct is often observable.

D. Dealing with Conflicting Ideas
____ Displays an appropriate willingness to state opinions and initiates constructive dealing with those opinions that conflict with other staff members.

Figure 9.2 Continued

___ Sometimes states opinions but only rarely becomes involved in a discussion with others that differ.
___ Does not state opinions and therefore never becomes involved in discussion with those whose opinions might differ.

E. Relationships with Co-workers
___ Supportive of co-workers and willing to share related professional experiences.
___ Usually seeks assistance and is supportive of co-workers.
___ Available for assistance and meeting for the purpose of learning but seldom initiates.
___ Will meet with co-workers for assistance when asked.
___ Seems uneasy and distant with co-workers.

F. Intra-Staff Decisions
___ Actively participates in decision-making process.
___ Occasionally involved in intrastaff decisions.
___ Does not contribute to decision-making process.

SOURCE: Adapted from a San Francisco State (1976) mimeo, found in Austin (1981).

Figure 9.2 Continued

similar shortcomings. Could a single orientation program properly prepare people to work in both Harvey's department and Sam's?

Updating refers to introducing staff and others to new facts, new performance criteria, changes in the client population or the problems being addressed by the agency, new technology, and so on. In the traditional one-on-one supervisory relationship, Millicent had discovered, the supervisor was responsible for updating the worker. Judging from what she knew of the All-Families Service Center, this was an unrealistic expectation. No supervisor could possibly hope to keep up-to-date on all pertinent issues, much less teach others all that they need to know. "This is an a area where the new staff development program that Bill may want me to set up will be crucial," Millicent realized. "It goes beyond *orientation* to new skill and knowledge development and overlaps with *upgrading*."

Millicent was quite correct. *Upgrading* goes beyond providing workers with new knowledge and skill. It aims at helping them optimize their full potential, freeing them to be creative, to continue growing and developing, to use all their available capacities or to develop new ones. It places responsibility squarely on the shoulders of the learner. The supervisor helps create the context, the atmosphere, and the opportunity for growth and development. But a

Exercise 9.2

Using Self-Assessment Tools

1. Look over the *Counseling Behaviors Checklist* adapted by Austin from a San Francisco State University internship assessment form. If you perform counseling tasks, score yourself in terms of your own personal self-assessment: *high*, *medium*, and *low* (h, m, l).

2. How would you modify the list for use in your own agency? You might consider its use by supervisors with their supervisees (both paid staff and volunteers), with your supervisor as a way of sharing your own self-rating (or for that matter, rating the supervisor), or with colleagues. Make the necessary changes, and discuss your modifications with others who might find it useful as well.

learning environment requires more than a supervisor's commitment. It requires an agency's full commitment.

In Kadushin's work, the third supervisory function is the "provision of support." This includes the "secondary leadership" role defined earlier by Kindelsperger. As Kadushin expands it, supportive activities include (a) *role modeling* performance (working under stress, being sensitive and emphatic, being assertive and independent); (b) *coaching* (helping the subordinant win at whatever he or she is working on, getting the team playing together, providing constructive criticism, motivating, and keeping an eye on the goal but not to the exclusion of process); (c) *trouble shooting* (opening up doors, providing new opportunities, making contacts); and (d) *resolving conflicts* (by heading them off, mediating disputes, finding creative alternatives, or helping each side develop empathy for the other).

Helpful as these concepts were, Millicent found the treatment of similar tasks in the Middleman and Rhodes book more to her liking. She reread their Chapter 5, which focused on "Nine Functions of Supervisors," and started making some notes, only to find the nine functions summarized in the last chapter. "Easier to xerox," she thought, and she got up. What she photocopied to discuss with supervisors at the agency appears in Figure 9.3.

The functions they listed were integrative (humanizing, managing tension, and catalyzing); assuring effective service delivery (which included teaching and career socializing as well as evaluating); and linkage (which included administrative tasks, advocating, and

Exercise 9.3

Who Does the Orienting?

1. In the figure below, you'll find a list of 10 orientation topics or issues (rows 1 through 10) and seven categories of persons who might be involved in providing orientation to new workers, beginning with (A) your supervisor. Think about the first three or four weeks you spent on your current job. Who provided you with orientation to each of the 10 issues or topics? Put a check (√) in the appropriate box. A large number of boxes may be left empty. That's OK. It's also OK if some entire rows or columns are left empty. Right now, we want to find out who provided orientation to what. Later, we'll examine whether the orientation was useful or not, and who else might have provided it. Note that there is an eleventh row and an eighth column (H) that do not have titles. Fill them in as appropriate.

	A. Your supervisor	B. Co-workers	C. A secretary or other staff members	D. Agency trainer	E. Agency administrator or personnel officer	F. People outside the agency	G. Agency clients	H.
1. Agency purposes and operations								
2. Department purposes and operations								
3. Administrative procedures								
4. Pay and benefit programs								
5. Supervision and the supervisory process								
6. Tasks and responsibilities of the tasks								
7. Power structure at the agency								
8. Clients and client population characteristics								
9. The community and neighborhood								
10. Agency resources and resource suppliers								
11.								

2. Now review your answers. Put a plus (+) next to the checkmark in the box where you thought the orientation was properly provided. Put a minus (–) where it was improperly provided. Why did you respond as you did?

3. Now circle the box (including whatever checks, pluses, or minuses might already be included within it) that appropriately reflects who (what person or persons) should be *primarily* responsible for each of the topics. If your response to this question is out of sync with what actually happened (good or bad), why might this be the case?

Exercise 9.4

Designing and Updating/Upgrading Inventory

Before moving on, take a few moments to think through the updating responsibilities. Look over **Exercise 9.3**. Redesign it to develop an inventory of topics or issues as well as persons who should be involved in the process. Now, complete the exercise of your own design, specifying who should have primary, secondary, or peripheral responsibility for updating and upgrading. Use the number (1) for primary, (2) for secondary, and (3) for tertiary or supplemental responsibility.

change-oriented activities). Although several of these task clusters might properly fit under administrative or educational responsibilities, Millicent thought that most of them articulated with the supervisor's supportive or enabling function. For example, in *humanizing work and the workplace*, supervisors may be involved in efforts to create and maintain conditions that promote human dignity (and in so doing, contributing to organizational stability). On an interpersonal level, they (should) demonstrate how the valuing of others and being valued by them leads to appreciating differences among staff members and the contributions that each can make to program or the organization. On the personal level, they (should) encourage acceptance and self-acceptance, thus freeing people to the best of themselves. By communicating a sense of caring, they (should) encourage interpersonal regard and engender the kind of trust that's necessary for people to take risks—risking themselves with others.

We propose the following practice principles to guide your supervisory efforts. You will find a general principle and several subcomponents for each of the nine functions introduced . . . as central imperatives forming the supervisory task. As you consider each of these, mentally add, "The supervisor should . . ." or "The supervisor will strive to . . ." as a lead to each statement.

1. *Humanizing–Make the workplace responsive to the human component of the organization.*
   - 1.1 Seek and provide opportunities for others' satisfactions and recognition.
   - 1.2 Model collaborative and cooperative behavior.
   - 1.3 Maximize egalitarian rather than hierarchical person-to-person relationships wherever possible.
   - 1.4 Attempt to see and appreciate the others' perspectives.
   - 1.5 Differentiate private messages from public ones and deal with the private messages in private.
   - 1.6 Help the others save face in the face of embarrassment.
2. *Managing tension–Attend to the imperatives of the professional and the organizational cultures in ways that do not compromise the ethical or the practical in terms of the values and norms of client, worker, organization, and profession.*
   - 2.1 Encourage the expression of and the dissipation of tensions.
   - 2.2 Recognize the conflicting interests, values, attitudes, and ideologies.
   - 2.3 Approach differences and conflicts as inevitable, as inherent in the organizational situation, and as often desirable.
   - 2.4 Mediate among different orientations and interests.
   - 2.5 Urge the development of some system of yield-and-prevail decision-making pattern.
3. *Catalyzing–Make the workplace an interesting, rewarding, and involving context for the delivery of services.*
   - 3.1 Inject excitement and enthusiasm whenever possible.
   - 3.2 Value novel and unusual ideas.
   - 3.3 Appreciate and acknowledge risking, revising points of view, and entertaining alternative perspectives.
   - 3.4 Encourage experimentation and "think time" for yourself and supervisees (for example, an opportunity each week to reflect and replan the work, or to consider alternative approaches and issues).
4. *Teaching–Create a work climate where the opportunity for learning and ongoing professional development is valued, available, and attainable.*
   - 4.1 Promote the acquisition of new knowledge and skills and the specialization (refinement) of known competencies.
   - 4.2 Encourage mutual exchanges of information among members of the work unit.
   - 4.3 Involve the supervisees in the determination of their learning needs.
   - 4.4 Make expectations explicit at the outset of the relationship in a participatory manner.
   - 4.5 Devise ways to meet these learning needs through individualized and unit-wide instructional formats.

Figure 9.3 Supervisory competence. *(continued)*

4.6 Connect your efforts with those of others in the organization whenever and wherever possible.

5. *Career socializing–Act as a role model to supervisees, as a person who exemplifies the ideals, values, and standards of the social work profession and the service mandate and mission of the organization.*
   5.1 Make your actions and the ways of pursuing the task imperatives congruent with your verbal and written directions and appeals.
   5.2 Know that in instances where actions and words are not congruent, the influential action "message" will make the greater impact.
   5.3 Act in ways that reflect understanding of the multiple careers of supervisees–agency, personal, professional–and the differentials among professional identities that diverse professional socialization imposes.
   5.4 Temper your assumptions about the normative expectations for role performance by sensitivity to differences between yourself and supervisees as influenced by gender, ethnic, racial, and age-related perspectives.
6. *Evaluating–Design evaluation procedures so that the process captures the unique and changing achievements of each supervisee.*
   6.1 Distinguish with supervisees those areas of managerial accountability and quality control where compliance is mandatory from those areas of the work where degrees of freedom for individual judgment and discretionary performance are valued.
   6.2 Establish a process of mutual feedback between yourself and supervisees and among the supervisees in ways that preserve dignity and promote wisdom.
   6.3 Determine performance objectives and other criteria for achievement in a participative way that reflects individual differences in education, experience, and difficulty of workload.
   6.4 Develop evaluative procedures, processes, and criteria that value interdependent work, collaboration with others, understanding others' work, problems, needs, and the "big picture" of organizational life.
7. *Administering–Mediate between agency objectives and worker activity–the critical task that brings credibility to your efforts and leverage for your permit of the other functions.*
   7.1 Be accountable for the competent execution of organizational productivity and efficiency needs and for the quality of service delivery.
   7.2 Translate the broad statements of organizational purpose into the concrete, operationalized components of priorities, assignments, and activities.
   7.3 Involve those responsible for the implementation of decisions in making the decisions that determine these activities.
   7.4 Delegate authority and responsibility for service delivery activities to the extent of your jurisdiction limits.
8. *Advocating–Seek to eliminate inequities and injustices that may have detrimental effects on workers and on agency goals.*
   8.1 Act persuasively on behalf of worker issues that pertain to the quality and quantity of service delivery.
   8.2 Focus energy on issues of fairness and justice within the agency, as well as within external groups and organizations in the larger service-delivery system.

Figure 9.3 Continued

8.3 Protect the supervisees from organizational assaults to professional or high-quality service delivery where possible, even when such a stance may result in unpopularity.

8.4 Support the promotion of well-qualified persons who have experienced discrimination (in terms of gender, race, ethnicity, or age) to positions of importance in the structure of the agency.

9. *Changing–Expect continuous fluctuations in the agency and its environment.*

9.1 Use your own and the workers' critical positions within the organization to influence these fluctuations in the direction of organizational development and enhancement.

9.2 Intiate collective efforts to move the organization to higher levels of functioning within the constraints imposed by the priority of service delivery.

9.3 Differentiate between short-term and long-term opportunities in terms of priorities, patterns, organizational arrangements, and intervention choices; and work strategically in both realms.

9.4 Help those who experience pain, loss, or dislocation during changes to find a new sense of value, self-worth, and competence.

SOURCE: Ruth R. Middleman and Gary B. Rhodes, *Competent Supervision: Making Imaginative Judgments*, © 1985, pp. 309-311. Reprinted by permission of Prentice-Hall, Inc., Englewood Cliffs, New Jersey.

Figure 9.3 Continued

Tension can be the result of pressures by a single force or a combination of forces, or by proto-forces tending to cause tension, tension beyond which an object or a person cannot be expected to stretch. The supervisor's *tension management* function may include identifying contradictions between individual interpretations and agency policies or expectations, spelling out the reasons for differences in interpretation or opinion among different staff members, restructuring work responsibilities to reduce complexity or increase order, engage others in problem solving that deals with pressure points, or perhaps just recognize the irreconcilable, to be able to live with it in the workplace.

As a *catalyst*, the supervisor adds some substance to a situation that permits a situation, a person, or a group to be transformed, or to speed up the process of being changed. It requires an encouragement of people and ideas, actions aimed at cutting through a maze (or through despondency) by showing a new direction, by morale and norm building. *Career socializing* focuses on more than vertical or horizontal career development. It deals with ethical choices, taking unpopular stands when they are in the best interests of the client, even if it means challenging agency policy. It means clarifying and examining the norms that have grown up about work, and challenging those norms when necessary. It means helping workers grow into a job and out of a job when they (even if they don't recognize it) are ready for a new stage in their development.

"These are tall orders for any supervisor," thought Millicent. "I wonder if we shouldn't be thinking of ways we can develop our supervisors, helping them become the supervisors they want to be. It might make some sense to start by finding out how people at the agency look at supervision, both those who are being supervised and those who are doing the supervising." There were two self-assessment exercises in the Middleman and Rhodes book that Millicent liked especially. We've included them as **Exercises 9.5** and **9.6**. Why not complete them before moving on?

* * * * *

Millicent finished her reading, gathered her notes, and went home to do some heavy thinking. Over the course of the weekend, she sketched out a brief summary report, spelling out what she thought were the appropriate responsibilities of supervisors in educating, supporting, and managing staff. She also sketched out those functions she thought might appropriately be lodged in the new personnel department that Bill had mentioned, for which Carl would be responsible. And she separated out those educational functions that might properly be assigned to a new staff development department. Before discussing her recommendations with Bill, she checked them out first with Carl, whose work might be affected by her recommendations, and with Yolanda, a supervisor whose judgment she trusted.

* * * * *

"I like what I see here, Millicent," Bill looked up after reading Millicent's recommendations. "But I want to go back to something that you said when we met last week. Remember you said something to the effect that we were losing control over the change process?"

"Well, I think it was just an old *habit*," Millicent remarked with a twinkle, "a habit of mind. You know I grew up in an organization that had a pretty rigid hierarchy of authority. Structure and accountability were pretty clear. Liberation theology may have liberated me a bit. But it wasn't until I really got into the supervision literature that I

Exercise 9.5

Your Working Style

Directions—The following items present situations that supervisors often encounter. Respond to each item according to the way you think you would most likely act. Put the appropriate letter to the left of each number, as follows: (A) always, (F) frequently, (O) occasionally, (S) seldom, or (N) never.

As a supervisor, I would:

1. Most likely help the workers by doing things for them
2. Encourage workers to go the extra mile
3. Allow them complete freedom in their work
4. Encourage the workers to follow certain routines
5. Permit others to use their own judgment in solving problems
6. Stress making the most of oneself all the time
7. Respond with help more readily when I know I am needed
8. Joke with workers to get them to work harder
9. Try to help the workers, even when they don't want it
10. Let workers do their work the way they think best
11. Be working hard to set a good example
12. be able to tolerate postponement and uncertainty
13. Speak for others if they have not been effective themselves
14. Expect others to keep working even when discouraged
15. Allow the workers to try out their own solutions to problems, even when I know these will not work
16. Settle conflicts between people
17. Get swamped by details
18. Present an individual's position to others if that individual is unclear
19. Be reluctant to allow new workers much freedom of action
20. Decide what should be done and how it should be done
21. Push people toward high-level functioning
22. Let some people have authority which I could keep
23. Think things would usually turn out as I predict
24. Allow people a high degree of initiative
25. Stick to the things I know how to do even when others want other things from me
26. Make exceptions to the rules for some workers
27. Ask workers to work harder
28. Trust workers to exercise good judgment
29. Schedule the work to be done

30. Not explain my actions
31. Persuade others that my ideas are to their advantage
32. Allow others to set their own pace
33. Urge people to keep aiming higher
34. Do things without consulting the workers
35. Ask the workers to follow standard rules and regulations

SOURCE: Ruth R. Middleman and Gary B. Rhodes, *Competent Supervision: Making Imaginative Judgments*, © 1985, pp. 349-352. Reprinted by permission of Prentice-Hall, Inc., Englewood Cliffs, New Jersey.

Scoring for Exercise 9.5

1. Circle the following numbers: 1, 4, 7, 13, 16, 17, 18, 19, 20, 23, 29, 30, 31, 34, 35.
2. Put a 1 outside all those circled numbers where you put S or N.
3. Put a 1 next to all those *uncircled* numbers where you put A or F.
4. Circle the 1 next to numbers 3, 5, 8, 10, 12, 15, 17, 19, 22, 24, 26, 28, 30, 32, 34.
5. Add up the uncircled 1's. This total is your T (*task*) score.
6. Add up the circled 1's. This total is your P (*people*) score.
7. Plot your P score on the supervisory orientations matrix (below) counting upwards 1 to 15; plot your T score according to the numbers 1-20. Connect these two values by drawing a line perpendicular to each number so that the two lines insert at a point.

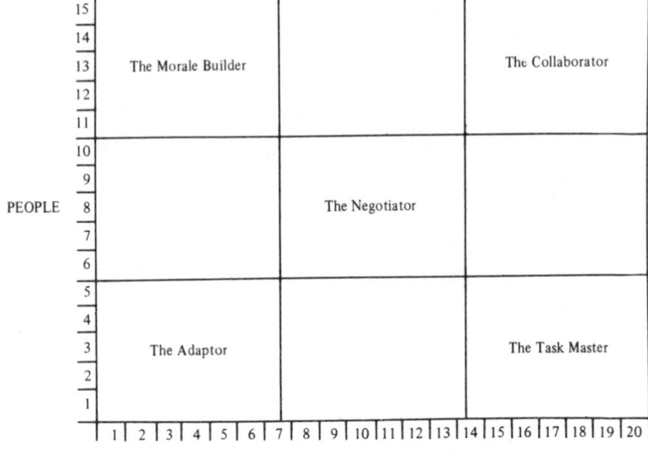

"In plotting your score on the supervisory orientation grid . . . , some of you may have found your score in a box without a label. The interpretation we have presented is our best estimate of the major orientations, and as such, it is not proven or absolute. Given the variability of configurations of context, task, and people, it is not unusual for some to end up in a blank box. To help those of you in this situation, we can offer the following ideas.

"If your point in an empty box is closer to one labeled box than to any of the others, you are probably oriented in the same direction as the pattern described for that labeled box. If your score is basically in the middle of an empty box, you are likely to vary your approach to fit the particular configuration of people, task, and context. For example, if you fall in the middle of the blank box in the upper center, you probably recognize that depending on the particulars you sometimes follow the pattern of the morale builder, sometimes the negotiator, and other times the collaborator. You can make this same self-assessment for each of the other blank boxes in relation to the labeled boxes that surround it.

"Finally, regardless of which box your score falls into, we suggest that you return to the questions and the scoring instructions to identify which questions and responses produced your location in the grid. For those of you who want to develop further ideas on how to modify your responses to fit a particular pattern, this reflective analysis may offer some clues."

Middleman and Rhodes explain that if your graph intersects boxes that are labeled, you can get a sense of your style by examining the following definitions:

> "*The task master*—You scored high on work and low on consideration for others. You may claim, "Nice guys finish last." The push is to get the work done well in the most direct and efficient manner, to sum up the situation quickly, decide what needs doing, and do it. The task master sees others as either effective or ineffective, right or wrong, with you or against you. You are highly persuasive, especially when in command, and you may evoke respect or fear. You value hard work, expect to be right, and are intolerant of roadblocks. You expedite and decide.
>
> "*The morale builder*—You scored high in concern for others, low in concern for the work. Your motto may be, "The important thing is not winning, but how the game is played." You enjoy personal friendships, avoid being critical, use personal loyalties, expect consideration, think positive, believe in team spirit, and use yourself to relieve tensions. You show consideration by shifting your opinion, and value peaceful, harmonious relations between people. You believe the work suffers if others are unhappy, angry, demoralized. You harmonize and accommodate.
>
> "*The negotiator*—This is a middle position, some concern for the task and for others—firm with tasks, fair with people. You think,

"You win some, you lose some," and "Don't rock the boat." You see life as a compromise, like to be practical, value reasonable solutions, argue skillfully, and influence by using diplomacy. You push to get things done, but only to a point; you are considerate of others, but not all the way. You concentrate on the immediate and get it out of the way as quickly as you can. You are strategic in managing information to strike the bargain, to do the expedient thing. You bargain and settle.

"*The collaborator*—You are very concerned about the task and the persons involved. Your motto is, "The most important part of an iceberg is that part below the surface." You expect conflict and believe it should be openly confronted. You believe people want to work hard, be involved, seek best solutions, are valuable resources, and can cooperate. You work for solutions that meet the situation and others' needs for respect and pride. You expect you might be wrong. You encourage emotional expression and full expression of opinions. You collaborate and go all out.

"*The adapter*—You are not concerned much for either the task or others. Mainly your concern is for yourself. Your motto is, "I may not become the administrator, but I'll not get ulcers." You value objectivity, usually go along with the majority, listen a lot, believe in live and let live, delegate as much as you can, and want to survive. You take a back seat, avoid the action, avoid taking sides, and try to get along with minimum effort. You delegate and go along with."

SOURCE: Ruth R. Middleman and Gary B. Rhodes, *Competent Supervision: Making Imaginative Judgments*, © 1985, pp. 349-352. Reprinted by permission of Prentice-Hall, Inc., Englewood Cliffs, New Jersey.

realized that authority, accountability, and consistency don't require rigid structures. What they require is a consistency in the process."

"You couldn't be more correct," replied Bill as he leaned back. "Bill," Millicent laughed. "You're leaning back again. What are you going to dump on me this time?" Bill laughed and adjusted his position. "Look, I'm sitting up straight," he said, "so I'll be straight with you."

"We've been talking as if the only personnel issues we should be concerned about are those that affect or are affected by paid staff," Bill said. "You mean we should also be thinking about the volunteers who work with clients or provide supportive services at the agency?" Millicent interjected. "Well, yes," Bill replied. "But there is another set of volunteers that also require development. They're not the

Exercise 9.6

Supervisor Preference Checklist

The following statements represent characteristics commonly found in the practice behavior of social work supervisors. These characteristics represent different supervisory approaches for which supervisees express varying preferences. On the scoring checklist that follows the list of statements, mark an X in the appropriate square for each statement, if it is broadly true that you would prefer this characteristic in your supervisor. If you think the statement does not reflect a characteristic you prefer, leave the space blank.

I PERFORM BEST WHEN MY SUPERVISOR:

1. Closely monitors the way I organize and carry out my work.
2. Has developed practice mastery from blending personal sensitivity and skill with social theory and interventions.
3. Emphasizes the organization and group role components of our relationship.
4. Expects me to learn by watching how he or she does the work.
5. Judges my performance on the basis of my skill in dealing with feelings.
6. Bends the rules and procedures when necessary.
7. Makes most of the decisions.
8. Stimulates my personal/professional development by sharing his of her personal insights into feelings and behavior of workers and clients.
9. Emphasizes both internal and external system forces in problem solving.
10. Gives me feedback on my work that focuses on specific directives for change.
11. Relates the way I organize and carry out my work to my own personality development.
12. Has developed practice mastery from combining practical experience with knowledge of social theory and interventions.
13. Emphasizes the task components of our relationship.
14. Expects me to learn by exploring my feelings and behavior with her or him.
15. Judges my performance on the basis of a mutually determined set of goals and objectives.
16. Uses a strict approach to rules and procedures.
17. Helps me gain insight into myself in making decisions.

18. Stimulates my personal/professional development by challenging me to integrate ideas from various sources.
19. Emphasizes agency regulations in problem solving.
20. Gives me feedback on my work that focuses on my expression of feelings in doing the work.
21. Allows me to organize and carry out my work pretty much on my own.
22. Has developed practice mastery from many years of job experience in the school of hard knocks.
23. Emphasizes the emotional components of our relationship.
24. Expects me to learn by mutual examination of my knowledge and skills in the light of contemporary social theory and interventions.
25. Judges my performance on how he or she would do my job.
26. Is responsive to my feelings about the enforcement of rules and procedures.
27. Encourages me to make most of my own decisions.
28. Stimulates my personal/professional development by sharing her of his fund of practical knowledge from prior personal experience as a worker.
29. Emphasizes the emotional forces involved in problem solving.
30. Gives me feedback on my work that focuses both on constructive criticism and on praise for work well done.

SOURCE: Ruth R. Middleman and Gary B. Rhodes, *Competent Supervision: Making Imaginative Judgments*, © 1985, pp. 337-338. Reprinted by permission of Prentice-Hall, Inc., Englewood Cliffs, New Jersey.

people we supervise, they're the people who supervise us, that is, who set the guidelines by which we operate and to whom we're accountable. I'm talking about members of the board and advisory committees to each of the departments and projects at the agency." "Bill, I think you're talking to the wrong person," Millicent responded. "No, I'm not. I'm talking to the right person, and you're it, Millicent. I've already spoken to members of the Executive Committee about a process of continued board development. It will mean the involvement of board members with supervisors and case workers and others at the program level in the agency. It'll also require some education, I mean real education, seminars and training days. We, the staff, I mean, may be accountable to them. But they are accountable in a more general way to the larger community. To do their job right, they need development too."

"And I suppose you want me to train the board as well as the staff?" Millicent asked. "I did have something like that in mind," Bill responded. "At least to work with me on board training and development. That is, after all, consistent with your work in community education, isn't it? If this really is going to be a competent and self-correcting agency, our board and committee people are going to have to be competent in decision making. And that means not only knowing how to make the decisions, but what to make decisions about. I really do need your help, Millicent. Look, I don't want you to give me an answer now. I'll give you a few more things to read." He laughed. "No, you won't have to go back to the library. Here are copies of the Executive Committee minutes in which we've talked about the need for board training. And here is a United Way of America pamphlet on *The Citizen Board in Voluntary Agencies*, and a manuscript by John Tropman at the University of Michigan on organizational governance and boards of directors. Look them over. And then let's meet again next week. Will 2:00 on Monday be OK?"

* * * * *

CITIZEN BOARDS

Like the board of a private corporation, boards of directors are at the apex of the authority structure in voluntary (nongovernmental) social agencies. Boards of directors are engaged in decision making. They have the legal responsibility, often under state statute, to act as collective entities that both represent the community and govern the organization for which they are responsible. Although no board operates in an ideal fashion, the ideal would be for it to hold the executive director and the agency employees accountable for proper fulfillment of their obligations, while they themselves are accountable to the larger community. Boards are trustees of civic purpose, and are legally responsible for overseeing that those purposes are achieved.

They are often responsible for selecting and evaluating the executive, and other key staff members. They often are subdivided into committees that deal with specific programs (in the Center's case, the Program Committee might include subcommittees that focus on the New Americans Project, the Group Homes Program, clinical services, protective services, and community education). The board's other committees include budget and finance, personnel, administration, and public and community relations. Each of the committees has specific responsibilities.

For example, the Center's Program Committee is responsible for overseeing existing programs, recommending new programs, and providing input from the community to the staff members engaged in program operations. The committee responsible for budget and finance oversees the budget and makes recommendations to the overall board for the budget's approval. It may engage in a wide variety of fund-raising activities (including making presentations on the behalf of the agency to the United Way and other federated bodies).

The committee responsible for administration examines the agency's procedures, communication patterns, and management structure with the view in mind of helping the staff to streamline or to restructure to be more effective. The committee concerned with personnel approves all new positions, the restructuring of tasks and responsibilities similar to those we discussed in the previous chapter, and would represent the larger board in negotiations with unions or other collective bargaining units, if such existed. Those board members involved in public and community relations help interpret the agency's missions and its programs and services. They often provide significant feedback to staff about the community's perceptions of the agency, or of community needs and special interests. They often are in a position to do so through their participation in a wide variety of other community activities and their memberships and various population subgroups throughout the community served by the agency.

This is undoubtedly the reason that Bill decided that development of the board and its members required as much attention and care as staff development. Staff members must be motivated and competent to make effective practice decisions. Board members must be motivated and competent if they're to make effective governance decisions.

INFLUENCE AND AUTHORITY

Authority refers to the power or right to give commands, enforce obedience, take action, or make final decisions. In the All-Families Center, final authority may be lodged in the board of directors, but as we have seen, it is dispersed fairly broadly throughout the entire organization. Power is, by implication, delegated from the community to the board, and delegated by the board to the executive director and other members of the staff. In fact, however, the power of each of the players is very much a function of the kinds of

Exercise 9.7

Examining Your Agency's Board of Directors

Does your agency have a board of directors? If not, complete this exercise by examining the relevant documents in another board with which you may be familiar——a church or civic organization, a local board of education, or some other citizens' group that has trustee responsibilities for an organization that provides services.

1. Locate and read the organization's bylaws. These define its purpose and its structure, and spell out the nature of its accountability and legal responsibilities.

2. How is the board organized? What kinds of committees does it have, and what tasks are assigned to each?

3. How are members elected or appointed to the board? How long are their terms? Are they appointed to committees? Do they go through a period of apprenticeship before being assigned to committees, or does committee participation precede full membership on the board?

4. Are board members expected to represent specific constituencies (say, the Black community, or the elderly) or are they expected to represent the general community interest?

5. What kinds of relationships exist between board members and staff, both formal and informal?

6. How do the staff members, the executive director, and others prepare community leaders and volunteers for effective participation on the board? Reexamine the discussion in this chapter on the functions of supervision. If you were the executive director or an agency responsible for board development, what kind of educational/facilitative activities would you conduct with the board? This is an interesting question that requires carefully thought. The board is, legally, in a superordinant position to the executive director. Yet the director and other staff members must invest a great deal of time in the board development if the board is to function competently.

7. Can you develop a list of board competencies that parallels the Middleman and Rhodes inventory of supervisory competence that appears in Figure 9.3 of this chapter?

resources they have at their command. Resources they *can* generate, and *will* use.

The word *power* generally refers to capacity or capability of performing or producing results. In the sense that it represents capacity, it implies "potential," and, in social terms, this means the potential to influence the actions or behaviors of others. Thus, clients and case workers both have some power over each other, as do supervisees and supervisors, and all other members of the enterprise (clerical staff, clinicians, community organizers, supervisory personnel, members of the board). The willingness of some persons to subordinate themselves, and some of their interests, to others, suggests that they are willing to give up some of their own individual power for something else, perhaps the greater collective power that is the result of concentration, working together within an organization. This power can then be used externally by the organization in its relationships to the environment, to clients, to funders, to other agencies. By pooling resources, and delegating power or accepting the authority of others, it is possible to achieve objectives that individuals, not acting in concert, would not be able to achieve.

Although power can be shared, it is always unevenly distributed, even in agencies like the All-Families Service Center, where considerable effort is made to disperse it broadly. Unequal distribution takes on legitimacy so long as subordinates agree that the more powerful individuals in the organization should hold power, and that they are using it in a fair and equitable manner. And that means not abusing power, not using it for personal gain when it should be used for the collective good or on behalf of some population in need (such as clients). The legitimate use of power is brought into question when its delegations and the acceptance of superordinate-subordinate positions are seen as self-serving rather than in the interest of the collective entity or its legitimate missions.

A person's power within the organization as a staff member, as a member of the board, and even as a client, can be maintained through the use of a variety of tactics. These are coercive, reward, expert, referent, and positional. *Coercive* tactics imply that one might threaten or actually use negative sanctions to assure compliance with one's wishes. For example, employees might threaten to strike, clients might refuse to come for appointments, a supervisor will submit a negative evaluation, a worker might imply that a desired benefit (e.g., a referral to another agency) will depend on whether or not the client agrees to fulfill certain obligations. As an example of an external threat, the United Way may imply or threaten a reduction in annual allocation unless the agency agrees to modify its services in some desired direction.

Reward tactics are just the opposite. They are reflected in the ability of one party to enable another to achieve some form of gratification, to acquire a desired benefit. Benefits might be a form of recognition, belonging, self-actualization, better salaries, advancement in the organization. Think of what we've already learned about the hierarchy of human needs. Can rewards or the penalties implied in coercive tactics be used to provide or withdraw resources necessary for persons to fulfill their needs?

When we talk about *expert* tactics, we're referring to the ability to get someone or some organization to do something based on the belief that expertise will lead to goals achievement. The more expert the supervisor, the more likely that staff members will subordinate themselves (be influenced). The more expert the executive director (knowledgeable and skilled), the more likely members of the board are to defer to his or her assessment or recommendation. Sometimes, expertise is reputational, as in the example of an outside consultant who might have disproportionate influence over the behavior of an organization's management because of his or her presumed expertise. A member of the staff who might have as much expertise but is not presumed to may have to expend a great deal more energy in his or her efforts to influence the behavior of others. Would consumers come voluntarily to the Center if they did not expect staff members to have the required expertise to provide desired assistance? By coming to the Center, by requesting help, they put themselves in at least a partially subordinate position, subject to the influence of the helping professionals at the agency.

The use of *referrent* tactics depends on the quality of relationships that exist among persons, among persons and organizations, or, for that matter, among organizations. Referrent power is based on mutual trust, often the result of earlier experience between the parties involved or with others who may be perceived as similar. Trust grows with each successive, successful experience. A person in need of family counseling may risk exposure because a friend had a successful experience at the Center. An agency may be willing to accept referrals from another, even if it has an over-full case load, because staff know they can depend on reciprocity from the first agency when they are in a pinch.

Power is also related to *position*, to the formal arrangements by which authority is delegated to persons or organizations performing designated and agreed-upon roles. Thus, the board is presumed to be in a position of power and authority over the executive, and the executive director is generally presumed to have more authority than department heads or supervisors in the agency. If this delegation of authority is accepted as legitimate, then the actions of incumbents who fill specific positions (so long as they do not go beyond their authority) are likely to be considered legitimate.

REVIEW AND TENTATIVE CONCLUSIONS

Power and authority in social agencies are broadly diffused. Legally, boards of directors in voluntary agencies bear ultimate responsibility for the agencies' programs and services. In fact, staff members share the primary responsibility for programs and services, and their relationships are frequently structured through a process of supervision.

(1) In social work, supervision has come to be defined as serving three major and interrelated functions: (a) the administrative, (b) the educational, and (c) the supportive.
(2) Administrative tasks include staff recruitment and selection, induction and placement, unit work planning, work assignment, work delegation, monitoring and reviewing, work evaluation or performance appraisal, coordination, administrative buffering, and community liaison.
(3) The educative function includes assessment, orientation, updating, and upgrading.
(4) The facilitative function includes role modeling, coaching, trouble shooting, and resolving conflicts.
(5) Boards of directors in voluntary agencies perform a trustee function for the larger community. They are legally accountable for the agency's programs and procedures, are responsible for policy determination, and for program review and development.
(6) The power and authority of board members, and of staff at various levels in the organization's hierarchy, are based on a number of sources: the ability to reward or to punish, expertise, referrent power, and position.

Exercise 9.8
Power and Influence

Think of your most recent supervisor, or relationships that you had with a member of an agency's board of directors (where you were a member of the staff).

1. Rank order the tactics that were used to influence (shape or control) your behavior:

   coercive
   reward
   expert
   referrent
   position

2. Undoubtedly you influenced that person as well. In a different color pencil or pen, indicate in order of importance or frequency those tactics you used to influence the other party.

3. Was the relationship balanced? Who tended to be more influential than the other? Around what kinds of issues?

4. Did each of you use the appropriate tactics? If so, explain. If not, what balance would have been more appropriate? Explain.

YOUR ADDITIONS

(7)

(8)

(9)

(10)

REFERENCES

Abels, Paul. (1977). *The new practice of supervision and staff development: a synergistic approach*. New York: Association Press.

Austin, Michael J. (1981). *Supervisory management for the human services*. Englewood Cliffs, NJ: Prentice-Hall.

Cook, K. S. (1977). Exchange and power in networks of interorganizational relations. *Sociological Quarterly, 18*.

Emerson, Robert M. (1962). Power-dependence relations. *American Sociological Review, 27*(1).

French, John, & Raven, Bernard. (1968). The basis of social power. In R. Cartwright & A. Zander (Eds.), *Group dynamics*. New York: Harper & Row.

Gambrill, Eileen, & Stein, Theodore J. (1983). *Supervision: A decision-making approach*. Newbury Park, CA: Sage.

Gitterman, Alex. (1972). Comparison of educational models and their influences on supervision. In Florence Kaslo et al. (Eds.), *Issues in human services*. San Francisco: Jossey-Bass.

Johnson, T. (1972). *Professions and power*. London: Macmillan.

Kadushin, Alfred. (1985). *Supervision in social work* (2nd ed.). New York: Columbia University Press.

Kindelsperger, Walter L. (1948). *The concept of primary and secondary leadership in supervision*. Unpublished manuscript prepared for the Personnel and Training Services of the YWCA National Training Board.

Lauffer, Armand. (1977). *The practice of continuing education in the human services*. New York: McGraw-Hill.

Lauffer, Armand. (1985). *Understanding your social agency* (2nd ed.).
Middleman, Ruth R., & Rhodes, Gary B. (1985). *Competent supervision: Making imaginative judgments*. Englewood Cliffs, NJ: Prentice-Hall.
Miller, Irving. (1971, 1977). Supervision of social work. In *Encyclopedia of Social Work* (16th & 17th eds.). New York: National Association of Social Workers.
Resnick, Herman & King, Shirley (1982). Shadow consultation. *Social Work*, (Jan./Feb.).
Reynolds, Bertha C. (1936). The art of supervision. *The Family*, June.
Reynolds, Bertha C. (1942). *Learning and teaching in the practice of social work*. New York: Rhinehart.
Shulman, Lawrence. (1982). *Skills of supervision and staff management*. Itasca, IL: Peacock.
Tropman, John E. (1986). *Organizational governance: Development and direction for boards of directors*. Unpublished manuscript, Ann Arbor.
United Way of America. (1983). *The citizen board in voluntary agencies*. Alexandria, VA: Author.
Williamson, Margaret. (1950). *Supervision: Principles and methods*. New York: Woman's Press.
Williamson, Margaret. (1961). *Supervision: New patterns and processes*. New York: Association Press.

Chapter 10

THRIVING ON CONFLICT AND CHANGE

Building the Future on the Past and Present

His selection of Carl Farrell to head the task analysis group was carefully reasoned. Carl, Bill Clapman knew, had been marking time. He needed a new challenge, something meaningful to do, a process he could see through from beginning to end. But Bill's decision to initiate the task analysis process wasn't motivated solely on the basis of his desire to remotivate Carl. Bill's real intent was to reenergize the agency. Organizations, like people, Bill knew from many years' experience, get set in their ways, and while this may be functional for a while—it makes it possible to handle challenges in routine ways—there's always the danger that rigidity can lead to rigor mortis.

The response to Sam's proposal had been the tipoff for Bill. When people get that defensive, he knew, it generally means that they are either too satisfied with what they've got (or what they've got going for themselves) or nervous about something. And he suspected that this "nervousness" (Bill didn't like to think of it as conflict) reflected a semiconscious awareness that it was time to make some major changes in the agency. In fact, some major changes had already been made. The New Americans Project was itself a departure, for both populations served and the kinds of services provided. And Harvey's operation, which Bill liked to think of as the agency's "left wing," was clearly breaking new ground. "If Harv keeps on getting additional contracts and grants," Bill mused, "he may be running the whole show around here." That didn't trouble Bill. What troubled him was that other units did not seem to be changing as much with the times or with the opportunities that presented themselves from time to time, or those opportunities that could be coaxed into being with some imagination and some energy.

But Bill wasn't the kind of administrator who liked to take the bull by the horns. "I'd rather coax the beast along." His style was not to confront others, but rather to help them confront the issues themselves. That's what he liked about the task analysis process. It forced people to examine what they did for what end. He saw this as the beginning of some major operational changes. "As people began to regroup tasks into definitions of how the job should be done, they were setting new standards for themselves. And as they regrouped tasks the way they wanted to see jobs structured, they began to think about new relationships between themselves," Bill reported at an NASW Symposium.

He was also aware that such changes were likely to generate, or perhaps the more appropriate word is "surface," dissatisfaction with things as they are. And that's precisely what Bill was after. "You have to be dissatisfied with the way things are and know it, or have some kind of vision of the way in which they could or ought to be, in order to want to change things. And you have to believe that the right changes can and *will* be made." He saw task analysis as leading to other innovations in the way in which the agency managed itself and the work of its workers.

Not that Bill Clapman had any illusions about the use of rational methods, technology, if you will, to improve the function of organizations. True, task analysis was primarily a rational method of allocating responsibilities and for holding people accountable for what they do. But Bill Clapman understood that accountability meant more than some rational configuration of tasks and clearly articulated performance criteria. Being accountable requires being clear about what one is expected to do, but it also requires being clear about the reasons for those expectations, and having a commitment both to purpose and to others with whom one works. Task analysis was no guarantee of commitment.

But it was a process, he had felt certain when he initiated it, that would free staff to examine what they do and how they do it, and ultimately to focus on a variety of issues that affect all agency functions. It had already led to job redesign and restructuring; recruitment, placement, and to reviewing staff salaries and benefits. Bill knew his organization and he knew his people. Organizations go through quiet spells, in which changes, if any, tend to be incremental and almost imperceptible. In those times staff are often reactive instead of pro-active. He also knew that organizations were sometimes not as responsive as they should be to changes in their internal and external environments. Finally, he was aware that organizations tend to segment, somewhat, as they grow, each unit or department developing a particular style or approach of its own . . . sometimes in response to different environments (just like members of a family respond to different environments) and sometimes as a way of avoiding internal confrontations when different values or perceptions of the possible are held.

For an organization to remain responsive to its environment, and to avoid overfragmentation, on one hand, and ossification on the other, it must periodically take stock. It was time, he felt, for the All-Families Service Center to go through such a stock-taking process. For several years now, the agency had struggled to maintain its own in a cutback environment, one in which each year saw the pool of financial resources for the agency's ongoing programs shrinking. But now, that environment was changing. Some new resources were becoming available. More important, there were new perceptions about appropriate practice interventions with newly targeted populations and changing ideas about the functions of organizations like the Center. Bill wasn't afraid of change. He welcomed it. But he wasn't about to get too far out in front of his staff.

Perhaps Bill's greatest strength as an administrator was that he trusted his staff. He sincerely believed that, given the opportunity, and a supportive environment, they would rise to any occasion that presented itself. And they would be able to deal with the conflicts and dislocations that are inevitable in any process of change.

DEALING WITH CONFLICTS IN THE AGENCY

Throughout these chapters, we've dealt with a number of sources of conflict within the organization. Conflict can be instrumental or expressive; or it can be ideological or operational. I'll explain.

The conflict that erupted briefly between Yolanda and some of her White colleagues was an example of *expressive* conflict (see Chap-

Exercise 10.1

Action Guidelines

Before moving on, let's see what we can learn from Bill Clapman. Go over his thought processes—those described in the preceding pages. Underline all the phrases and thought fragments that deal with conflict and change.

In the space below, rewrite all those items you underlined in the form of action guidelines or practice principles. For example, if you underlined part of the paragraph that immediately preceded this exercise, you might rewrite it as

"Given the opportunity and a supportive environment, staff will be able to deal with the conflicts and dislocations that are inevitable in any change process."

Use additional paper if necessary. Find and rewrite at least 10 action guidelines. Compare those you generated with those produced by colleagues who have also read this material. Which ones are similar, which ones are different? Why?

Exercise 10.2

Sources of Conflict

1. Review Bill's thought processes once again. This time, record as many of the *sources* of conflict he alluded to as you can find. Use additional paper, if needed.

2. Now think back on the preceding chapters. What other conflicts do you remember? What were their sources? This may take some time. Recall the kinds of issues we explored (gender, age and racial or ethnic identity; career choices; professionalization; collegiality; ethical dilemmas; supervision and authority; and so on). Use additional paper, if needed.

Keep your "source" inventories. You'll have occasion to refer to them soon.

ter 2). It was the result of the accumulation of tension and a need to release hostile feelings. It may have also been the result of error and ignorance on her part, and on the part of others. Sam's response to "defeat" at the meeting of the agency's supervisory staff was also perceived by him in expressive terms. It was perceived by others, however, both expressively and instrumentally. *Instrumental* conflict tends to be marked by opposing practices or goals.

Instrumental conflict may be further perceived as either ideological or operational in nature. When it is defined as a conflict in basic values, it becomes ideological, and decisions are made (the conflict is resolved or one side wins) on the basis of what people perceive to be "right" or "wrong." When the conflict, however, is perceived to be operational in nature, it may be resolved on the basis of perceptions of effectiveness and ineffectiveness. Sam was defining a problem operationally, while others were perceiving it both operationally and ideologically.

Conflict may also be defined as inherent or induced. *Inherent* conflicts arise from irreconcilable differences in a given situation. For example, while the conflict was not perceived as intense, there was clearly a conflict between Betsy, Cyndi, Mike, and Mary Jo's identity as students and their identification with their supervisors and work units. It was resolved by reducing student identity and increasing departmental identity. Conflicts can also be *induced* artificially for strategic purposes.

Induced conflict is purposive. Differences may be highlighted so as to promote recognition of alternatives that might otherwise remain hidden from view. It might also be used to increase coherence within a particular group. Could Sam have used conflict more purposefully, or more strategically? Was Bill employing an induced conflict strategy (or setting one up) when he initiated the task analysis process?

The presence or absence of conflict will vary from agency to agency and from time to time. Around any given issue, there may be a great deal of conflict or virtually none. For example, when everyone agrees that a procedure is correct or that a particular population deserves expanded services, one might find consensus on both means and goals. By definition, such consensus would reflect an absence of conflict. In such circumstances, an appropriate strategy would be to bring the consenting parties together for purposes of developing a plan of action.

There may, however, be considerable difference of opinion, perhaps even indifference to the issues at hand. Under such circumstances it wouldn't do to bring the interested parties together, because they are basically disinterested. But highlighting the issue, developing a critical consciousness of it, may lead to interest and commitment. Much of Millicent's work as an adult educator, and more recently as a staff developer, is aimed at generating just such interest and commitment.

When there is clear disagreement on goals or procedures, conflicts of interest may be present. If these are intense, it may do no good to ignore them. It may be more appropriate to line up support on one side in order to attempt to beat the opposition. In some agencies this may be possible. However, in the All-Families Service Center, using a contest strategy of this sort would clearly be a violation of agency norms. Sam could not have won any battle perceived of as conflictive in nature. The collegial nature of decision making could not accommodate it. Conflict, if it were to be reconciled, had to be dealt with indirectly and resolved informally. The collective stake of the staff in preserving a climate of cooperation, collegiality, and professionalism did not permit any other means of resolving conflict.

In other agencies, a different set of mechanisms might exist. These could include arbitration or decision making by those in higher levels of authority, structured and open debates on differences of opinion regarding appropriate practices or value stances or the creation of third-party interventions to mediate conflicts including use of appeal procedures.

I don't mean to imply by this discussion that conflict is unnatural to an organization. On the contrary. Conflict is normal to all social institutions. Without conflicts of interest and perspectives, one would hardly expect organizations to change, grow or develop. Conflict is only destructive if there are no ways to handle it, and if it leads to disintegration rather than integration. By integration, I mean the way in which elements in a social organization become connected so as to give unity to the total organization.

The All-Families Service Center is clearly characterized by a great deal of diversity in its services, yet it maintains a considerable degree of integration in its sense of mission and professionalism. The diversity in program and services, in fact, may be an instrument of such integration, permitting staff to pursue a wide variety of intervention approaches, and thus minimizing the conflict that might arise if they had to argue out the benefits of one approach or another within a single staff grouping. It is only when the practices in a particular unit seem to contradict or conflict with the practices of another (as in Sam's example) that conflict surfaces and becomes intrusive.

Exercise 10.3

Analyzing Conflict Situations

Review the notes you made for **Exercise 10.2.**

1. Identify a conflict situation that was defined by one or more parties to the dispute as *expressive*, while it might have been perceived as *instrumental* by others. Describe it below.

   If all the parties had defined it in the same way, would it have been dealt with differently? Think first in expressive, then in instrumental, terms. How different? Why so?

2. Identify another situation in which conflict may have been *inherent* but was perceived as *induced*. What is the basis for this perception? Review what you learned about perception in Chapter 5. Explain.

   What were the consequences of this perception?

Are there other situations in which conflict was purposefully induced? How, by whom? What processes were set in motion? Were they properly managed? How could the management of this conflict situation have been improved? To what end?

3. Now locate an example of a conflict that may have been interpreted in operational terms by some but in ideological terms by others. Which interpretation was more accurate? How so? Would a conclusion to the situation (perhaps a resolution, perhaps an acceleration of the conflict) have been different if everyone had agreed to one or the other interpretation? Describe and give your reasons for your conclusion.

4. Think about your own agency experiences. On a separate sheet of paper, use questions 1 through 3 to analyze instrumental-expressive, inherent-induced, and ideological-operational conflicts you have experienced.

5. How frequently do these conflicts occur in your place of work? How intense are they? How long do they last?

   Rate each of the conflict situations you have described.

   VF (very frequent), F (frequent), NF (not frequent)
   VI (very intense), I (intense), NI (not intense)
   VL (very long), L (long), NL (not long)

Instrumental Conflicts	Expressive Conflicts
Inherent Conflicts	Induced Conflicts
Ideological Conflicts	Operational Conflicts

ROLE RELATIONSHIPS AND CONFLICTS

Some conflicts are induced by differences in perception about how roles are or should be performed. Roles are the structural building blocks of any organization or social system, so an understanding of roles is central to our understanding of both conflict and change. An understanding of tasks and job descriptions is no substitute for comprehension of roles and role-relationships.

A staff member's own perceptions and interpretations of what is expected for effective role performance affects behavior. This is called a *filtered process*, which, to a certain extent, distorts the messages being sent by others. Perhaps the proper word is not *distort*. Perhaps the appropriate word is *shape*. For example, your supervisor may ask you to call a client who is suffering a crisis. It's almost 5:00, closing time. After about 60 minutes of trying, you finally reach the client and offer help. But your supervisor may have intended that you call during office hours, because it is "unprofessional" to call after hours. An after-hours call might generate inappropriate expectations in the future. The apparent "double bind" is not uncommon when expectations are unclear.

"If I'm going all out for my client, it gets me into trouble," you might conclude. "Next time, I'll just follow the rules, and to hell with the client." What you might not have understood is that the supervisor was concerned about the client but had a different idea about how the professional helping role should be performed. Nevertheless, you were placed in a bind, unsure of his or her expectations, feeling damned if you do and damned if you don't. We'll get back to this point in a moment.

The people with whom a role incumbent interacts in the performance of the tasks associated with that role make up what sociologists such as Robert Merton call a "role set." Each of the members of the role set performs tasks associated with his or her own roles in ways that articulate with a filtered perception of how the role should be performed. Sources of interpersonal conflict in an agency are often found in the different perceptions of the role by members of the role set. For this reason, solutions to job performance problems can often be found in an analysis of the role/role set interactions.

For example, Ali's job, that of receptionist, exists beyond the life of the role occupant. This is a major stabilizing factor for the organization. If Ali were to leave, someone else in that role, however, might attempt to modify the way the receptionist's role is performed. If the new receptionist behaved very differently from Ali, one might expect the initial response of other staff members to be to give the new role incumbent cues to appropriate behavior. Regardless of the role incumbent, however, substantial portions of the role, and the tasks associated with it, often remain unchanged. Nevertheless, individuals do perform particular roles differently from others placed in the same position. To understand this point, think about actors in a play.

Roles are generally established and defined in the script, but different actors will bring different styles, interpretations, and experiences to the same role. The role will never be portrayed by two performers in exactly the same way. What one actor does with the role may also be affected by how other actors play their roles, or by how the director wants the script interpreted. Consider also a staff role previously occupied by a person who did everything he or she was told, but no more. Assume that a new person now occupies the same role but imbues it with a great deal more energy and willingness to do whatever will help the agency.

Would not the new incumbent reshape the expectations of others? Someone else in Harvey's role might perform it quite differently. Harvey, as we defined him earlier, is a climber, a builder. Someone else might be much more conservative, focusing on the managing of what is, rather than expanding it to what it might be. Although the basic job description might remain the same, the new department head might have very different ideas about appropriate tasks, dress, style, and so on. As the new person settles into the job, the expectations of others are likely to change to accommodate the new incumbent's definitions.

If everyone in an agency lived up to current role expectations and made compatible role demands on others, there would be few problems in interpersonal and organizational relationships. Unfortunately, things don't happen this way. Role conflict occurs when contradictory expectations exist for role performance, and when living up to one set of expectations makes compliance with another difficult if not impossible. There are several sources of role conflict. Robert Kahn and his associates have defined these as intersender, person-role, interrole, and intrasender conflicts.

Intersender role conflicts occurs when the person occupying a role is confronted with conflicting expectations from two or more significant others, creating a situation such that the fulfillment of one expectation makes it difficult or impossible to satisfy others. In any work situation, a particular role incumbent may be subject to contradictory expectations "sent" by other members of the role-set: the agency's administrative director, a person's direct supervisor, co-workers at the agency, subordinates, a union or its representatives, others outside the agency whose expectations have an impact on role performance (clients or workers at other agencies); or members in the worker's affective network (such as a spouse or friends). When the expectations of one of these groups or individuals conflict with the expectations of another, an intersender role conflict exists.

A *person-role* conflict is of a somewhat different order. It occurs when expectations associated with a particular role violate the moral values, needs, or aspirations of the role incumbent. For example, Sam feels that Asian and Arab Americans should be treated in a special or different way. But other members of the staff feel that they should not be treated differently from other agency clients. Several of the agency staff members feel that task analysis may be impossible or inappropriate with regard to certain staff positions, but this conflicts with Carl's sense of order. Carl faces yet another conflict. He has never been able to integrate his jazz musician self into his professional self. He deals with this by not dealing with it, by keeping both selves discrete and separate. When a person is required to behave in ways that conflict with his or her basic sense of self, the person-role conflict can be acute. Yolanda, as we have seen, deals with this by turning her Black self off and her professional (White) self on when she reaches the agency.

Interrole conflicts occur when expectations attached to one role conflict with the expectations of the same individual when performing another role. For example, in his role as department head, Harvey must make sure that appropriate standards are maintained in the group homes that his department is required to oversee and license. This may require close monitoring and supervision of his staff. On the other hand, Harvey's style is such that he encourages the staff to be innovative and creative. If he overemphasizes his administrative role, he is likely either to alienate his subordinates or limit their autonomy. On the other hand, if he encourages them to be innovative and expansionary, their regulatory functions (and his) may suffer.

Finally, *intrasender* role conflicts occur when the expectations of a significant other are themselves contradictory or conflicting. This is the double-bind-type conflict we examined earlier. To satisfy one expectation would make it virtually impossible to satisfy another. Carl may be under such pressure at the moment. His boss wants him to develop more rational and measurable job descriptions. But at the same time, he doesn't want Carl's work to upset existing relationships within the agency. Yolanda is always under such pressure. Her husband, Reggie, wants her to be a successful social work administrator in the White world, but he also wants her to be at home when he needs her, and that means being culturally Black in her interpersonal and womanly role at home.

There are two other terms that might bear some explanation: *role ambiguity* and *role overload*. These may not lead directly to conflict, but, like conflict, they do lead to stress. Role ambiguity occurs when a person occupying a particular role receives inadequate information from others regarding role-related performance. It becomes difficult to satisfy the expectations of significant others when those expectations are not made known. Here we are not speaking about being pulled in opposite directions by unknown forces. Rather, we are speaking about inadequate knowledge about what is required.

To a certain extent, Carl's assignment was ambiguous, and his boss hoped that by assembling a task force, the ambiguities might be resolved. In order to deal with the ambiguous assignment, Carl decided to consult with more knowledgeable peers about their thoughts on the assignment. Carl's effort to identify the critical issues that had been raised in those individual meetings reflected his efforts to cut through the ambiguity.

Role overload refers to a situation in which an individual is confronted with a large number of expectations and finds it difficult, if not impossible, to satisfy all of them in a given period. If someone were to ask Harvey why he works so hard, he would not likely respond by defining himself as a climber or a workaholic. Yet his evenings are often taken up with business: catching up on office work or preparing for conferences the next day. He's often on the go during the work day, even using his breakfast time to meet with staff or make hurried visits to group homes.

Many of Harvey's lunch hours are devoted to additional meetings with staff and with representatives of other organizations with whom Harvey hopes to establish interagency linkages. He also meets with people who may possess information that will lead to new grant possibilities and the expansion of the programs for which Harvey is responsible. The demands on Harvey's time are often beyond those to which he can effectively respond. The result is an occasional slipshod performance, particularly in areas that he feels are not critical at the moment. For example, oversight of group homes may be of secondary importance, and hurried site visits may occur only when time permits.

Now I'd like you to examine some of your own experiences in light of these concepts.

Conflicts create pressure. And pressure requires a response. The response may lead to rigidification, what Bill referred to as *ossification*—becoming bonelike. But bones can splinter, no matter how resilient. A more appropriate response to pressure may be movement; and movement leads to change.

SOME PLAIN TALK ABOUT CHANGE

Social workers have a thing about change. They often refer to themselves as "change agents," aiming some of their intervention efforts at "change targets," whether these are individuals, groups, organizations, communities, programs, or policies. They are often involved in the development of policies for social change, and lobbying for legislative changes. They tend to be aware of changes in the environment, in the forces that lead to the creation of problems for their communities, clients, agencies, and themselves. Much of the social work literature focuses on how change occurs, the effects of change, the planning and managing of change, and the stabilization or freezing of change processes only to start a new change process all over again.

One might even conclude that social workers are preoccupied, obsessed with change. Although all professions are affected by and concerned with change, it is social work's major concern, its principal business, the profession's core activity.

This doesn't mean that all change is necessarily to the good, or that social workers know how to analyze it properly, plan it, manage it, or evaluate its outcomes. This chapter has been about change, some of which was initiated internally, some of which was responsive to pressures from the environment or opportunities available within it. Although we've examined only a few of the change efforts underway at the All-Families Service Center, these efforts share some characteristics that are associated with a great many successful agencies (and, by implication, successful change efforts). By "successful," I

Exercise 10.4

Identifying Sources of Role Conflict and Ambiguity

1. Below you will find the key terms we have just analyzed together. For each one, describe a situation of role conflict, role ambiguity, or role overload that you or someone else you are familiar with has experienced or is currently experiencing.

   a. intersender role conflict

   b. person-role conflict

   c. interrole conflict

d. intrasender conflict

e. role ambiguity

f. role overload

2. There are several approaches that might be used in resolving role conflicts, ambiguity, or overload. These include (1) clarification of ambiguity; (2) conformity to one or another of the conflicting expectations; (3) performing at some level of compromised behavior that represents an attempt to conform to more than a single expectation; and (4) avoidance of conforming to any but one's own internal expectations. Using this scheme, select one or two of the problem situations you described above and spell out how you might resolve the problem. Would this approach also work for the other problem situations? Why or why not?

mean those changes that enable the organization to achieve its mission, even if the nature of that mission must adapt (change) in response to new challenges and opportunities.

Bill Clapman was apparently aware that complacency, even stagnation, can suddenly creep into what is otherwise an effective and developing organization. He could, as do some administrators, have decreed changes from the top down. But that is not Bill's style. The directions of change, innovation, if you will, and the processes that must be set in motion so that change is both purposeful and functional, Bill felt, must be shared broadly within the organization.

Bill saw his role as one of helping to set change processes in motion, empowering others to take responsibility for change, and managing the process in a low-key manner. He was less concerned with the ultimate directions that the change efforts might take than with the involvement and commitment of staff and others to the process. Bill did not believe that successful change efforts necessarily require master blueprints. His actions suggest that he perceived staff at all levels in the organization as intelligent, productive, and capable of sharing in the solving of organizational problems, and in setting the directions of change.

One might assume that he also was aware that individuals or departments might sometimes be parochial in their viewpoints. Perhaps that is why he supported a change process that involved representatives of all departments in the task analysis process. And once this process was set in motion, he encouraged its continuation both at the work unit or departmental levels (for example, in Sam's and Harvey's departments) and at the overall organizational level (with the emergence of more flexible work patterns).

In contrast with Bill's approach, you might be interested in looking at what Rosabeth Moss Kanter defines as "rules for stifling innovation" in her recent book *the Change Masters* (1984). I've adapted them as "rules for stifling innovation in a social agency." You'll find these rules below.

The rules, Kanter suggests, reflect a culture and an attitude that make it both unattractive and difficult for people in an organization to take initiative in the solving of problems and the development of innovative solutions to them. By disempowering people, or cutting them adrift, it reduces the likelihood that they are likely to take the risks that must be associated with any change process.

(1) Suspect any new idea that comes up from the ranks, both because it is new and it comes from below.

(2) Make sure everyone in the chain of command signs off on any new ideas.
(3) Have new ideas thoroughly reviewed . . . challenged and criticized within and across departments; accept only those that have survived the gauntlet.
(4) Keep people on their toes by sparing the praise and criticizing freely.
(5) Encourage people to deal with problems at their own levels by treating reports of problems as symptoms of failure.
(6) Insist on careful accounting and accountability procedures; make sure that anything that can be counted is . . . and frequently.
(7) Make all major decisions on policy or programmatic changes centrally, at the top; don't let people know what they are going to be until the decisions are finalized (better to spring it on them rather than let them muck up the works).
(8) Limit access to information, lest it fall in the wrong hands; make sure that only those who can justify their need for it get the data they request.
(9) Delegate unpleasant tasks; get lower level people to participate in cut-back and layoff decisions or in program curtailments.
(10) Remember that the higher up in the organization you may be, the more you know about what ought to be done and how.

Venturing into the unfamiliar is almost always risky. People are unwilling to take risks if they might lead to loss of support, whether the support is external from funders or internal from one's colleagues and friends at the agency. You'll recall McClelland's discussion of the need for achievement (*n* Ach). Well, people also have, according to McClelland, a need to avoid failure (*n* AF). And when one departs from known practice, one often increases the likelihood of making a mistake, being in error. All of us like to stand on "safe ground." And sometimes we're willing to stand on familiar ground, even if it's not all that safe.

Some organizations are more likely to encourage risk-taking, and with it innovation, than others. Some observers suggest that the following four factors influence the extent to which workers are likely to take risks in promoting, managing, and implementing change. First, there must be an expectation, built into the normative or cultural system in the agency, that staff will be pro-active toward the environment. Environment in this case is what some sociologists refer to as the *organization-set* or *task environment*. It is made up of all the organizations and other environmental elements that have a direct impact on the agency's ability to achieve its missions. We've mentioned some of these elements before. They include funders, auspice providers and legitimaters, consumers, collaborating organizations (such as other agencies with which clients are exchanged). Some agencies try to close themselves off, protect themselves from the influence of elements in the task environment. But others are more pro-active, engaging in open exchanges, many of their own initiation.

Harvey's department is pro-active almost to a fault. The most rapidly growing, in some ways most dynamic program division in the agency, it was successful in generating new programs and projects every year, and moving the agency into new and untried territory. But Harvey and his staff's actions also required a supportive rather than a punitive reward system. On a formal basis, rewards included expanded responsibility, rapid promotions, and the accompanying financial remuneration for key staff members. On an informal basis, rewards included recognition from colleagues and peers, and a sense of accomplishment.

It was just plain motivating to work in Harvey's department, if you liked to be autonomous, if you wanted to get quick and immediate feedback about the outcomes of your efforts, and if you liked the feeling that what you did was important, that it counted. That the staff's efforts sometimes resulted in failure (not all grant applications were successful) was perceived as just part of reality. If Harvey were given to clichés, he might have concluded that "nothing ventured, nothing gained."

Risk-taking also requires a support system. To a large extent, Bill modeled the support that he expected other staff members to provide their colleagues and subordinates. But he backed up the moral and intellectual support with real resources. For example, when he originally asked Carl to head the task force on task analysis, he provided Carl with both time and help (in the form of Mary Jo's assistance). Although Sam was initially frustrated by the rejection of his paraprofessionals proposal, he found enough support in his relationships with Harvey and federal officials to find an alternative way of achieving his goal of the greater involvement of new Americans in their own self-help.

Risk-taking requires both the availability and the accessibility of necessary resources. Resources are all the means and commodities necessary to achieve an objective. They may include concrete resources such as money (e.g., grant or contract awards), facilities, and equipment, and ephemeral resources such as knowledge and expertise, commitment, plus time and energy. These were apparently sufficient, available, and accessible for those changes described in this chapter. In fact, in some ways the change processes increased the likelihood of the continued availability of these resources.

JOURNEY INTO THE FUTURE

Despite these good prospects, Bill wasn't altogether satisfied with the change processes at the agency. "We're moving," he thought to himself, "but now that we've greased the wheels, we have to make sure we're on the right track." Bill was a word associator. He hated his own clichés—"on the right track" is something he would have winced at had he said it out loud. But to his "mind's eye"—"ouch, another cliché," it suggested an "image of a journey," a "trip along a road," an effort to go in a "certain direction." He let himself visualize other images suggested by the "right track" and "mind's eye" analogues. "Direction," "drift," "end of a journey," "goal," "movement in time," "getting there," Bill jotted the words on his ever-present yellow pad. "Perhaps Millicent was right," he considered, recalling their discussion prior to his asking her to do some reading on supervision. "We may be losing control over the direction of the change process."

To correct for the problem of "drift," Bill decided it might make sense to have a board-staff workshop "to examine where we've come from" and "to where we're moving." He discussed the idea with Millicent, who suggested they bring in a consultant from the University. On the pages that follow, I've outlined a series of exercises[1] developed for the workshop by the consultant. Look them over. Complete them, much as the members of the staff and board of the All-Families Service center might have. They will take you beyond the Center to your own agency and its future.

REVIEW AND TENTATIVE CONCLUSIONS

Nice work. Let's review what we learned in this chapter.

(1) Agencies are not conflict-free. Conflicts may take on expressive or instrumental forms. *Expressive* conflict is often the result of accumulated tension, whereas *instrumental* conflict relates more to differences in ideological or operational approaches to practice. Some

Exercise 10.5

Decades of Change*

1. Characterize each of the preceding decades in the United States. Jot down words that come to mind. For example, for 1900-1910 you might think "rural society," or "mass immigration from Europe," or for 1930-1940 you might jot down "Great Depression," "New Deal," and so on.

1900-1910 ______________________________
1910-1920 ______________________________
1920-1930 ______________________________
1930-1940 ______________________________
1940-1950 ______________________________
1950-1960 ______________________________
19601970 ______________________________
1970-1980 ______________________________
1980-present ______________________________

2. Do you see any trends? What are they?

3. Now characterize what is to come.

Rest of ______________________________
the decade ______________________________

1990-2000 ______________________________
____

2000-2010 ______________________________
____

*These exercises can be done alone or as a brainstorming session in a large group. Participants might be assigned to record the image words on newsprint-size sheets of paper, one for each decade.

Exercise 10.6

Designing Area Scenarios of the Future

Working alone, with a partner, or in small groups (each assigned to a different "arena"), design two scenarios for each of the *arenas of change* listed below. Build on what you learned in the "Decades of Change" exercise, but this time focus in on your own locale (community, city, county, and so on)—the area served by your agency.

Pick a year to describe—say the year 2000, or a date 10 years from today. Then design an "optimistic" picture of the future—the "best case" scenario—this is not what you would *like* to see happen. It is what is *likely* to happen, could happen, if things go right for the area. And then design a "worst case" scenario that shows what could happen if things go sour. Be as realistic as you can in both cases.

Arenas of Change (one per group)

1. The Local Economy
   (industrial development, rural, farm economy, employment-unemployment, women in the work force, age-related issues, impact of technology)

2. Demographics and Land Use
   (population size and density, demographic composition, in- and out-migration, consensus and conflict issues around land use)

3. Social and Political Values
   (personal values, community values—equity, justice, communal versus individual responsibility, attitudes toward government and roles of other social institutions, nature of political activism and focus of concern, political-social ideologies)

4. Types and Severity of Social-Health Problems
   (health, mental health, educational, substance abuse, criminal justice related, and so on)

5. Services Available
   (public and private mix, local support and commitment, including financial—i.e., levels of giving in dollars and time).

Share the information. What does it suggest as practice arenas for the agency? Are there areas of service it is not now involved in but should consider, others that will be more or less significant?

Exercise 10.7

Imaging the Agency

1. *Impressions.* Complete the following sentences.

   a. When I first heard of the agency, I thought of it as ________________________________ .

   b. The first time I walked into the agency (or called the agency), I ________________________________ .

   c. When I think of the agency's programs, the following images come to mind ________________________________ .

   d. When I think of the agency staff, I ________________________________ .

   e. My affiliation with the agency ought to ________________________________ .

   f. The role I expect to be playing in the year 2000 at the agency is ________________________________ .

   g. The agency really should go out of business if ________________________________ .

2. *Developmental Stages.* Now think of the agency going through a number of developmental stages. Use a separate sheet of paper to jot down your answers. If you are working in a small group, one member should record the answers.

   a. Who was involved in its conception?
   b. What happened during its infancy (years)?
   c. What happened during its childhood (years)?
   d. Has it lived through adolescence? If so, when, and what happened? If not yet, what would have to happen to make the adolescent period least traumatic and most productive for future development?

e. What kinds of adult periods should it prepare for? When will it be entering them?
f. Can you envision a period of old age, disengagement, retirement, new challenges? Death? What would the circumstances be?

3. *Discovery Trip.* Visit the agency at some future date—say 10 years from now, the year 2000, 2010. What do you find? Describe it in detail. What is missing? Make sure you deal with issues of *conflict* and *change*. Record your discoveries.

conflicts are *inherent*, built into a situation, whereas others are *induced* and then purposefully brought into the open so that issues can be dealt with.

(2) When expectations about role performance are either unclear, contradictory, or excessive, several possibilities exist: role conflict (expressed in intersender, person-role, interrole, and intrasender conflicts), role ambiguity, or role overload. These can be resolved through clarification, conformity, compromise, avoidance, or refusal to accommodate.

(3) Social agencies, like all organizations, change in response to pressures from their external and internal environments. External pressures may come from suppliers of resources and legitimacy as well as from consumers of agency services (even when consumers are not organized, but their needs are argued by staff) and from other organizations whose coooperation is necessary for achievement of the agency's mission.

(4) Internal pressures may be generated by those who hold key positions within the organization. Their change-oriented efforts may be motivated by dissatisfaction with things as they are or a vision of something better, and often are focused on some problem to be resolved or condition to be ameliorated.

(5) Change requires some risk-taking, and when those risks are expected to be shared (along with responsibility for the change process) by staff at all levels within the organization, the following factors may contribute or detract from the willingness to take risks:
   (a) the extent to which the agency takes a pro-active stance toward its environment,
   (b) the nature of the formal and informal reward system,
   (c) the nature of support for individuals and groups or units within the agency for engaging in change efforts, and
   (d) the availability and accessibility of resources necessary to plan and implement a change effort.

Exercise 10.8

Scenarios for Preferred Agency Futures

Time now to design scenarios of the *preferred* future. Refer back to what you already know about the area in which the agency provides services (**Exercise 10.6**), the findings of your *discovery trip* (**Exercise 10.7**), your thoughts on conflict and change (**Exercises 10.2**, **10.3**, and **10.4**), and review earlier exercises that are relevant to the issues you want to explore.

Issues for scenario building that draw on material focused on in the book:

a. conditions leading to improvements in work-related satisfaction, motivation, and effort
b. interpersonal relations, related to personal identity, race-ethnicity-culture, gender, and so on.
c. career development, growth opportunities
d. professionalism, professional ethics, and values
e. supervision, staff, and organizational development
f. the agency's authority structure

Other issues for scenario building, discussed in the book:

a. programs and services, populations to be served
b. resources needed, resource development, sources of supply

Your additions:

a.

b.

c.

Pick one or more of the above to work on. If the exercise is conducted in a large group, break into dyads or triads, each building a scenario around a different area of concern. Record the scenarios on large sheets of newsprint. Share them on completion. Which scenarios articulate well with each other? Which are out of sync? How can they be better integrated? Make necessary adjustments.

Exercise 10.9

Goal Attainment Scaling

Each of the scenarios you designed in **Exercise 10.8** includes a number of implied goals. Goals are statements of intent. They tell you where you want to go, provide a vision of the "end of a journey," as Bill Clapman put it.

1. List all the goals that you found in each scenario. Make sure that they include a target date: the time by which the goal will be achieved. Use additional sheets of paper.

2. Now rank-order these goals in terms of *desirability* or *importance* to the agency.

3. Next to each goal, put a *feasibility rating*. VF = very feasible; F = feasible; NS = not sure; NF = not feasible; NAF = not at all feasible. Cross out those goals that are rated as NF or NAF.
4. Now take any of the goals that rate high on feasibility and rank high on desirability or importance and develop an outcome or performance measures scale. It is relatively easy to do.

Goal statement ____

____

____

____

Much higher than expected	
Better than expected	
Acceptable and expected	
Not as good as expected	
Below expectations or acceptability	

For example, if your acceptable and expected outcome for these goals is

"To increase participation in staff meetings by________"

An acceptable outcome might be:

"At least 75% of the staff will participate in the discussions, half will have suggested items for the agenda, and at least 25% will assume responsibility for leading the discussions or presenting data relevant to agenda items."

What might be more than acceptable (yet realistic)? Less than expected or acceptable?

YOUR ADDITIONS

Since you've helped write this chapter by doing the exercises, your additions are likely to be extensive.

(6)

(7)

(8)

(9)

(10)

NOTE

1. Many of these exercises were suggested by Edward Lindemann and Ronald Lippit (see the references for this chapter).

REFERENCES

Ayers, Robert, & Nachamkin, Beverly. (1982). Sex and ethnic differences in the use of power. *Journal of Applied Psychology, 67*(4).

Bennis, Warren G. (1966). *Changing organizations*. New York: McGraw-Hill.

Brager, George, & Holloway, Stephen. (1978). *Changing human service organizations: Politics and practice*. New York: Free Press.

Cohen, Lynn R. (1982). Minimizing communicative breakdowns between male and female managers. *Personnel Administrator*, October.

Coser, Louis A. (1957). Social conflict and the theory of social change. *British Journal of Sociology*, September.

Costello, Thomas W., & Zalkind, S. S. (1963). *Psychology and administration*. Englewood Cliffs, NJ: Prentice-Hall.

Dahrendorf, Ralf. (1958). Towards a theory of social conflict. *Journal of Conflict Resolution*, Spring.

Hasenfeld, Yeheskel. (1983). *Human service organizations*. Englewood Cliffs, NJ: Prentice-Hall.

Havelock, Ronald G. (1970). *A guide to innovation in education*. Ann Arbor, MI: Center for Research on Utilization of Scientific Knowledge, Institute for Social Research.

Kanter, Rosabeth Moss. (1983). *The change masters*. New York: Simon & Schuster.

Kettner, Peter, Daley, John M., & Nichols, Ann Weaver. (1985). *Initiating changes in organizations and communities: A macro practice model*. Monterey, CA: Brooks/Cole.

Lauffer, Armand. (1978). Social planning at the community level. Englewood Cliffs, NJ: Prentice-Hall.

Lindemann, Edward B., & Lippitt, Ronald O. (1979). *Choosing the future you prefer*. Washington, DC: Development Publications.

Lippitt, Ronald, Watson, Gene, & Westley, B. (1958). *The dynamics of Planned Change*. New York: Harcourt, Brace.

Merton, Robert. (1957). *Social theory and social structure*. New York: Free Press.

Nadler, David A., & Tushman, Michael L. (1983). A general diagnostic model for organizational behavior: Applying a congruence perspective." In J. Richard Hackman et al., *Perspectives on behavor in organizations*. New York: McGraw-Hill.

Niehoff, A. H. (Ed.). (1966). *Handbook of social change*. Chicago: Aldine.

Pincus, Allan, & Minahan, Anne. (Eds.). (1979). *Social work practice: Model and methods*. Itasca, IL: Peacock.

Poza, Ernesto J. (1985). Comprehensive change making. *Training and Developmental Journal*, February.

Resnick, Herman, & Patti, Rino J. (1980). *Change from within: Humanizing social welfare organizations*. Philadelphia: Temple University Press.

Rogers, Everrett M., & Svenning, L. (1969). *Managing change*. Washington, DC: U.S. Office of Education.

Thompson, James D. (1960). Organizational management in conflict. *Administrative Science Quarterly*, March.

Tjosvold, Dean. (1984). Making conflict productive. *Personnel Administrator*, June.

Walter, Richard. (1969). *Interpersonal peacemaking*. Reading, MA: Addison-Wesley.

Warren, Roland L. (1977). *Social change and human purpose: Toward understanding and action*. Chicago: Rand McNally.

Zander, Alvin. (1962). Resistance to change: It's analysis and prevention. In Warren G. Bennis, Kenneth D. Benne, & Robert Chin (Eds.), *The planning of change: Readings in the applied behavioral sciences*, New York: Holt, Rinehart, & Winston.

EPILOGUE

Epilogues are sometimes found at the end of a novel or play, rarely in a professional book. But because there was a certain amount of drama involved in the relations between the staff members discussed in this volume, and between them and the work setting, I thought you might like to know what happened to each person.

* * * * *

Harvey Marcus got the grant he applied for in Chapter 1, and two more in the next two years. Both he and Millicent were considered for the job of associate executive director when that position became vacant; Harvey didn't get it. At the time, expansion possibilities for his own department were becoming increasingly limited. So when an opportunity for a top-level administrative position opened up in the state department of social services, Harvey, with some reluctance, left the All-Families Service Center. Two of his subordinates left with him.

Billie Jean became department head for the community placement and group homes program. She put greater emphasis on procedures than Harvey and less on promotions. The department was now more carefully managed, with attention given to certification and oversight. But some of the excitement of the old days under Harvey's leadership left with him. Within a couple of years, other staff members either moved into different positions within the agency or left to take jobs elsewhere.

* * * * *

Yolanda Stephenson continued to perform professionally and competently. In a multiracial setting, conflicts that affected both her professional and her personal life were not so easily resolved. A year after the incidents recorded in this book took place, Yolanda and Reggie had a child, a girl. Being a mother created some additional role conflicts, but the rewards were well worth the strains.

Her entire career, she realized, was an exercise in overcoming strains and stereotypes. Both Blacks and women in America are expected to play subservient, supportive roles. They're not expected to be in leadership positions, or in positions of providing guidance and direction to Whites (whether they be clients or subordinates at work). She was prepared to accept the contradictions and to deal with them throughout her professional life. Her daughter, she hoped, would grow up in a different America.

* * * * *

For Carl Farrell, success at working with a team of other staff members gave him an entirely new outlook on his work and his position in the agency. "For the first time, I began feeling like I was an integral part of the team. It feels good." He continued playing jazz in the evenings but found that work was increasingly becoming more jazzy. That is, there were all kinds of opportunities for "improvising and orchestrating," as he put it.

When the task force's work was completed, Bill Clapman had asked Carl if he would be willing to continue to supervise the accounting department and also take on a new role as the agency's personnel director." At last I'm a social worker," Carl laughed to himself. "I'll do it if we give Mary Jo a permanent job as my assistant." Mary Jo had stayed on at the agency after completing her field placement for the year that the task force was doing its work. For her, the new position meant not only security but an opportunity to continue helping to shape programs and services by devoting her efforts to improving the quality of work and work life at the agency.

* * * * *

Sam Mansouri never did get to hire the paraprofessionals for whom he had advocated. The opposition to the idea was just too strong. Paraprofessionals did not fit the agency's ideological climate, even though he felt there was a significant contribution they might make, particularly in his own department. Nevertheless, Sam found other ways to achieve the same objectives.

He and his staff devoted a considerable amount of energy to the development of self-help groups among the Vietnamese and Chaldean populations served by the New Americans Project. Sam was able to negotiate with the federal government for the responsibility of allocating funds from his grant to these groups. In turn, they were able to hire people from among their own populations to manage a variety of self-help activities. They received much technical assistance and consultation from Sam's staff.

* * * * *

Alberta Schmid's work on the task force opened up all kinds of new opportunities for her. At first, the gratification of working with professionals on the staff, and the increase in self-esteem that this brought her, led her to consider leaving the agency to earn a bachelor's degree in social work. But about that time, the American Federation of State, County and Municipal Employees began to organize the clerical staff at the Center.

Ali's knowledge of the tasks performed by different staff members and of the structure of the agency resulted in her being sought out by the union organizer. And her good relationship with the clerical staff led to her election as shop steward. Getting the professional degree was placed on the back burner. "It's something I might do someday," she told her father. "But not know, there's just too much to do at work."

* * * * *

Millicent Kapinski accepted the offer to become the agency's associate administrative director, albeit with some reluctance. Being an administrator didn't quite fit her own self-image, but the respect she gained from others, and the opportunities the new position offered her to help give direction to the agency's programs in areas that complemented her own critical consciousness, made up for some of the satisfaction she had derived from interacting directly with clients and others in the community.

* * * * *

That's their story. What about yours?

APPENDIX A:
THE NASW CODE OF ETHICS

(Passed by the 1979 Delegate Assembly. Implementation set for July 1, 1980)

PREAMBLE

This code is intended to serve as a guide to the everyday conduct of members of the social work profession and as a basis for the adjudication of issues in ethics when the conduct of social workers is alleged to deviate from the standards expressed or implied in this code. It represents standards of ethical behavior for social workers in professional relationships with those served, with colleagues, with employers, with other individuals and professions, and with the community and society as a whole. It also embodies standards of ethical behavior governing individual conduct to the extent that such conduct is associated with an individual's status and identity as a social worker.

This code is based on the fundamental values of the social work profession that include the worth, dignity, and uniqueness of all persons as well as their rights and opportunities. It is also based on the nature of social work, which fosters conditions that promote these values.

In subscribing to and abiding by this code, the social worker is expected to view ethical responsibility in as inclusive a context as each situation demands and within which ethical judgment is required. The social worker is expected to take into consideration all the principles in this code that have a bearing upon any situation in which ethical intervention or conduct is planned. The course of action that the social worker chooses is expected to be consistent with the spirit as well as the letter of this code.

In itself, this code does not represent a set of rules that will prescribe all the behaviors of social workers in all the complexities of professional life. Rather, it offers general principles to guide conduct, and the judicious appraisal of conduct, in situations that have ethical implications. It provides the basis for making judgments about ethical actions before and after they occur. Frequently, the particular situation determines the ethical principles that apply and the manner of their application. In such cases, not only the particular ethical principles are taken into immediate consideration, but also the entire code and its spirit. Specific applications of ethical principles must be judged within the context in which they are being considered. Ethical behavior in a given situation must satisfy not only the judgment of the individual social worker, but also the judgment of an unbiased jury of professional peers.

This code should not be used as an instrument to deprive any social worker of the opportunity or freedom to practice with complete professional integrity; nor should any disciplinary action be taken on the basis of this code without maximum provision for safeguarding the rights of the social worker affected.

The ethical behavior of social workers results not from edict, but from a personal commitment of the individual. This code is offered to affirm the will and zeal of all social workers to be ethical and to act ethically in all that they do as social workers.

The following codified ethical principles should guide social workers in the various roles and relationships and at the various levels of responsibility in which they function professionally. These principles also serve as a basis for the addjudication by the National Association of Social Workers of issues in ethics.

In subscribing to this code, social workers are required to cooperate in its implementation and abide by any disciplinary rulings based on it. They should also take adequate measures to discourage, prevent, expose, and correct the unethical conduct of colleagues. Finally, social workers should be equally ready to defend and assist colleagues unjustly charged with unethical conduct.

I. THE SOCIAL WORKER'S CONDUCT AND COMPORTMENT AS A SOCIAL WORKER

A. Propriety—The social worker should maintain high standards of personal conduct in the capacity or identity as social worker.

1. The private conduct of the social worker is a personal matter to the same degree as is any other person's, except when such conduct compromises the fulfillment of professional responsibilities.

2. The social worker should not participate in, condone, or be associated with dishonesty, fraud, deceit, or misrepresentation.

3. The social worker should distinguish clearly between statements and actions made as a private individual and as a representative of the social work profession or an organization or group.

B. Competence and Professional Development–The social worker should strive to become and remain proficient in professional practice and the performance of professional functions.

1. The social worker should accept responsibility or employment only on the basis of existing competence or the intention to acquire the necessary competence.

2. The social worker should not misrepresent professional qualifications, education, experience, or affiliations.

C. Service–The social worker should regard as primary the service obligation of the social work profession.

1. The social worker should retain ultimate responsibility for the quality and extent of the service which that individual assumes, assigns, or performs.

2. The social worker should act to prevent practices that are inhumane or discriminatory against any person or group of persons.

D. Integrity–The social worker should act in accordance with the highest standards of professional integrity and impartiality.

1. The social worker should be alert to and resist the influences and pressures that interfere with the exercise of professional discretion and impartial judgment required for the performance of professional functions.

2. The social worker should not exploit professional relationships for personal gain.

E. Scholarship and Research–The social worker engaged in study and research should be guided by the conventions of scholarly inquiry.

1. The social worker engaged in research should consider carefully its possible consequences for human beings.

2. The social worker engaged in research should ascertain that the consent of participants in the research is voluntary and informed, without any implied deprivation or penalty for refusal to participate, and with due regard for participants' privacy and dignity.

3. The social worker engaged in research should protect participants from unwarranted physical or mental discomfort, distress, harm, danger, or deprivation.

4. The social worker who engages in the evaluation of services or cases should discuss them only for professional purposes and only with persons directly and professionally concerned with them.

5. Information obtained about participants in research should be treated as confidential.

6. The social worker should take credit only for work actually done in connection with scholarly and research endeavors and credit contributions made by others.

II. THE SOCIAL WORKER'S ETHICAL RESPONSIBILITY TO CLIENTS

F. Primacy of Clients' Interests–The social worker's primary responsibility is to clients.

1. The social worker should serve clients with devotion, loyalty, determination, and the maximum application of professional skill and competence.

2. The social worker should not exploit relationships with clients for personal advantage, or solicit the clients of one's agency for private practice.

3. The social worker should not practice, condone, facilitate, or collaborate with any form of discrimination on the basis of race, color, sex, sexual orientation, age, religion, national origin, marital status, political belief, mental or physical handicap, or any other preference or personal characteristic, condition, or status.

4. The social worker should avoid relationships or commitments that conflict with the interests of clients.

5. The social worker should under no circumstances engage in sexual activities with clients.

6. The social worker should provide clients with accurate and complete information regarding the extent and nature of the services available to them.

7. The social worker should apprise clients of their risks, rights, opportunities, and obligations associated with social service to them.

8. The social worker should seek advice and counsel of colleagues and supervisors whenever such consultation is in the best interest of clients.

9. The social worker should terminate service to clients, and professional relationships with them, when such service and relationships are no longer required or no longer serve the clients' needs or interests.

10. The social worker should withdraw services precipitously only under unusual circumstances, giving careful consideration to all factors in the

situation and taking care to minimize possible adverse effects.

11. The social worker who anticipates the termination or interruption of service to clients should notify clients promptly and seek the transfer, referral, or continuation of service in relation to the clients' needs and preferences.

G. Rights and Prerogatives of Clients–the social worker should make every effort to foster maximum self-determination on the part of clients.

1. When the social worker must act on behalf of a client who has been adjudged legally incompetent, the social worker should safeguard the interests and rights of that client.

2. When another individual has been legally authorized to act in behalf of a client, the social worker should deal with the person always with the client's best interest in mind.

3. The social worker should not engage in any action that violates or diminishes the civil or legal rights of clients.

H. Confidentiality and Privacy–The social worker should respect the privacy of clients and hold in confidence all information obtained in the course of professional service.

1. The social worker should share with others confidences revealed by clients without their consent only for compelling professional reasons.

2. The social worker should inform clients fully about the limits of confidentiality in a given situation, the purposes for which information is obtained, and how it may be used.

3. The social worker should afford clients reasonable access to any official social work records concerning them.

4. When providing clients with access to records, the social worker should take due care to protect the confidences of others contained in those records.

5. The social worker should obtain informed consent of clients before taping, recording, or permitting third-party observation of their activities.

I. Fees–When setting fees, the social worker should ensure that they are fair, reasonable, considerate and commensurate with the service performed and with due regard for the clients' ability to pay.

1. The social worker should not divide a fee or accept or give anything of value for recieving or making a referral.

III. THE SOCIAL WORKER'S ETHICAL RESPONSIBILITY TO COLLEAGUES

J. Respect, Fairness, and Courtesy–The social worker should treat colleagues with respect, courtesy, fairness, and good faith.

1. The social worker should cooperate with colleagues to promote professional interests and concerns.

2. The social worker should respect confidences shared by colleagues in the course of their professional relationships and transactions.

3. The social worker should create and maintain conditions of practice that facilitate ethical and competent professional performance by colleagues.

4. The social worker should treat with respect, and represent accurately and fairly, the qualifications, views, and findings of colleagues and use appropriate channels to express judgments on these matters.

5. The social worker who replaces or is replaced by a colleague in professional practice should act with consideration for the interest, character, and reputation of that colleague.

6. The social worker should not exploit a dispute between a colleague and employers to obtain a position or otherwise advance the social worker's interest.

7. The social worker should seek arbitration or mediation when conflicts with colleagues require resolution for compelling professional reasons.

8. The social worker should extend to colleagues of other professions the same respect and cooperation that is extended to social work colleagues.

9. The social worker who serves as an employer, supervisor, or mentor to colleagues should make orderly and explicit arrangements regarding the conditions of their continuing professional relationship.

10. The social worker who has the responsibility for employing and evaluating the performance of other staff members should fulfill such responsibility in a fair, considerate, and equitable manner, on the basis of clearly enunciated criteria.

11. The social worker who has the responsibility for evaluating the performance of employees, supervisees, or students should share evaluations with them.

K. Dealing with Colleagues' Clients–The social worker has the responsibility to relate to the clients of colleagues with full professional consideration.

1. The social worker should not solicit the clients of colleagues.

2. The social worker should not assume professional responsibility for the clients of another agency or a colleague without appropriate communication with that agency or colleague.

3. The social worker who serves the clients of colleagues during a temporary absence or emergency should serve those clients with the same consideration as that afforded any client.

IV. THE SOCIAL WORKER'S ETHICAL RESPONSIBILITY TO EMPLOYERS AND EMPLOYING ORGANIZATIONS

L. Commitment to Employing Organization—The social worker should adhere to commitments made to the employing organization.

1. The social worker should work to improve the employing agency's policies and procedures, and the efficiency and effectiveness of its services.
2. The social worker should not accept employment or arrange student field placements in an organization which is currently under public sanction by NASW for violating personnel standards or imposing limitations on or penalties for professional actions on behalf of clients.
3. The social worker should act to prevent and eliminate discrimination in the employing organization's work assignments and in its employment policies and practices.
4. The social worker should use with scrupulous regard, and only for the purpose for which they are intended, the resources of the employing organization.

V. THE SOCIAL WORKER'S ETHICAL RESPONSIBILITY TO THE SOCIAL WORK PROFESSION

M. Maintaining the Integrity of the Profession—The social worker should uphold and advance the values, ethics, knowledge, and mission of the profession.

1. The social worker should protect and enhance the dignity and integrity of the profession and should be responsible and vigorous in discussion and criticism of the profession.
2. The social worker should take action through appropriate channels against unethical conduct by any other member of the profession.
3. The social worker should act to prevent the unauthorized and unqualified practice of social work.
4. The social worker should make no misrepresentation in advertising as to qualifications, competence, service, or results to be achieved.

N. Community Service—The social worker should assist the profession in making social services available to the general public.

1. The social worker should contribute time and professional expertise to activities that promote respect for the utility, the integrity, and the competence of the social work profession.
2. The social worker should support the formulation, development, enactment and implementation of social policies of concern to the profession.

O. Development of Knowledge—The social worker should take responsibility for identifying, developing, and fully utilizing knowledge for professional practice.

1. The social worker should base practice upon recognized knowledge relevant to social work.
2. The social worker should critically examine, and keep current with, emerging knowledge relevant to social work.
3. The social worker should contribute to the knowledge base of social work and share research knowledge and practice wisdom with colleagues.

VI. THE SOCIAL WORKER'S ETHICAL RESPONSIBILITY TO SOCIETY

P. Promoting the General Welfare—The social worker should promote the general welfare of society.

1. The social worker should act to prevent and eliminate discrimination against any person or group on the basis of race, color, sex, sexual orientation, age, religion, national origin, marital status, political belief, mental or physical handicap, or any other preference or personal characteristic, condition, or status.
2. The social worker should act to ensure that all persons have access to the resources, services, and opportunities which they require.
3. The social worker should act to expand choice and opportunity for all persons, with special regard for disadvantaged or oppressed groups or persons.
4. The social worker should promote conditions that encourage respect for the diversity of cultures which constitute American society.
5. The social worker should provide appropriate professional services in public emergencies.
6. **The social worker should advocate changes in** policy and legislation to improve social conditions and to promote social justice.
7. The social worker should encourage informed participation by the public in shaping social policies and institutions.

APPENDIX B: NATIONAL ASSOCIATION OF BLACK SOCIAL WORKERS CODE OF ETHICS

In America today, no Black person, except the selfish or irrational, can claim neutrality in quest for Black liberation nor fail to consider the implications of the events taking place in our society. Given the neccessity for committing ourselves to the struggle for freedom, we as Black Americans practicing in the field of social welfare set forth this statement of ideals and guiding principles.

If a sense of community awareness is a precondition to humanitarian acts, then we as Black social workers must use our knowledge of the Black Community, our commitments to its self-determination and our helping skills for the benefit of Black people as we marshal our expertise to improve the quality of life of Black people. Our activities will be guided by our Black consciousness, our determination to protect the security of the Black community and to serve as advocates to relieve suffering of Black people by any means necessary.

Therefore, as Black social workers we commit ourselves, collectively, to the interest of our Black brethren and as individuals subscribe to the following statements:

I regard as my primary obligation the welfare of the Black individual, Black family and Black community and will engage in action for improving social conditions.

I give precedence to this mission over my personal interests.

I adopt the concept of a Black extended family and embrace all Black people as my brothers and sisters, making no distinction between their destiny and my own.

I hold myself responsible for the quality and extent of service I perform and the qualilty and extent of service performed by the agency or organization in which I am employed, as it relates to the Black Community.

I accept the responsibility to protect the Black community against unethical and hypocritical practice by any individuals or organizations engaged in social welfare activities.

I stand ready to supplement my paid or professional advocacy with voluntary service in the Black public interest.

I will consciously use my skills, and my whole being, as an instrument for social change, with particular attention directed to the establishment of Black social institutions.

ABOUT THE AUTHOR

ARMAND LAUFFER is Professor of Social Work at the University of Michigan, where he teaches courses in administration, staff development, and community planning. He received his doctorate at Brandeis University and has spent several years on the faculties of the Hebrew University and Haifa University in Israel as a visiting professor. He now consults with Ben Gurion University.

Co-Editor of the Sage Human Services Guides and Sage Sourcebooks for the Human Services, Lauffer has written a number of other professional books.

For Sage:
Careers, Colleagues, and Conflicts, 1985
Understanding Your Social Agency (2nd Edition), 1985
Grantsmanship (2nd Edition), 1984
Grantsmanship and Fund Raising, 1984
Assessment Tools, 1982
Getting the Resources You Need, 1982
Health Needs of Children (with Roger Manela), 1979
Resources for Child Placement, 1979
Volunteers (with Sarah Gorodezky), 1977

Other books in print:
Strategic Marketing for Not-for-Profit Organizations, 1984 (Free Press)
Community Organization for the 1980s (ed., with Edward Newman), 1982 (SDI)
Doing Continuing Education and Staff Development, 1978 (McGraw-Hill)
Social Planning at the Community Level, 1978 (Prentice-Hall)
The Practice of Continuing Education in the Human Services, 1977 (McGraw-Hill)
The Aim of the Game, 1973 (G.S.I.)
Community Organizers and Social Planners (with Joan L. Ecklein), 1971 (John Wiley)

NOTES

NOTES

NOTES